ENGLISH DEMOCRATIC IDEAS
IN THE
SEVENTEENTH CENTURY

CAMBRIDGE
UNIVERSITY PRESS
LONDON: Fetter Lane

NEW YORK
The Macmillan Co.

BOMBAY, CALCUTTA and
MADRAS
Macmillan and Co., Ltd.

TORONTO
The Macmillan Co. of
Canada, Ltd.

TOKYO
Maruzen-Kabushiki-Kaisha

ENGLISH DEMOCRATIC IDEAS
IN THE
SEVENTEENTH CENTURY

BY

G. P. GOOCH, D.Litt., F.B.A.

SECOND EDITION

WITH SUPPLEMENTARY NOTES
AND APPENDICES BY

PROFESSOR H. J. LASKI

CAMBRIDGE
AT THE UNIVERSITY PRESS
1927

PRINTED IN GREAT BRITAIN

PREFACE

TO THE FIRST EDITION

THE ESSAY out of which the present work has grown obtained the Thirlwall Prize in 1897. My thanks are due to the Adjudicators for permission to recast and expand it.

The design of the following Essay is to serve both as an illustration of English History in the seventeenth century and as a contribution to the history of political ideas. English political thinking from the Reformation to the opening of the eighteenth century can be divided broadly into what may be called the Monarchical and the Democratic; for even among the more oligarchic systems of thought there is a democratic element. The former has been already adequately portrayed. An attempt is now for the first time made to relate the story of the latter.

Within the limits of an Essay covering so wide a field, it is impossible to do more than direct the attention to the salient points of the story. The justification for the treatment of the two middle decades of the century at what may at first sight appear disproportionate length is to be found both in the volume and the quality of the ideas which then made their appearance.

My best thanks are due to Lord Acton and Mr S. R. Gardiner for suggestions and criticism.

The chief abbreviations are the following:

    C. S. P. = Calendar of State Papers.
    T. P.   = Thomason Collection of Pamphlets.
    C. S.   = Camden Society Publications.
    A.-C. L.= Anglo-Catholic Library.

When no details are given, the reference is to the single or the standard edition of a work.

March 1898

PREFACE

TO THE SECOND EDITION

THE FIRST edition of this book was published in 1898 and went out of print in 1906. That its usefulness to students was not exhausted was shewn by the high price quoted for second-hand copies and by the appearance of a pirated edition in America in 1912. The desire for a new edition was often expressed by friends and correspondents; but owing to my absorption in later periods of history I was unable to keep in close touch with the progress of seventeenth century studies, and unwilling to reprint without expert revision. The reappearance of the essay is due to the encouragement and practical help of Professor Laski, who kindly volunteered to bring the bibliographical references up to date and to contribute some appendices. I also desire to record my gratitude to the Syndics of the University Press for offering to publish the new edition. My own share in the enterprise has been limited to verbal corrections of the text.

G. P. G.

February 1927

CONTENTS

CHAPTER I

The Origin of Modern Democratic Ideas

I

THAT department of modern political thought which may be broadly called democratic takes its rise in the sixteenth century. The spirit of the Reformation, neutralising where not moulding the teaching of its leaders, was individualistic[1]. Though it might be going too far to say, with Montesquieu[2], that Catholicism has an innate affinity with Monarchy and Protestantism with Republicanism, the idea that underlies the exaggeration is to some extent correct. The true nature of the Reformation is found not in its intention but in its result. To its philosophic tendency, moreover, was added an historical influence. Its appeal to Christian antiquity as a model issued in familiarisation with the democratic organisation of the early Church.

That these tendencies were not noticed or were angrily denied by the accredited spokesmen of Protestantism was of slight importance. In his famous letter to the German princes[3], Pope Adrian asked if they could not see that under the name of liberty these children of iniquity were seeking to throw off all obedience. King Francis used to declare that 'cette nouveauté' tended to the destruction

---

[1] Cp. Hegel's *Philosophy of History*, 433–4; Hinrichs' *Politische Vorlesungen*, I. etc. [On the political thought of the Reformation generally see R. H. Murray, *The Political Consequences of the Reformation*; G. de Lagarde, *L'Esprit politique de la Réforme*; J. N. Figgis, *From Gerson to Grotius*. H. J. L.]

[2] *Esprit des Lois*, XXIV. 5.

[3] Laurent, *Droit des Gens*, VIII. 500.

of Monarchy[1]. And from the bosom of the movement, the Peasants' War and the rising of the Anabaptists gave evidence that some of its fundamental principles had been seized.

Luther himself at first held no definite political opinions; but with the need of defending his movement against its own excesses, this indifferentism was laid aside[2]. In one direction alone did he authorise, nay, insist upon, rebellion. 'The Pope,' he wrote in 1545, 'is a mad wolf against whom the whole world takes up arms without waiting for the command of King or Magistrate. And all who defend him must be treated like a band of robbers, be they Kings, be they Caesars[3].' The teaching, however, of the first authoritative exposition of the tenets of the new movement is of a very sober character[4]. And yet in Melanchthon, the principal author of the Confession of Augsburg, we find the first signs of the bursting of the bonds. With Luther the recognition of Natural Right is far from clear; but in the scheme of his colleague, the magistrate's claim to obedience is thwarted by that of the Law of Nature. Although it was left for others to carry on the tradition to Grotius, the recognition of the principle itself was of no small importance. And it was worked out democratically enough by Melanchthon himself in the test question of the lawfulness of killing tyrants[5]. Injuries which were not flagrant should be for-

[1] Hundeshagen's 'Einfluss des Calvinismus auf die Ideen vom Staat,' *Kleinere Schriften*, II.

[2] *Tischreden, Von der Obrigkeit der Fürsten.* [On Luther's political opinions see R. H. Murray, *Erasmus and Luther*; E. Ehrhardt, *La Notion du Droit Naturel chez Luther*; L. H. Waring, *The Political Theories of Martin Luther*; J. Binder, *Luther's Staatsauffassung.* H. J. L.]

[3] Bossuet, *Variations*, Livre VIII. § 1.

[4] Augsburg Confession, Ranke's *Deutsche Geschichte*, VI. 89.

[5] A collection of the passages in Melanchthon's works relating to political principles appeared in England under the title of 'A Civil Nosegay,' 1550.

given; but no magistrate might command anything contrary to the Law of Nature. Private citizens might slay usurpers and even cruel officers under special provocation. With Bullinger, on the contrary, whose authority in some countries surpassed that of any other reformer, we return to an almost unqualified doctrine of submission. God had many ways to set us free; our duty was only to repent. Sometimes He would stir up valiant men to displace tyrants. Of forms of government, though it was useless to dispute which was the best, Democracy was certainly the most perilous[1].

In Political Philosophy the Reformation is most fully represented by Calvin. Not only was he the one leading reformer who had enjoyed the training of a jurist, but he alone was called on to apply his political principles to the actual conduct of government. It has been, however, a matter of lively controversy from Calvin's day to our own as to the real extent of his democracy; for, though it possesses a certain superficial clearness, his system is as full of inconsistencies and confusions as that of Hobbes.

The famous chapter in the *Institutes* on Civil Government[2] opens with the remark that rule is necessitated by the fanaticism of those who try to overturn order and live like rats in straw, pell-mell, and by those who unduly extol the power of princes. It is as natural and necessary as food. 'Those who maintain that restraint accords not with the Christian law betray their pride and arrogate to themselves a perfection of which they do not possess the hundredth part.' Some form of government being clearly necessary, it is a more difficult matter to determine which form is best; indeed, having regard to circumstances, it is almost im-

I quote from this convenient summary. Cp. the remarks of Kaltenborn, *Vorläufer des Hugo Grotius*, 211–17.

[1] Decade II. Sermon 6, ed. Parker Society, I. 309–22; cp. his equally cautious answers to Knox's questions, Knox's *Works*, III. 221–6.

[2] *Institutes*, Bk. IV. c. 20.

possible. But if the author were pressed to indicate a preference, it would be for an aristocracy, either pure or modified by some element of popular control. In the famous discussion of the duty of obedience to bad rulers is to be sought the key of some of the most momentous incidents in modern history. Calvin admits that the natural feeling of the human mind is to hate tyrants; but with his usual contempt for natural instincts, he makes it an evidence of respect to God to obey princes, 'by whatever means they have so become, and though there is nothing they less perform than the duty of princes. For an unjust ruler fulfils the purposes of God by punishing the people for their sins. If we remember that the worst kings are appointed by the same decree as the best, we shall never entertain the seditious thought that a king is to be treated according to his deserts, and that we are not compelled to act the part of good subjects to him because he does not act the part of a good king to us. Are not wives bound to husbands and children to parents?' But rulers, it may be objected, owe duties to those under them. To this Calvin replies, as the Stuarts were afterwards to reply, that they are responsible to God alone, and that revenge is not committed to men.

It might seem as if there was nothing that could bend this iron teaching. But at this point two qualifications are introduced, involving what is hardly less than a *volte-face*. Vengeance, the author has just told us, is not for men, to whom, indeed, no command has been given but to suffer and obey. But we learn that he has been speaking of private individuals alone; and that where magistrates have been appointed to curb the tyranny of the ruler, to suffer it is to betray the liberty of the people. Such a right was possessed of old by the Ephors and Tribunes and is perhaps exercised to-day by the Three Estates. But, as Calvin's critics pointed out, no civilised nation was without some such machinery as he had indicated, and his elaborate inculcation of obedience provided therefore no effective guarantee against sedition.

The first qualification, then, of unvarying submission is that which allows a people's accredited representatives to voice its discontent, and allows a nation to resist as a nation[1]. But the second is still more far-reaching. The readers of the *Institutes* were instructed to withhold obedience when incompatible with obedience to God. They were indeed subject to their rulers, but subject only in the Lord. Had God resigned His own rights to certain mortals in appointing them to rule over their fellows? And Calvin only refrains from saying that the Bible was to decide when the duties of the Christian conflicted with the duties of the subject because his meaning was too obvious to need stating. But when politics and theology were inseparable, and when each individual found in the Bible what he desired to find, Calvin's authorisation made each man the judge in his own case of conscience.

It is thus perfectly plain from the *Institutes* that the nation might resist as a nation and the individual as an individual. But it is equally certain that Calvin had no desire that the qualifications should override the thesis. We shall only read him aright if we figure to ourselves the proclamation of the duty of submission by a herald in the market-place, and the whispering of the right of resistance in the by-lanes of the city. For Calvin dedicated his *Institutes* to Francis, as Beza tells us, 'pour luy faire entendre que faussement et calomnieusement ses plus loyaux sujets estoient chargés des crimes d'hérésie et de rebellion[2].'

This interpretation is confirmed in various ways. In the first

[1] This is wholly omitted in the discussion of the question of obedience in the Commentary on Romans xiii.

[2] Beza's *Histoire Ecclésiastique des Eglises Réformées*, I. 37, ed. 1883.

place, whenever Calvin was invited to decide on definite issues, he counselled non-resistance. When, for instance, Knox and Goodman published books in Geneva, he took the utmost pains to dissociate himself from them and told Elizabeth that he strongly disapproved of their doctrines and had prohibited their circulation[1]. In an even more important case, the famous letter to Coligny in reference to the conspiracy of Amboise reveals the tendency not to take advantage of his own teaching[2]. In the second place, Calvin had a very low opinion of the Plebs. In many passages of the Fourth Book of the *Institutes* the cup is withdrawn from the very lips of the people. The election of a minister, for instance, is, of course, to be made with the consent and approbation of the congregation; but he is careful to add that the pastor must preside, 'in order that the multitude do not proceed with precipitancy or in tumult[3].' Excommunication, again, can only take place with the consent and knowledge of the whole Church; it must be done, nevertheless, 'in such a way that the multitude have not the chief power in its determination[4].' Finally, he was of opinion that human nature had a tendency to obedience, or, as he phrases it, the minds of all men had the impression of civil order, and therefore, being by nature a social animal, man was disposed by instinct to cherish and preserve society[5].

But do what he could, Calvin was unable to convince the

[1] Calvin to Cecil, *Zurich Letters*, I. 34–6; cp. Beza to Bullinger, I. 131, Parker Society.

[2] Laurent's *Droit des Gens*, VIII. 511, 12. But cp. Bossuet, *Variations*, Livre x. § 33.

[3] *Institutes*, IV. c. 3.

[4] IV. c. 12.

[5] II. c. 2. [For the full statement of Calvin's views on obedience consult (i) *Sermons sur le cinquième Livre de Moïse*; (ii) *Commentaire sur Samuel*. For his general views see Hans Baron, *Calvin's Staatsanschauung*; Cadix, *L'État et ses Rapports avec l'Église après Calvin*. H. J. L.]

world of his sincerity[1], though some of his critics were ready to confess that the scholars had gone far beyond their master[2]. And as we trace the development of the theory and practice of resistance through the next century, we shall convince ourselves that, despite his guarded reservations, the teaching of Calvin, even though we do not care to describe it with Mignet as the 'religion of insurrection,' made steadily for popular right[3].

The tendency of Reformation teaching now became unmistakeable. The *De Jure Magistratuum*, with some reason attributed to Beza, was so far in advance of Calvin's own position that its publication was forbidden by the Senate as unseasonable, though it was admitted to contain nothing but the truth[4]. And, finally, Pareus may close the list of the theologians. The famous explanation of the verse in Romans was to be more quoted than any other single passage from the political teachings of the Reformers. Henceforward it was competent for Calvinists to believe that St Paul intended the office and not the officer to be guaranteed against destruction.

Modern Democracy is the child of the Reformation, not of the Reformers. Of the latter, inconsistency is the chief characteristic. Not only is the man not the doctrine, but the doctrine itself is found to contain much that its author never could or never

[1] Barclay's *De Regno et Regum Potestate adversus Monarchomachos*, 7, ed. 1600; Blackwood, *Adversus Buchananum*, 13, ed. 1581.

[2] Heylyn, *Tracts*, ed. 1681, 652, 3; but see also his *History of the Presbyterians*, ed. 1672, 435.

[3] 'Voilà des colombes et des brebis,' cried Bossuet scoffingly, 'qui n'ont eu partage que d'humbles gémissements et de la patience ! Mais il n'était pas possible qu'on soutînt longtemps ce qu'on n'avait pas dans le cœur.' Laurent, VIII. 512.

[4] MSS. Records of Geneva, in McCrie's *Life of Melville*, I. 427–8; cp. Baum's *Beza*, III. 54, 'Le nom mesme de Béze est épouvantable à nos ennemis.' Morel to Calvin.

cared to find in it. Omitting its political and moral causes, the
Reformation largely owed its origin to the enunciation of two
intellectual principles, the rightful duty of free inquiry, and the
priesthood of all believers. Its justification could be found in no
others. And this practical necessity of keeping the philosophical
basis of the religious revolution well in view led, as it could not
fail to lead, to the application of cognate principles to other de-
partments of thought. Free inquiry (though those who invoked
it intended that it should mean nothing more than the right for
each to read the Bible for himself, yet punished many of those
who did so) led straight from theological to political criticism,
and the theory of universal priesthood indicated the general direction of the investigation. The first led to liberty; the second to
equality.

The importance of the fact that the principles of modern democracy, however distorted by a theocratic bias, advanced under
the wing of the Reformation, is difficult to exaggerate. In the
emancipation of the people the Reformation played a part it is
impossible to overlook. So far from being hostile to the principles
with which it was associated, the theocratic element in truth pro-
tected and even fostered them. For without the fighting power
which they derived from their patron and ally, they would have
failed to make any progress in an age where the struggle of creed
was the dominant factor of national life. And with the decline
of the theocratic spirit, the popular basis came ever more clearly
into view.

II

From those who wrote of politics indirectly to those who treated of them professedly is but a step.

Anticipations of democratic thought begin very early in French history; but though there was much to point the way to the most revolutionary teaching, there had never been such an outbreak as that which accompanied the rise of the Huguenots. For, on the one hand, the working-classes in their revolts had urged their claims with no theoretical basis except a few generalities which they took for axioms; and, on the other, the teaching of the pulpit, however apparently democratic, contained throughout an explicit or implicit reference to Papal or theocratic pretensions. During the twelve years preceding the great Massacre, the Huguenots are still content with attacking the government of favourites[1]; and even after the Civil Wars have begun, the pretence that the king is a prisoner is still maintained in order to allow the rebels to disown the name. They teach the doctrines of historical Constitutionalism. They express equal aversion for absolutism and anarchy. They declare the existence of a body of rules which form a constitution, not indeed written but traditional. A series of events, however, nay, a single event, might make it inevitable that they should adopt far more audacious principles[2].

The notoriety of the king's share in the origination of the Massacre of St Bartholomew, though Charles assured the Swiss Protestants that it was an accident[3], brought into prominence the

[1] Beza's *Églises Réformées*, I. 241, 2.
[2] 'Tout prince qui voudra régner sans être controllé par la parole de Dieu, il faut qu'il extermine les Huguenots. Car ils sont gens qui pour la gloire de Dieu foulent aux pieds toute gloire des hommes, même des princes.' Polenz, *Französischer Calvinismus*, III. 1, D'Aubigné.
[3] Gaberel's *L'Église de Genève*, II. 316, 17.

radicalism latent in the earlier teaching of the reciprocal engagement of King and People. The change of front that was forced on the Huguenots was explained in a sentence of De Mornay's: 'L'état s'est ébranlé depuis la journée de St-Barthélemy, depuis, dis-je, que la foi du prince envers le sujet et du sujet envers le prince, qui est le seul ciment qui entretient les états en un, s'est si outrageusement démentie[1].' The existing Constitution had been weighed and found wanting, and a discussion of political principles by the injured party became inevitable. This discussion took two forms.

The author of the *Franco-Gallia* illustrates the connection of the Reformation with Huguenot political thinking in a very remarkable way. Hotman's career as a teacher of law and a diplomatist had made his name and writings familiar in Germany[2]. He was on terms of intimacy with Sleidan and Peter Martyr; Calvin had come to Strassburg to hear him lecture; and he was a constant correspondent of every reformer of note. His part in the actual march of events had been no less important. He had counselled the Conspiracy of Amboise, and on its failure had dispatched the famous letter to Le Tygre de la France[3]. He had been designed as a victim of the great Massacre; and the event condemned him to leave his country for ever.

The prefatory dedication declares that the author has been induced to write by the miseries of the times, and by observing that nobody attempts to assuage but rather seeks to inflame the passions of his countrymen. Hotman's panacea is the return of the country to what he supposed to be the ancient constitution.

[1] Weill, *Les Théories sur le Pouvoir royal pendant les Guerres de Religion*, 81.

[2] Cp. Besson's *Fischart*.

[3] Dareste's *Hotman*, 1–48.

His book at first glance seems merely a grave treatise on French history, and his proposals and opinions require to be gleaned from the general story. Before the Roman occupation, Gaul was the country of perfect liberty[1]; and she invited the Franks to assist her to throw off the Roman yoke when it became intolerable[2]. The first two dynasties saw the restoration of the golden age of freedom; for hereditary succession was merely a custom[3], and the first of the duties of the 'sacro-sanctum concilium' was the creation and deposition of kings[4]. The people, too, were consulted in legislation and were only bound by such laws as they had sanctioned[5]. The laws themselves were administered with perfect justice[6]. The accession of the third race, with its entire cessation of the National Council[7], marked the commencement of an era of degeneracy, which became rapid with the creation of the Peers and Parlement, the rise of the lawyers[8] and the growth of absolutism. For a nation to be governed by the nod of a single man was worthy not of men but of beasts[9].

It is not a book of republicanism. The author respects hereditary Monarchy and is content if the rights of the nation are preserved and the old traditions maintained. But the very conservatism of the position, and the historical basis on which it affected to rest, made it all the more dangerous a missile against the *régime* of the day.

The historical side of the Huguenot teaching had been put with rare power by Hotman and created the profoundest im-

---

[1] Ed. 1574, c. 1.   [2] c. 4

[3] c. 5–7.   [4] c. 11, 82.

[5] 92.   [6] 151, 2.

[7] c. 16, 17.   [8] c. 20.

[9] 'Quod regna unius regis arbitrio et nutu gubernantur, rectissime Aristoteles animadvertit eam non hominum sed pecudum gubernationem esse.' 71.

pression. The *Franco-Gallia* had demanded the old constitution. The most remarkable piece of philosophical politics produced by the Huguenot movement represents a profoundly different attitude of mind; for the *Vindiciae contra Tyrannos* pleaded for the rights of man. Though Bayle's dissertation[1] was long supposed to have proved the authorship of Languet beyond possibility of cavil, an attempt has recently been made to reverse the time-honoured judgment[2]. But even if Duplessis-Mornay were the actual author[3], so close was their intimacy[4] that the work would have scarcely less claim to represent the thought of the disciple of Melanchthon and the correspondent of Philip Sidney[5].

The keynote is struck by the explanation in the Preface that the object of the work is to replace the State on its true basis, from which it had been removed by Macchiavelli, and that this is to be found by the application of certain moral axioms to the problems which arise from the relationship of rulers and subjects. The syllogistic method, for it is little else, is announced in the very wording of the query as to whether it is necessary to obey the command of princes when it conflicts with the Law of God[6].

[1] 'Dissertation concernant le livre de Junius Brutus,' *Dictionnaire Critique*, xv. 124-48. [On the *Vindiciae contra Tyrannos* cp. the translation of 1689, edited with an Introduction by H. J. Laski, where the more recent discussion of its problems is considered. H. J. L.]

[2] By Lossen, in the *Sitzungsberichte* of the Bavarian Academy, 1887.

[3] Cp. *Mémoires de Mme Duplessis-Mornay*, 81.

[4] Mornay, *Œuvres*, ii. 80-4, etc.

[5] There can be little doubt that, like many of the most famous Huguenot writings, the authorship was joint. There are evident traces of two hands; and while the classical vein may come from him who had tasted of the Renaissance, the Biblical element may well be attributed to the young Huguenot. The almost hopeless confusion of the dates of composition and publication confirms this view of dual workmanship.

[6] Ed. 1648, 1-19.

The second question[1] is whether the people may resist an infringement of the Divine Law; and the answer reveals the influence both of the teaching of the *Institutes* and the later inspiration of the St Bartholomew. It is the right and duty of the entire body of the officers of the nation to resist, and even of the principal men in provinces and towns. But God has not put the sword into the hands of private men. With the third query[2] we pass to the broader question of resistance to the oppression and ruin of a state by the prince; and here the fullest exposition of the Huguenot theories is to be found. The people, we read, established kings, and put the sceptre into their hands[3]. And God wishes that kings should acknowledge that, after Him, they hold their power and sovereignty from the people, that they may not imagine that they are formed of matter more excellent than other men. For kings are merely the administrators of the Commonwealth; the pilot is not the owner of the vessel. Since the people only submitted to the curtailment of liberty in the expectation of special profit, and dynasties are only tolerated to avoid certain evils, if the medicine prove worse than the disease it must be stopped. So far from derogating from a king's dignity to have his will bridled, nothing is more royal than to be ruled by good laws. If he disobey them he is no less guilty of rebellion than any other individual. Furthermore, he may not make new laws; he does not possess the power of life and death, and he may not pardon. The name of king does not denote a possession or an usufruct but an office and a stewardship[4]. All kings covenant

[1] Ed. 1648, 19–45.   [2] 46–135.
[3] Yet the text-books, till recently, have contained statements such as the following: 'Locke a le premier ressaissi au nom de la liberté la doctrine d'un contrat primitif.' Lerminier, *Philosophie du Droit*, 287.
[4] 'Regis nomen non hereditatem, proprietatem, usumfructum sed functionem et procurationem sonat.'

to keep the laws, and history tells us of no states worthy the name where there was not some such covenant. Finally, where a Christian people is afflicted by its prince, it is the duty of neighbouring princes to come to its assistance[1].

It will have been noticed that whereas the method of Hotman was inductive, that of the *Vindiciae* is deductive. And it is from this that the latter derives its importance. It is the first work in modern history that constructs a political philosophy on the basis of certain inalienable rights of man. For this reason its relevance was not confined to France. It was utilised by, even if not specially composed for, the United Provinces[2], was quoted to justify the trial and execution of Charles I[3], and reprinted to justify the Revolution of 1688. Its faults however are obvious. Like all other Calvinist treatises, confusion is introduced by attempting to combine the theories of the divine and human origin of Government. The introduction of a Contract, again, though appearing to simplify the relations of governor and governed, merely serves to complicate it, unless some fixed mode of interpreting the covenant is suggested. Further, though the sovereignty of the people is admitted, nay, insisted on, the sovereignty of the majority is tacitly denied where it might endanger the supposed interests and liberty of a part. In a word, the capital flaw of the book is in its method; and yet it was essential that an appeal should be made to the Law of God and Nature as well as to tradition, essential that it should be proclaimed that the right to freedom and self-government rests on philosophical and ethical as well as on historical grounds.

With the death of Anjou in 1584 and the commencement of

---

[1] 135–48.   [2] Lossen, *op. cit.*
[3] *People's Right briefly asserted*, 7, T. P. vol. 538; Canne's *Golden Rule*, 12, T. P. vol. 543, etc.

the real power of the League, the Huguenots swung round to a more conservative creed, and their philosophical position is to some extent occupied by their opponents[1]. Regicide teaching was heard of no more. Indeed, between the Politiques and the Huguenots there was now little difference[2]. The same veneration for the historic royalty; the return to the position that the patience of Christians should be more longsuffering than that of others; the distrust of the plebs; the conviction that resistance should be undertaken solely by the States-General; so much at least was common ground[3]. But the *rapprochement* was in large measure rendered possible by the impression that Huguenot theories had made on that school of political thinkers.

What, then, is the final judgment on the political philosophy of the Huguenots? In the first place, despite the common impression that it was republican[4], every prominent member of the party accepted monarchical government[5]. Though the Huguenot doctrine would suit a republic, the proposal to transform the government was not made. The single exception, if, indeed, he deserves to be called an exception at all, is La Boétie. But although the

[1] Cp. Barclay, *De Regno*; addressing Boucher, he remarks: 'Magnam partem ex Bruto paene ad verbum descripsisti,' 387. It is significant that this work should attack writers of both communions indifferently.

[2] The *Vindiciae* was often disowned and attributed to a Romanist hand; cp. James I, 'Defence of the Right of Kings,' *Works*, 1616, 480; and Haag, *La France Protestante*, VI. Art. 'Languet.'

[3] Bodin, *La République*, Livre VI. ch. 4, especially 937–948, 971–2, ed. 1580.

[4] Polenz, III. 186; Martin, IX. 387; etc.

[5] With the rank and file it was sometimes otherwise. When the name of the king was mentioned, relates Monluc, the Huguenots would burst out, 'Quel Roy? Nous sommes les roys, nous. Estuy-là que vous dictes, nous luy donnerons des verges.' He adds, 'Ilz tenoient ce langaige partout!' *Mémoires*, II. 362. Satires were also written against the 'Republicans.' Lenient's *La Satire en France au 16ème siècle*, II. 44.

Contre-un was printed in the company of Huguenot pamphlets, and was eagerly read by Huguenots, it cannot fairly be taken as a specimen of their opinions at any time, much less at the date of its composition in 1548[1]. The author drew his inspiration from antiquity, and pleaded not so much for republicanism as for an individualism almost amounting to anarchy[2]. The century was sincerely royalist. It is one of the capital differences between the political philosophy of France in the sixteenth and of England in the seventeenth century, that, though starting from the same premises, the English alone pressed on to their logical outcome[3]. The contribution of the Huguenot theorists to practical politics was their demand that the sovereignty of the people should be expressed in the machinery of government in some definite way. The cry for the States-General owed its rise and its strength to them. Under Henry II not a voice was raised in their favour; under Francis II they were recommended only because the king was a minor; and L'Hôpital himself did not regard them as an essential element in the government. But from the moment of the Massacre every writer urges their summons, not merely to extricate the nation from an *impasse*, but because the sovereignty of the people is a fact and can express itself in no other way. They are no longer to constitute an expedient of emergency, but to take their place in the normal life of the nation. The teaching

[1] Yet the mistake has been made. Weber writes positively that it proves the circulation of republican ideas in 1548. *Der Calvinismus im Verhältniss zum Staat*, 53.

[2] 'Si d'aventure il naissoit aujourd'hui quelques gents, touts neufs, non accoutumez à la subjection, si on leur presentoit ou d'estre sujets ou vivre de liberté, à quoi s'accorderaient-ils?' ed. 1891, 51.

[3] It is significant that Davila's *Civil Wars* should be the 'Vade Mecum' of Hampden; Warwick's *Memoirs*, 240. The connection of the Huguenot movement is purely with the early phases of the English Civil War.

infects the Catholics[1], and remains the banner of liberal thinkers till the whole nation surrenders to Henry IV.

In a word, the Huguenots never went beyond a liberal interpretation of Constitutional Monarchy. To contend that their spokesmen are the contemporaries of 1789[2] is merely childish. Though it is unfair to declare the teaching of the Huguenots was that the people should effect the revolution and the nobility profit by it[3], it is impossible to find any thinker who may be described as consistently democratic[4]. Hotman, who, almost alone, speaks for universal suffrage, grants the king a liberal allowance of power and respects the hereditary principle. The authors of the *Vindiciae,* who, contending for the legislative power of the States-General, almost reach the doctrine of the separation of powers, have little confidence in the people, whom, with their memory filled with the scenes of the Massacre, they describe as a raging beast[5]. Their stopping short may be accounted for partly by the fact that they lived in a monarchical country, and hoped for more from the accession of the Protestant candidate with large prerogatives than from the uncontrolled expression of the will of the people, and partly because they had, as it were, to begin further back in the agitation for reform and to fight for much that their English colleagues had obtained long before. And, finally, we must remember that the Huguenots were unquestioning disciples of Calvin. The great movement of Independency in religion, which was to Calvinism what Calvinism was to Catholicism, only grew up in the interval between the civil wars of France and the civil wars of England.

[1] Cp. the League Manifesto of 1583, Ranke's *Französische Geschichte,* I. 294, 5.
[2] Haag, *La France Protestante*, Art. 'Languet.'
[3] Baudrillart's *Bodin,* 63.
[4] Cp. Louis Blanc, *La Révolution Française*, I. 84.   [5] Belua.

G   2

III

In both the great schools of political thought of the Middle Ages, the Imperialists and the Ultramontanes, championship of some form of popular rights may be detected[1]. Though the jurists who rallied to the cause of Louis of Bavaria are usually described as the earliest democratic thinkers of modern Europe, they pleaded, with the exception of Marsilio[2], more for the claims of the king than of the people, and, so far from being the founders of the theory of the sovereignty of the people, were the authors of the doctrine of divine right[3]. It is indeed the writer of the *Defensor Pacis*, Leopold of Babenberg and Nicolas of Cusa, alone of those who may be called the secular thinkers, who claim a place in the history of liberal political thought[4].

Some theory of popular rights again is often to be met with in the writings of the Curialists and Ultramontanes. Aquinas, for example, declared that a king who betrays his trust loses his right to obedience, and that it is not rebellion to depose and kill one who is himself a rebel. But though this be their undoubted right, the Angelic Doctor thinks the people's interest best served by so diminishing the royal prerogative that it cannot be abused, and therefore counsels a limited or elective monarchy, an aristocracy of merit, and a certain mixture of democracy which allows all

[1] Bezold's 'Lehre von der Volkssouveränetät während des Mittelalters,' *Sybel's H. Z.* Band 36; Gierke's *Althusius*, Kap. 3; Jourdain's *Excursions Historiques et Philosophiques*, 511–59.

[2] *Defensor Pacis*, especially Bk. I. 12, 13; in Goldast's *Monarchia*, vol. II.; cp. Riezler's *Literarische Widersacher des Papstes*.

[3] Figgis' *Divine Right of Kings*, ch. 3.

[4] The author of *Somnium Viridarii*, of course, belongs to the number; Goldast, II. 107–11, etc.; but it was only a pamphlet, though an influential one.

posts to be filled by popular choice. Three hundred years later Lainez, the spokesman of the newly founded Order of the Jesuits at the Council of Trent, reaffirmed the doctrine that all power springs from the people, and added that, although it be shared among the officers of the State, the community did not thereby deprive itself of it[1]. The logical issue of this attitude is of course that there is no finality about any form of government.

The march of events in France gradually led to teaching of a similar character becoming the political creed of a large number of Catholic publicists[2]. The death of Alençon, by bringing within sight the accession of Henry of Navarre, opens the third period of the political teaching of the Civil Wars, as the Massacre had opened the second. Did not the theories of the Huguenots furnish arms to the Catholics, who formed the majority of the people, for the exclusion of Henry of Navarre and the election of Guise? In the midst of the fight they exchanged rapiers, affairs, in Bayle's phrase, having pirouetted, and forgot their antecedents of yesterday. The democracy of the League, declares its historian, equalled and perhaps surpassed the democracy of the Huguenots[3].

By his ability, his learning, his ceaseless activity and his immense influence, Boucher stands out from the ranks of his fellows[4],

---

[1] Ranke, 'Zur Geschichte der politischen Theorien,' *Abhandlungen und Versuche*, 227. [On the Jesuits and their political views cp. Figgis in *Proceedings of Royal Historical Society*, 1900. H. J. L.]

[2] There is little of it in the League Manifesto of 1576, D'Aubigné's *Histoire Universelle*, v. 101; and it was of course never shared by the Politiques. Their position was clearly stated by Pasquier, *Œuvres*, ii. 128, 635–7, etc.

[3] Labitte, *La Démocratie chez les Prédicateurs de la Ligue*, LXXIV., and *passim*. This excellent monograph fully deserves the eulogy of Sainte-Beuve, Lenient, and indeed, all its critics.

[4] 'Un borgne gouvernait tout Paris comme un petit roi.' L'Estoile, *Journal*, v. 49.

and his attack on Henry III contains the summary of his philosophy. The cry that the king is subject to no laws is detestable[1]. It is also unreasonable, for kings are made by the people, who retain the supreme power, and are set up for public convenience. For this reason, the people possess the right of life and death over the king, since violators of public faith are unworthy to rule. But no more is the rabble to be supreme[2]: the true majesty of the State is to be looked for in the Orders and the Estates[3].

During the composition of the work the author witnessed the execution of the project it suggested. The coincidence was so remarkable that Boucher was commonly considered to be joint author with Clément of the assassination itself[4]. But whether or not the scheme sprang so directly from his brain, there can be no question that the incident may be traced to the teaching of which he, D'Orléans and Lincestre were only the most distinguished exponents. In order to compass their purpose they were driven into maintaining the sovereignty of the people and supporting the elective principle. As far indeed as actual theory goes, there is no reason to suppose that the preachers of the League had convictions different from those of the Curialists of the Middle Ages, since their objects were in great measure the same. But whereas it was found sufficient in the former case to declare the offence of the king against the Church without a hint that he had broken faith with the people, in the later period even the fanatical Boucher himself is compelled to fortify his position by declaring that the people are the masters, and that it is their right

---

[1] *De Justa Abdicatione Henrici III*, ed. 1589, I. c. 3.

[2] 'De confusa turba quae belua multorum capitum est,' *De Justa Abdic.* I. c. 9.

[3] III. c. 8.

[4] Bayle, *Boucher*. The preachers however compared it to the glories of the Incarnation and Resurrection. L'Estoile, v. Août, 1589.

and duty to make use of their sovereignty. The Ultramontanes were at bottom pure indifferentists in political philosophy, and attacked and championed rival theories in turn as it suited their purpose. It is not therefore as a genuine expression of radicalism that the teaching of Boucher and his brother-preachers is of importance, but in the testimony it bears to the influence of the Huguenot philosophy. For had not some form of democratic thought been in the ascendant, the opportunists would never have become its champions. And far from ending with the League, it spread from France through Europe, and passed from sermons into treatises.

The *De Rege* of Mariana presents in its most systematic form the radicalism of the Ultramontanes. Its author[1] was a man of wide culture and deserved his reputation of being the chief of Spain's historians. Moreover the book, appearing with the flattering imprimatur of the Provincial[2], came with the whole weight of the Order of the Jesuits behind it.

Alone of the theorists of the century Mariana discusses the origin of Society, and anticipates Hobbes in his description of the State of Nature. Civil society springs from the failings of mankind[3]. Despite the announcement in the title of the second chapter that the government of one is the more excellent, the author declares that, though under monarchy order is better preserved, the difficulty of keeping within bounds one who wields the power of life and death and has force at his disposal is very serious. But though a monarchy often degenerates into tyranny, he considers that its advantages are as a whole outweighed by the unity of its

---

[1] Ribadeneira, *Bibl. Script. Soc. Jesu*, 476, 7, ed. 1676.
[2] Ed. 1605. 'Noster Regem iis moribus, iis praeceptis instruit quae eo loco digna sunt.'
[3] 1–17.

policy. Mariana is indeed no more a republican than were the Huguenots. If monarchy there must be, in the next place, shall it be hereditary and elective? Originally, as was natural enough, those who were to rule over all were chosen by all[1]. But degeneracy set in, writes the author, sliding over the awkward break between the age of reason and the age of the Philips, and the best form that can now be devised is a union of both. If therefore the public weal dictates the preference of some member of the family not in the direct line, there is no reason why the substitution should not be effected. But hereditary rule may be as popular as any other form of government, and the ruler may be questioned and if unreasonable deposed; for no prince has ever been entrusted with so much power that the people have not retained still more[2]. If the oppressor be in addition an usurper, philosophers and theologians concur in teaching that he may be assassinated without the formalities of an express consent from the citizens[3]. The lawful king, in like manner, after neglect of warning, subjects himself to the chances of retaliation. For why should the public interest or the inviolability of religion be endangered by a single man[4]?

The details of Mariana's work strengthened the impression which, from its representative character and the fame and ability of its author, it would in any case have produced. It was not the enunciation of the sovereignty of the people nor of the right of deposition that startled the world, but the concession of the privilege of vengeance to the individual. Although writers of both Churches were in agreement as to the right of slaying a tyrant,

[1] *De Rege*, c. 3.
[2] 'Respublica ita in principem jura potestatis non transtulit ut non sibi majorem reservavit potestatem,' 57.
[3] c. 7.   [4] 59.

and many approved the deposition of a lawful king, no Protestant
had ever hinted at the lawfulness of regicide for any individual
who persuaded himself that it was deserved. The preachers of
the League had, of course, approved it; but they implicitly confined the authorisation to religious grounds. But Mariana, though
his teaching was purely sectarian, does not explicitly narrow its
application to any particular field.

The reception of the *De Rege* reveals the extent to which
ultra-democratic notions had ramified in the Catholic Church.
The book was openly bought in the streets of Paris. The first
noteworthy attack came from Coton, the Jesuit Confessor of
Henry IV, in 1606, and a meeting in Paris in the same year
disowned the teaching with equal decision[1]. The famous *Anti-
Coton* thereupon hurled back a collection of the political utterances of the Jesuits, proving that the tenets which Coton disclaimed on behalf of his Order were held by its most illustrious
spokesmen. Despite the serried mass of quotations, Coton repeated
his denial, which was confirmed by other writers. The issue of
the second edition in Mainz, in 1605, brought the book pro-
minently before the Protestant critics, and the reapplication of
its chief theory in 1610 once more concentrated attention on
Jesuit teachings[2]. Even if Ravaillac did not say he had drawn
his inspiration from Mariana, he appealed to Jesuit doctrines
with which, though in all other branches of knowledge utterly
ignorant, he was sufficiently familiar. The Parlement at once
burnt the *De Rege*, and the University did its utmost to muzzle
Jesuit teachers. The immediate effect of this outburst of indig-

---

[1] [More remarkable even than Coton's defence of his Order is the *Anti-
Mariana* of Michel Roussell (1610), and there is material of great importance in Godefroy's *Mercure Jesuite*, Part I. (1631). H. J. L.]

[2] Cp. Sarpi's *Lettere*, II. 105.

nation was that the General felt himself compelled authoritatively to disclaim the principle of tyrannicide. None the less, a few years later, the doctrine was again proclaimed with unabated vigour[1].

Closely related to, though independent of, the peculiar tenets of Mariana, was the teaching in relation to the English oath of allegiance. As long ago as 1583 Cardinal Allen had hurled back Burleigh's charge of treason. But with the rise of the League, the same revolutionary transformation of thought takes place in England as occurred along the whole line. The Gunpowder Plot marks the triumph of the new politics. The equivocations of Garnet were promptly extolled by Bellarmine. To this 'blowing of the bellows of sedition' the English Solomon rejoined[2]. The controversy reached its height in 1609–11, and nearly the whole of Europe was involved in it[3].

Of any independent and disinterested belief in the sovereignty of the people, or in the wider principles of liberalism, we may acquit the heated spirits of the sixteenth and seventeenth century Ultramontanes. The reference, implicit where not explicit, to sectarian interests paralyses the effectiveness of the plea. It would not be true to say that they positively disbelieved in the propositions of which they became the temporary champions. The conflict of opinion proves that the Order as a whole neither be-

[1] Backer's *Bibliographie de la Compagnie de Jésus*, V. 559, 60; Bayle, *Mariana*, Note H; Jeremy Taylor's 'Sermon on the Anniversary of Gunpowder Plot,' *Works*, VI. 581–605. Cp. Krebs' *Politische Publizistik der Jesuiten*, 40–68; and above all, Reusch's 'Lehre vom Tyrannenmorde,' in his *Beiträge zur Geschichte des Jesuitenordens*.

[2] James' *Works*, 259–85.

[3] Krebs, 139–68; Reusch, *Der Index der verbotenen Bücher*, II. 327–41; Döllinger's *Bellarmin*, etc. [On the Oath of Allegiance and the controversy it aroused the best discussion is C. H. McIlwain's Introduction to his reprint of the *Political Works of James I*. H. J. L.]

lieved nor disbelieved in them[1]. In comparison with the importance it attached to the triumph of Ultramontanism, every other
cause paled. At once pure indifferentists and acute opportunists,
its members caught up the first weapons that came to hand. That
the discussion of Mariana's teaching confined itself to the acceptance or rejection of his more extravagant propositions shews how
little attention was paid to the broader features of his system.
The controversy on the oath of allegiance, confining itself in
like manner to a single aspect of the relation of subject and
sovereign, confirms the impression that this school of thinkers
almost wholly neglected the disinterested consideration of political
principles. Their chief importance lies in the fact that they gave
further currency to a set of opinions that had been gathering
strength for half a century.

It would be difficult to exaggerate the closeness of the connection between the opinions that we have been studying and
those with which we shall now have to deal. The political ideas
to which the religious wars in France had given rise continued
to circulate in England long after they were forgotten on the
Continent. The writings of the Huguenots were studied and
quoted by the forerunners of the great democratic thinkers of
the middle of the seventeenth century, and were to become in-
timately known to those thinkers themselves. The pages of the
Ultramontanes, again, were continually searched by Protestant
controversialists, and by those eager to discredit the positions of
their Puritan opponents by exhibiting their similarity to the
contentions of the hated Jesuits.

[1] Tyrannicide is not among the charges of the *Lettres Provinciales*.

CHAPTER II

The Growth of Democratic Ideas in England before the Seventeenth Century

I

THE more learned among the democratic thinkers of the seventeenth century were as well aware of their debt to their English as to their continental predecessors.

The earliest writer to whom reference is made by the adherents and opponents of later democracy is Wyclif[1]. And indeed Wyclif set in motion a number of ideas which were not only revolutionary in themselves but were charged, and with some reason[2], with connection with the first great uprising of the people in English history. In the *Civil Lordship* we read that the righteous man is lord of the world, not only spiritually but actually[3]. But there are many righteous, and the universe must therefore be held in common. No title, hereditary or elective, furnishes a sufficient basis for lordship without the possession of Grace. The good man, however, is not at liberty to claim what he does not possess; he may not disobey the civil ruler because he is unworthy. Christ Himself yielded obedience[4]. But the *De Officio Regis* tells

---

[1] A Dr Creighton, writing in 1650, attributed all the heresies and treasons of the time to his teaching, Cal. Clar. S. P. III. 90; cp. Barclay, *De Regno et Regum Potestate adversus Monarchomachos*, ed. 1600, 167, 8; and Bossuet, *Variations*, Livre VI. § 156.

[2] Lechler will not allow any connection whatever, *Wyclif and his Predecessors*, II. 226–9. The case is more fairly stated in Poole's *Illustrations of Mediaeval Thought*. [See also H. B. Workman's masterly *John Wyclif*, 1926. H. J. L.]

[3] *De Civili Dominio*, ed. 1884, c. 7–13.   [4] c. 28

us that the king is nevertheless strictly bound to observe justice[1], and that if he become a tyrant he may be resisted, provided there is a reasonable hope of the opposition proving successful[2].

Not only were Wyclif's political works written before the revolt of 1381, but such an application of his teaching never occurred to him. Ball, however, declared that he had sat at the feet of Wyclif for two years and learnt his heresies from him[3], and the historians of the time attribute his opinions to the same source[4]. At any rate, the leaders of the Peasants' Revolt of 1381 were the first to apply socialistic theories to actual affairs. Efforts have been made to prove that they were men of studiously moderate views[5]. And indeed it is impossible to believe the story of Walsingham[6] that Wat Tyler desired the execution of all persons connected with the law, on the ground that after their death a plebiscite would be able to arrange all things afresh. But there is no reason to suppose that such were not the wishes of the more hot-headed of his followers; and Jack Straw's[7] confession, whether genuine or extorted, admitting the intention of killing the king and rooting out the propertied classes[8], might doubtless have been signed by many. But the most authentic relic of the philosophy of the insurrection is the sermon of John Ball at Blackheath, partially preserved by Walsingham[9]. Taking

[1] Ed. 1887, c. 4.
[2] *De Civili Dom.* c. 28, 'Si esset verisimile hominibus per subtraccionem temporalis juraminis destruere potestatis tyrannidem vel abusum, debet ea intentione subtrahere,' p. 201.
[3] *Fasciculi Zizaniorum*, 273, 'Per biennium erat discipulus Wyclif, et ab eo didicerat haereses quas docuit'; etc.
[4] Walsingham, II. 32, 'Docuit perversa dogmata perfidi J. W.'
[5] Maurice's *Ball, Tyler and Oldcastle.*
[6] I. 464, 'De Superbia W. T.'
[7] Walsingham, II. 9–10.   [8] 'Cunctos possessionatos.'
[9] II. 32–4, 'De John Balle, Presbytero.'

as his text the well-known distich about Adam and Eve, he
went on to prove that in the beginning all were created equal
by nature, and that subjection had been introduced by oppression.
The time had now come once again to enjoy the liberty for
which they had so longed. By slaying their lords[1] and the lawyers, they would reach a liberty without inequalities of title, rank
or power. In place of the incitement to bloodshed, Froissart
substitutes an appeal to the king, which consorts better with the
character of the speaker[2].

In the seventeenth century Wyclif's works were lying forgotten in MSS. at Prague and Vienna. The earliest writer to
whom the apologists of the English revolution habitually appeal
is the great constitutionalist of the fifteenth century. There is
not much political philosophy in Fortescue; indeed, the constant
tendency of his work is to slide from general discussions into
criticism of the constitution or devising means for its amendment.
Nevertheless his significance in the history of English thought
is hardly diminished by the fact that he was only indirectly a
thinker at all. It was of great importance two centuries later
that our first exclusively political writer should have taken up a
position of liberal constitutionalism and conceded the fundamental
principle of democracy, the Sovereignty of the People. Kingly
power, he teaches, is good, though it was originated by wicked
men[3]. The best form of Monarchy is limited or 'politic[4].' For
no nation ever formed itself into a kingdom with any view but
thereby to enjoy what it had more securely than before[5]. Moreover, when God ordained the governing of the world, He created

---

[1] 'Majores.'
[2] Ed. Buchon, II. 156.
[3] 'De Natura Legis Naturae,' c. 10, *Works*, ed. Clermont.
[4] *Absolute and Limited Monarchy*, ch. 1; *De Lege Naturae*, cc. 23, 26.
[5] *De Laudibus Legum Angliae*, c. 14.

the Justice by which it should be governed[1], the Law of Nature, to which civil laws are only auxiliary[2]. To assist the sovereign in maintaining this law, a council should be given him, the members of which should only be displaced by the will of the majority[3].

The next mile-stone tells a very different tale. Whether the more revolutionary passages of the *Utopia* express More's real convictions it is of course no longer possible to decide. But it is beyond controversy that the publication of the story of Ralph Hythloday in 1516 opened the chapter of modern socialism. The importance of the book lies above all in the freedom with which it criticised the principles which nearly all political treatises assume. Undesirous of leading by a parade of axioms to a justification of the existing condition of things, it rested for the first time on the assumption that society might be conceived in some radically different form. While the Reformers were calling on the civil powers to arm against the down-trodden peasant of Germany, More was pleading the cause of the workers. The essence of his system, alone of writers before Winstanley, is that the author does not content himself with assigning the sovereignty to the people. Social and political arrangements are tested by the convenience and claims of the working-classes. The recognition of the community as a moral organism, the proclamation of the right and duty to work, the state organisation of production, the abolition of coinage,—each of the articles of his creed set a train of speculation in motion. It is surely extravagant to regard a work which is so remarkable as a mere intellectual exercise[4].

[1] *De Lege Naturae*, c. 38.   [2] *ib.* c. 5.
[3] *Absolute and Limited Monarchy*, ch. 15.
[4] Kett and his followers merely fought against enclosures. Russell, *Kett's Rebellion*. To call them Communists, with Froude, IV. 441, is to pretend to more knowledge than we possess.

II

The earliest English political writer produced by the Reformation was a dignitary of the Church. The little treatise of Poynet[1], bishop of Winchester, attracted a good deal of attention both on its appearance and subsequently, and is of great importance in the history of democratic thought. Half a century after publication, Gentilis thought it necessary to reply to it[2]. The Opposition of 1642 reprinted it before any other pamphlet. Moreover it was considered by John Adams[3] to constitute by itself the first period of English political thought, and pronounced by him to contain all the essential principles of liberty that were to be found in Sidney and Locke. Owing to the Fall of Man, says Poynet, God instituted a number of laws, among which was one that whosoever should shed the blood of man should forfeit his own life[4]. For not only are kings equally subject with all men to God's laws, but they are bound by positive laws, with which they may not dispense without the express permission of their authors[5]. Each command must therefore be carefully scrutinised, and, if it be cruel or evil, it is not to be performed at all. But how is a bad ruler to be treated? The Gentiles held it lawful to kill their tyrants, and Ehud and Jael are commended in Scripture. Besides if the Church may depose a pope, how much more may kings be deposed by the State. For all laws and usages testify that kings have their authority from the people. Above all, the Law

[1] *A Short Treatise of Politique Power.*

[2] Mohl's *Gesch. u. Lit. der Staatswissenschaften*, I. 334. [Tudor political theory awaits its historian. There is an interesting if hardly profound essay by L. Einstein, *Tudor Ideals*. McIlwain, *op. cit.*, draws attention to its importance in an appendix. We know, particularly, too little of the English monarchomachs, especially Robert Parsons. H. J. L.]

[3] *Works*, VI. 3, 4.   [4] Ed. 1642, T.P. vol. 154, c. 1.   [5] c. 3, 4.

of Nature, grafted in the hearts of men, 'taken, sucked and drawn
in out of Nature,' declares that it is natural to cut away an in-
curable member which, being suffered, would destroy the whole
body[1]. Ambition and guile being characteristics of princes[2], the
wise should suspect their promises and mistrust their words.

Scarcely less remarkable is the treatise, How Superior Powers
should be obeyed and wherein they may be lawfully and by God's
word resisted, the work of Christopher Goodman, once Lady
Margaret Professor, the companion of Knox at Frankfurt and
Geneva and his lifelong friend. In the gloomy months of 1558,
when Calais had fallen, the exiled divines, believing the people
at last ripe for insurrection, called on them to rise and throw off
their yoke[3]. Most men, writes Goodman, have taught the unlawfulness of disobedience in all cases, but what evils have come
on England lately through yielding to ungodly rulers[4]! It is the
duty of the Councillors to bridle the government; but if they
are cowardly, the common people may resist. It is not enough to
refuse obedience; it is both lawful and necessary actively to
withstand ungodly magistrates. When they become blasphemers
of God and oppressors of their subjects, they are no more to be
regarded as kings, but as private men, and are to be condemned
and punished by the Law of God[5]. Wyatt[6], to take an example,
was no rebel, but fought for a cause both just and lawful.

It is remarkable that, in these two political tracts, the theo-

---

[1] c. 6.　　　　　　　[2] p. 70.

[3] The Queen, as if the ordinary laws had no existence, proclaimed that
any one found in possession of the works of Knox or Goodman should be
executed by martial law; and, even after Mary's death, Goodman dared not
return to England for many years, so angry did her successor grow at the
very mention of his name. Zurich Letters, I. 21.

[4] Ed. 1558, 28-30.

[5] 191.　　　　　　　　　　　[6] 209-12.

logical issue is strictly subordinate to the wider claims and interests of the national life. The works of Poynet and Goodman
were of course in the first place inspired by the fact that Mary's
religion was not theirs; but the principles introduced to defend
the national religion are utilised to ensure the preservation of
every department of national well-being.

The accession of Elizabeth was the signal for the cessation of
political thinking. Sir Thomas Smith's *Commonwealth of England*
may be taken as representing the ordinary attitude of thoughtful
minds at that time towards the more general problems of politics[1].
'My map,' says Sir Thomas, 'is unlike Plato and Xenophon and
More,—feigned commonwealths such as never were nor shall be,
—vain imaginations, fantasies of philosophers, to occupy their
time and to exercise their wits[2].' We find, accordingly, little but
an account of the English constitution and its working. He recognises, indeed, that since governments should be fitted like
boots, mutations of governments are natural; but he considers
that innovation is always a hazardous matter, and recommends
obedience to the orders of a government which a man finds already established[3]. The old feudal views of land triumph over
the newer doctrines of popular right. A Commonwealth is a
society of which the members are united by covenants among
themselves; but labourers, poor husbandmen, copyholders, artisans,
merchants, and those that own no free land, have no account
made of them[4].

---

[1] Sir Thomas Chaloner's *De Republica Anglorum Instauranda* is of little
value. It presents the ordinary monarchical tenets of time, 221, etc. ed.
1579.

[2] *The Commonwealth of England*, 283, ed. 1633.

[3] p. 20, 8.

[4] 69. From the Catholics alone did anything of a different character
proceed. But from the authors of the *Treatise on the Succession* (Parsons

The conduct of the Parliaments of the reign, in the next place, exhibits the interesting spectacle of a stout determination to have their way on questions of importance combined with a tacit understanding that first principles shall be let alone. In replying to the first address she received, urging her to marriage, the Queen declared that such conduct did not become them, who were born her subjects, nor herself, considered as an absolute princess[1]. A few years later, the Commons were again chidden for 'mixing themselves with matters that did not appertain unto them[2].' A compact, however, to avoid closer definitions could not be maintained for ever, and in 1586 Wentworth asked a number of questions of fundamental importance. 'The want of knowledge of the liberties of this Council doth hold and stay us back....Is not this Council a place for any member freely and without the control of any or danger by the laws to alter any of the griefs of the Commonwealth[3]?' The Queen's answer was given in 1592, when the Lord Keeper informed the House that Liberty of Speech was granted 'in respect of the Aye or No, but not that everybody should speak what he listed[4].' It was repeated by Bacon in the great debate on Monopolies in 1601. 'For the prerogative of the prince, I hope I shall never hear it discussed. The Queen hath both enlarging and restraining power; she may set at liberty things restrained by Statute and may restrain things which be at

probably shared in its composition, Backer's *Bibliographie des Jésuites*, VI. 333, but cp. Oliver's *English Jesuits*, 162, 3) we can only expect the familiar Jesuit teachings. The opportunism is obvious (ed. 1643, 45, etc.); but when the popular Tudor is succeeded by the unpopular Stuart, every fragment of opposition teaching will be gathered up, and Parsons' *Tract* among the first. Clement Walker accused the army leaders of republishing it when they desired to 'put down Monarchy,' *Hist. of Indep.* I. 115; cp. Hacket's *Williams*, II. 201.

[1] Camden's *Annals*, 1559.   [2] D'Ewes' *Journals*, 135.
[3] D'Ewes, 411.   [4] D'Ewes, 469.

G

liberty[1].' The debate, however, ran so high that Cecil declared
he had never known such an occasion. And yet criticism, so great
was the skill of the Queen, never passed into hostility. The mutilated Stubbs was speaking for the vast majority of his countrymen
when he declared that 'he would rather lose both hands than fall
in his prince's thought for a subject suspect of doubtful loyalty[2].'
We must therefore inquire whether in the ranks of the new religious bodies any opposition that does not masquerade in the
trappings of loyalty is to be found.

III

While Mary sat upon the throne, democratic utterances had
been heard from members of the English Church; but from her
sister's accession they were heard no more. 'Our common teaching,'
wrote Jewel, in his *Apology*, 'is that we ought so to obey princes
as sent of God, and that whoso withstandeth them withstandeth
God's ordinance. And this is well to be seen both in our books
and in our preachings[3].' A similar philosophy was expounded in
the *Homilies*[4].

With those Churchmen who desired to modify and to inno-
vate, it was not very different. The malcontents before Cartwright, indeed, agitated for little more than an abolition of
vestments. The First Admonition to Parliament merely declared
that the combination of civil with ecclesiastical offices was against
the word of God, and protested that there was no intention of
taking away the authority of the civil magistrate[5]. Cartwright's
pamphlet went further, selecting the reading of prayers and

---

[1] *Occasional Works*, III. 26–8.
[2] Harrington's *Nugae*, I. 153, ed. 1804.
[3] *Apology*, Part 4.   [4] 'On Wilful Rebellion.'
[5] *Admonition to Parliament*, ed. 1572, unpaged.

homilies and the disuse of excommunication for special censure[1]. There was, however, no desire to meddle with the office of the magistrate, nor, indeed, with anything but the admonition and excommunication of the obstinate[2]. Some justices were desirous to have a quarrel with the Precisians, as they were called, for their conscience; but the author wished the government might find better subjects[3]. An organisation supplemental to that already in operation was outlined in the following year; but so little danger was seen in the movement that Travers was assisted by Burleigh in his candidature for the Mastership of the Temple. Cartwright himself strongly expressed his disapproval of the Marprelate Tracts, and, when Barrow blamed him for not leaving the Church, replied that separation was unjustifiable[4]. The few 'classes' that were formed had but a short life, and the party as a party disappeared about 1590[5].

But though the movement itself passed away without leading to disturbance, the dangers inherent in it were not unobserved. Though the Prophesyings had been regarded by certain prominent Churchmen as complementary, not antagonistic, to the work of the Church[6], their opinion of the Puritan movement was not

[1] *Second Admonition*, ed. 1572, pp. 21, 39, 47.   [2] *ib.* 3.
[3] *ib.* 26, 61. Cp. Bacon on the Controversies of the Church. 'They are charged as though they denied tribute to Caesar and withdrew from the civil magistrate the obedience they have ever performed and taught.' *Occasional Works*, I. 89.
[4] Hooker, however, saddled the malcontents with the indirect origination of separatists. 'The foolish Barrowist deriveth his schism by way of conclusion, as to him it seemeth, directly and plainly out of your principles. Him therefore we leave to be satisfied by you from whom he hath sprung.' *Ecclesiastical Polity*, Preface, chs. 8, 9. Cp. Sutcliffe's *Ecclesiastical Discipline*, 165, ed. 1591.
[5] Shaw, 'Elizabethan Presbyterianism,' *English Historical Review*, Oct. 1888.
[6] Strype's *Grindal*, 482–4, etc.

generally shared by the rulers in Church and State. 'All that these men tend towards,' wrote Parker to Burleigh, 'is the overthrow of all of honourable quality and the setting a foot a Commonwealth, or a popularity[1].' The Queen was of the same opinion: 'There is risen a sect of perilous consequences,' she wrote to James, 'who would have no kings but a presbytery....Suppose you I can tolerate such scandals[2]?' Moreover, a drama was being acted in Scotland that to the keen eyes of authority portended mischief. The influence of the teaching of the Scotch Reformers on the thinking of the seventeenth century was so considerable that we must look at it with some care.

Although the full tide of democratic thought in Scotland only begins to flow with the struggles of the Reformation, anticipations are not infrequent in earlier times. When the Pope declared against Bruce, the Scots replied that Providence, the Laws, and customs of the country and the choice of the people had made him their king, and that if he betrayed his country, they would elect another. They cared not for glory nor riches, but for that liberty which no man renounces till death[3]. Two centuries later, the national sentiment was again strongly expressed in John Major's *History of Britain*. In his discussion of the claim of Bruce he remarks that it is impossible to deny that a king holds from his people the right to rule, for no other can be given him. The people might therefore deprive their king of all authority,

---

[1] Strype's *Parker*, II. 323; cp. Sutcliffe's *Ecclesiastical Discipline*, 143–6.

[2] *Correspondence of Elizabeth and James VI*, 63, 4, C. S. There is a remarkable passage in Bancroft's *Dangerous Positions*. 'Hereby it shall appear to our posterity that if any such mischiefs shall happen, they were sufficiently warned,' 183, ed. 1593. Cp. Owen's *Herod and Pilate reconciled*, ed. 1610, 46–57. [Material of great importance in relation to the Puritans under Elizabeth will be found in Peel's edition of the *Second Parte of a Register*. See also A. F. Pearson, *Life of Thomas Cartwright*. H. J. L.]

[3] Cp. Barbour's *Bruce*, ed. Spalding Club, 54–6, 280–5.

when his worthlessness called for it, even if his legal claim was faultless, and might appoint another without any claim. In any ambiguity, the decision of the people should be final[1]. But the king is only to be deposed where it is indisputably best for the State[2]. The chief ground, however, on which Major may claim to be the 'first Scotch Radical,' as he has been dubbed by Masson, is found in his great pupils, Knox and Buchanan.

It is well known that Knox's acceptance of the doctrinal principles of the Reformation was very gradual. The development in his political philosophy was no more rapid. Writing in 1552, in the quiet days of Edward VI, to his congregation at Berwick, we are at the first stage[3]. 'Remember always that due obedience be given to magistrates, rulers and princes, without tumult, grudge or sedition. For however wicked they are in life, or however ungodly their precepts, ye must obey them for conscience' sake, except in chief points of religion, not pretending it by violence or the sword, but patiently suffering[4].' Two years later, in the beginning of Mary's reign, but before the horrors of persecution appeared, Knox, foreseeing what was shortly to follow, wrote to ask Bullinger whether it was necessary to obey a magistrate who enforced idolatry and condemned true religion, and whether one should join a 'religious nobility' in opposition. He received the vague reply that it depended on circumstances[5]. A third stage is reached in 1557 when, stirred to indignant horror at the auto-da-fés of Mary and Henry II, he champions the imprisoned

---

[1] 213–15, ed. Scotch Hist. Soc.; cp. 158–61.   [2] 215–20.
[3] In 1548 his teacher Balnave had written, 'Give thy prince his duty; and whatever he chargeth thee concerning temporals, inquire not the cause. Look not to his vices but to thy own. Disobey him not; howbeit he be evil, grudge not thereat but pray for him.' Hume Brown's *Knox*, I. 94, 5.
[4] Lorimer's *Knox Papers*, 259.
[5] *Works*, ed. Laing, III. 221–6.

Huguenots. 'To speak my conscience, the regiment of princes is this day come to that heap of iniquity that no godly man can brook office or authority under them. For in so doing he shall be compelled to oppress the pure. And what must follow hereof but that either princes must be reformed or else that all good men depart from their service and company[1]?' In the following year appeared the *Address to the Nobility of Scotland*. 'The common song,' writes Knox, 'is that we must obey our kings, be they good or bad, for God hath so commanded....But it is not less than blasphemy to say God commanded kings to be obeyed when they command impiety[2].' In the same year Knox blew the first *Blast of the Trumpet against the monstrous Regiment of Women*, especially of Mary, denying her right as a woman to the crown of England[3].

In the *Second Blast*, outlined directly afterwards[4], the final form of Knox's creed is reached. 'No oath or promise can bind the people to obey and maintain tyrants against God; and if they have ignorantly chosen such as after declare themselves unworthy of the regiment of the people of God, most justly may they depose and punish them.' It is hardly surprising that Elizabeth should have refused the dedication of Calvin's Commentaries on Isaiah, on the ground that such books were published in Geneva; for, as Cecil said, of all men Knox's name, if it was not Goodman's, was most odious at Court. And indeed Calvin's letter to Cecil[5], of January, 1559, and Beza's to Bullinger in 1566[6], shew how far Knox had outstripped his Genevan masters. From these principles Knox never flinched, and in his *History of the Reformation* they

---

[1] *Apology for the French Protestants imprisoned*, IV. 327.
[2] *Works*, IV. 496, 7.
[3] IV. 369, etc.
[4] IV. 539, 40.
[5] *Zurich Letters*, I. 34–6.
[6] *ib.* I. 131.

are constantly avowed. His famous discussion with Maitland[1] is a significant example. He was in the habit of praying for Mary, he informs us, in the following way: 'O Lord, if thy pleasure be, purge the heart of the Queen from the venom of idolatry and deliver her from the bondage of Satan.' The formula was hardly flattering, and Maitland remonstrated with him on its use and on his opposition to the Queen, reminding him that he had the most famous men in Europe against him. 'And with that[2] he began to read with great gravity the judgment of Luther, Melanchthon, Bucer and Calvin,' by which, however, Knox was not greatly affected. He had slowly groped his way to the position he held, believing it to be indicated by the principles of the Reformation itself. And it was to this position that his irresistible influence succeeded in bringing his Church and his country. The *Second Book of Discipline*, published in 1578, told a tale widely different from that of the first composed eighteen years before[3]. When Elizabeth asked the Scotch Commissioners on what grounds they had deposed their queen, they replied by a quotation from Calvin. It would have been more appropriate if they had selected a passage from the writings of Knox.

When Buchanan published his *De Jure Regni* in 1579, the battle in Scotland had been fought and won[4]. But in the history of political thought, and in actual influence on the period immediately following, Buchanan bulks more largely than Knox. This was the work that frightened Heylyn[5]; this was that 'criminal

[1] *Works*, II. 428–54.
[2] 442.   [3] Cp. Buckle, *History of Civilisation*, III. 97–9.
[4] The Scotch soldiers who fought in the armies of Henry of Navarre, and the French Protestants who settled in crowds in Scotland, reinforced the teaching of the bolder clergy. Michel's *Ecossais en France*, II. 117–28, etc.; James Melville, *Diary*, 314, 418, and *passim*.
[5] *Tracts*, 687.

book' of which, a century after its appearance, the royalist
historian of the Civil Wars could not speak without fear[1]. Denounced by Blackwood in 1581 and by Barclay in 1600, it remained dangerous enough to be burnt by the University of Oxford
in 1683[2]. The pupil of Major at St Andrews, the fellow-student
of Knox, the victim of Beaton, the heretic driven by persecution
to and from Bordeaux, Paris and Coimbra, the author of the
Detectio[3] could not fail to construct his theory at least in part
from his own experiences. But it is its author's European reputation rather than its originality of thought that gives the *De
Jure Regni* its unique importance.

The cause of human association was not merely utility, says
Buchanan, but one far more ancient and venerable, a far more
sacred bond of community, the instinct of nature[4]. The discords
of men, however, made it necessary to choose a king, the community corresponding to the human body, civil commotions to
diseases, and the king to a physician. In giving him the authority,
the people should prescribe the form of his government. The
king deriving his entire authority from the law, absolutism must
be opposed, since the Scripture expressly commands that wicked
men should be cut off, without any exception of rank. For when
Paul inculcated obedience to the higher powers, he did not prescribe the conduct of men living under different circumstances.

[1] Heath, *Chronicle*, 528.
[2] Ranke's judgment, 'Er bezieht sich bei weitem mehr auf positive
schottische Satzungen als auf allgemeine Menschenrechte,' was certainly
not that of the sixteenth and seventeenth centuries. *Abh. u. Versuche*, 225,
6. For instance, Barclay writes: 'Licet inscriptio libri est apud Scotos
tamen de jure regni illic disputat et rationum momenta extendit latius et
omnes omnino Reges comprehendit.' *De Regno*, 7.
[3] Hume Brown's *Buchanan*.
[4] Ed. 1680, 12.

If the king govern well he is to be obeyed, be he lawful king or usurper[1]. When Maitland in the Dialogue ejaculates that he seems unduly severe on kings, Buchanan replies that, in awarding his praise, he does not look so much to the form as to the equity of government[2]. And indeed this seems accurately to describe the moderate character of the treatise. The danger of the book, however, lay precisely in its applicability. Its teaching was of such a kind that circumstances could change it into radicalism without let or hindrance.

Despite the personal opinions of the young king, and despite the condemnation of the tenets of his old tutor which he extorted from a packed assembly, the principles of Knox and Buchanan became immoveably fixed in the mind of the people. Andrew Melville, after the death of Knox the most influential man in the Church, set the example of delivering lectures at St Andrews on the relation of the people and their rulers expressive of the same tendency[3], and informed the king that Knox and Buchanan were his best friends[4]. And the lament of King James to his son shortly before leaving his northern home shews that he recognised the hopelessness of stemming the tide. 'Some fiery-spirited men in the Ministry got such a guiding of the people in the time of confusion that, finding the gust of government sweet, they began to fancy a democratic form. And never was there a faction in my minority but they were of it. I was calumniated in their sermons not for any vice in me but because I was a king, which they thought the highest evil. For they told their flocks that kings and princes were naturally enemies to the Church[5].'

[1] 131.   [2] 23.
[3] McCrie's *Melville*, ii. 26.
[4] James Melville, *Diary*, 313.
[5] 'Basilicon Doron,' *Works*, 160, ed. 1616. Much violent talk was undoubtedly heard. A sermon was sent over to the Low Countries proclaiming

IV

Since the accession of Queen Elizabeth, a stream of Dutch refugees had flowed into England, among them Anabaptists, Familists, Mennonites and members of various other unorthodox religious bodies[1]. But their numbers being so small, their cohesion so imperfect, and their object merely that of finding an asylum, the foreign settlements offered no opposition to the ruling powers and created no alarm.

With the Brownists, on the contrary, it was very different. Robert Brown[2] had been a pupil of Cartwright, but finding his master's views too narrow, he endeavoured to organise churches in Cambridge, London, Norwich and other places, in accordance with his own[3]. On being expelled by the Bishop, he crossed over to Holland, and in 1582 published a series of works containing the first systematic statement of Independent principles. In his *Reformation without tarrying for any*, he urged that it was useless to wait till the civil power should undertake a reform. In his *Order for studying the Scriptures* he insisted that it was a sin not to avoid the ungodly communion of false Christians, especially of wicked preachers and hirelings. In his *Life and Manners of all true Christians*, he sketched the lines on which the reformation should be conducted[4]. The latter work contains the first defence

that all kings were the children of the devil, and that it was therefore idle to pray for James. Brandt's *Reformation in the Low Countries*, ed. 1720, I. 456.   [1] Camden's *Annals*, 1559, etc.

[2] Fuller's *Church History*, v. 62–70; Dexter's *Congregationalism*, 61–128; Hanbury's *Independents*, I. ch. 2.

[3] Thorndike considered Brown had been led to his democratic theories chiefly through the influence of Morel and Ramus in the English Universities. 'Right of a Church in a Christian State,' ch. 2, *Works*, A.-C. L. I. 445, 6.

[4] These three books were published at Middelburg. I quote from these editions, the only ones known. The two former are without paging.

written by an Englishman of a full measure of religious liberty, a generation before Busher and half a century before Roger Williams. Cartwright and Travers had insisted on the election of ministers by the congregation and on the sovereignty of the general body of the faithful. To these principles Brown added that the magistrate was to have no ecclesiastical authority whatever. This notion struck at the root of the idea of a National Church, and involved a complete separation between the domains of religion and politics. A Church consisted of 'true Christians united into a company, a number of believers who place themselves under the government of God and Christ[1].' All true Christians were kings and priests[2]. In civil matters Christians were to be obedient to their superiors, to 'esteem, honour and serve the magistrates[3]'; but the ideal of religious life was a voluntary association of individuals in a body independent of every other.

The significance of the scheme lay in the fact that the religious life of the individual centred in an organisation of a purely democratic nature. If any seven make a church, wrote Thorndike later, we are plainly invited to a new Christianity[4]. The thought of the Brownist became saturated with democratic principles. And, indeed, though the duties to superiors are set forth at length, it is on the assumption that they are chosen by the will of the people[5]. The implications of the teaching[6] were at once perceived, and several people suffered death for possessing the book, though, as Raleigh remarked in Parliament, it was impossible to punish them all[7].

[1] Brown, *Life and Manners*, 2.   [2] *ib.* 59.   [3] *ib.* 132–71.
[4] 'Principles of Christian Truth,' *Works*, A.-C. L. II. 152, 403.
[5] 115–17.
[6] The 'processes' of some Brownists are printed in the *Egerton Paper* 166–79, C. S. The tone is decidedly intransigent.
[7] D'Ewes' *Journals of Elizabeth*, 517. Cp. Camden, *Annals*, 1583.

Fuller consigns Brown to the grave with the pious wish that his opinions had been interred with him[1]; and for the moment it seemed that this was to be the case. In England, except for a little colony of Independents in Southwark, no organised non-conformity remained after the rise of Whitgift; and in 1592, Bacon could write 'they were, at their height, a very small number of silly and base people, here and there in corners dispersed, and now by the good remedies suppressed and worn out so that there is scarce any news of them[2].' These opinions, however, were too much in accordance with the spirit of the age to escape the most gigantic development. The case of Harrington, who let his son be educated by a Puritan 'to sicken him of Puritanism,' with the result that the lad joined the ranks of his teacher, was typical[3]. The development, however, proceeded along the lines laid down not by Brown but by Barrow. To the disciple it seemed that his master's teaching erred as much on one side as that of Calvin or Cartwright on the other. Relations of mutual sympathy and support between different congregations were by no means to be despised, and some degree of control by the pastors and Council of Elders should form an essential part of the Independent system[4]. What had proved impossible in England was put into practice in Holland ; and this migration was one of the principal factors of the democratic thought of the seventeenth century, involving as it did the inoculation of certain English religious bodies with Dutch ideas and Dutch ideals.

[1] v. 70.   [2] 'Observations on a Libel,' *Occasional Works*, I. 104–6.
[3] Harrington's *Nugae*, vol. I. Park's *Life*.
[4] Dexter, 131–202, was the first fully to indicate Barrow's importance; Hooker, however, had already identified the sectaries with the name of Barrow, not of Brown. *Ecclesiastical Polity*, Preface, ch. 8. [The text here is probably too strong; cp. Burrage, *The Early History of the Dissenters* ; R. G. Usher, *The Rise and Fall of the High Commission.* H. J. L.]

The United Netherlands, by their recent history and their actual condition, formed an object-lesson the significance of which it was impossible to overlook. A nation had solemnly deposed its king and had issued a Declaration of Independence, basing the justification on the breach of contract by the sovereign[1]. Undaunted by the efforts of the strongest monarchy and the most skilful generals in the world, the inhabitants of a small district had triumphed over the oppressor and were now enjoying the fruits of their victory. And there were many reasons for England to turn her eyes in that direction.

What served to arouse interest and admiration more than perhaps anything else was the almost incredible prosperity of the country. From the time that Gresham sent home glowing accounts of the opulence that met his gaze[2], report had followed report. Guicciardini's enthusiastic work appeared in an English dress[3], and the story was re-told by Fynes Moryson[4]. Raleigh could hardly find words to express his admiration for the enterprise of the people who 'of nothing màde great things,' or his dismay at the inferiority of his countrymen[5]. Works composed by or relating to the Dutch quickly found translators and readers[6]. In 1618 the Venetian ambassador wrote that there was not a single person who was not in comfortable circumstances[7]. And these happy

[1] Gachard, *Études sur l'histoire des Pays-Bas*, vol. II. *La Déchéance de Philippe II.*

[2] Burgon's *Gresham*, I. 377–91, etc.

[3] Ed. 1593, especially 60–73.

[4] *Itinerary*, 93–8, 283–91.

[5] 'Observations concerning Trade and Commerce with the Hollanders, *Works*, vol. VIII., especially 356–75.

[6] Chamberlain's *Letters*, 19, C. S.; *Stationers' Registry*, vol. 3, *passim*.

[7] Pringsheim's *Wirthschaftliche Entwickelung der Niederlanden*, 61. Even Winwood was forced to admit the prosperity: Winwood's *State Papers*, I. 362, 3.

circumstances became connected in many minds with the principle of self-government which was applied in every department of the national life. Many years later, Hobbes enumerated the envy of the Dutch cities as one of the causes of the English revolution. 'London and other towns of traders, having in admiration the great prosperity of the Low Countries, after they had revolted from their monarch, were inclined to think the like change of government here would produce like prosperity[1].'

Of great importance, in the second place, was the religious condition of the Low Countries. At the time when the English colonies were planted, Calvinism had triumphed both in dogma and discipline. In the majority of states it was determined that the limits of religious liberty should be narrow[2]; but in Holland, above all in its capital, a more liberal spirit prevailed[3]. Such limitations as there were, however, did not exclude the various bodies that had grown up outside the national church, such as those of Menno, Nicolas and David George. Being unmolested themselves and seeing many different sects co-existing in a flourishing Commonwealth, the settlers were led insensibly to the formation of tolerant opinions[4]. In the work which repre-

[1] Hobbes, *Behemoth*, 1.; cp. Howell's *Dodona's Grove*, 19, T. P. vol. 19, and the remarkable passage in Crashaw's Sermon before the Lord Lawarre, Governor of Virginia: 'are not the Hollanders become for their valour, government, wealth, power and policy, even the wonder of nations?' 49, 50, ed. 1610.

[2] Dudley Carleton's *Letters*, 1616–20, 42 and *passim*.

[3] Even here, however, it was not perfect. Brandt's *Reformation in the Low Countries*, II. 15, etc.

[4] The Scotch Presbyterians sometimes attended Independent services. Stevens' *Scotch Church of Rotterdam*, ch. 1. The crusade against the Arminians was in large measure political. The Catholics, who were about half the population, lived for the most part unmolested: Motley's *Barneveldt*. The only important exceptions were the Jansenists: Neale's *Jansenist Church of Holland*, ch. 5.

sents the best mind of the country, a liberal religious policy is supported on grounds of political and economic advantage[1].

But there was a third lesson to learn. It was inevitable that the struggle should lead in Holland as elsewhere to a discussion of political principles. The youth of the country were instructed in democratic principles from the chairs of Danaeus and Franciscus Junius in the new University at Leyden[2]. The courtly Leicester was shocked by the talk and methods of his allies[3]. But it was not until the work of Althusius, a German Calvinist, that a reasoned defence of their action was forthcoming; for though the principles of freedom were chanted in the hymns and embodied in a constitution by St Aldegonde[4], he produced no political treatise, while Lipsius in renouncing his Protestantism renounced also such liberal principles as he had ever professed[5]. The *Politica methodice Digesta* appeared in 1603, and was largely rewritten for the second edition of 1610[6]. The novelty of the work is to be found less in the teaching of the Sovereignty of the People, or of the Social Contract, or of the Separation of Powers, than in the republican framework into which he builds the democratic ideas which were common property. Unlike that of Mariana and Hobbes, Althusius' theory of the origin of society lays the basis of a truly popular system. Man is born for Society[7]. The efficient cause of political association lies in the compact of the citizens; but the final cause is the convenience and well-being of the

---

[1] *Mémoires de Jean de Witt*, pt. 1. ch. 9.

[2] Siegenbeck's *G. der Leidsche Hoogeschool*, I. 34, 35, 54.

[3] *Leicester Correspondence*, 312, 367, etc. C. S. Cp. Motley's *United Netherlands*, II. 115–35.

[4] Quinet's *St Aldegonde*, 45–95.

[5] Lipsius' *Politica* is at once a counsel to rulers and an attack on the people. See especially 67–70, 200, 201, ed. 1594.

[6] Gierke's *Althusius*, 1–36.

[7] Ed. 1610, c. 1.

community. Each province has its ecclesiastical and secular estates, and the entire country forms a confederation[1]. The government is shared between the supreme magistrate and the ephors, who choose, watch and if necessary depose the chief magistrate[2]. The justification of opposition is to be found primarily in the nature of the compact, no obligation lying on the subject to obey any exercise of power other than that expressly granted to the ruler[3]. Besides, the ephors are specially constituted to prevent him from not exceeding his rights. For the People and the Ephors are greater than he whom they have set up. Without this defence against tyranny, the license of the ruler would go beyond all limits. He may be slain when in defiance of all law he is accomplishing the destruction of the state, provided other remedies are not to be found[4]. And yet, as in all thinkers before the English revolution, Althusius, with all his confidence in 'The People,' has but scanty respect for the Plebs. Democracy seems to him to detract from the dignity and majesty of the State[5]. The representatives are to be chosen only among the influential and wealthy in order that their attachment to the public weal may be beyond suspicion. As a whole the system is aristocratic[6]. But in the concatenation of political ideas, the aristocratic superstructure is easily lost sight of and the democratic substratum easily borrowed.

To a place in the development of democratic thought, Grotius,

---

[1] c. 7.   [2] c. 13.   [3] c. 38, p. 658, etc.

[4] 'Uno in casu interfici jure potest, quando furiose spretis omnibus legibus exitium regni molitur, atque alia remedia non dantur,' 678. His authority was of course quoted to justify the execution of Charles I. Canne's *Golden Rule*, 11, T. P. vol. 543; *The Original and End of Civil Power*, anon., 22, T. P. vol. 554.

[5] c. 23, 'De natura populi,' gives fullest expression to his views.

[6] The less liberal elements are repeated and exaggerated in his disciple Boxhorn. Beauverger's *Tableau de la philosophie politique*, 81–94.

like Hobbes and Spinoza, has only an indirect claim. His teaching is full of inconsistencies. Yet no thinker who starts with the sociability of human nature[1] issues in absolutism. No writer who finds the origin of Natural Law in human nature, in right reason and in the will of God, who maintains that God Himself cannot change it[2], who believes that its tenets may be discerned with hardly less precision by the mind than external objects by the senses[3], and who teaches that positive law should be dictated by Natural Law, can logically construct a system in which human activities will not find free play. No writer who declares that nations as well as individuals are bound to act justly, and that liberty of conscience is a right, can approve a State where the general well-being is sacrificed to the vices of an individual. The appeal to moral axioms must in the long run lead to a liberal theory of politics.

Man's principal characteristic and privilege, declares Grotius, is freedom, and the form of government may therefore be chosen by the people[4]; and all agree that sovereigns are not to be obeyed when they order anything contrary to Natural Law or God's commands[5]. We are not bound to watch in silence the violation of laws which the ruler has sworn to observe, nor the alienation of national territory, nor to suffer a government notoriously adverse to the public welfare. Such a ruler may be deposed and even killed[6]. Again, in a mixed government it is even more the duty than the right of each branch to maintain its share of power[7]. It is yet more surprising to learn that communism was

---

[1] *De Jure Belli et Pacis*, Prolegomena, § 6.
[2] I. i. § 10, § 16.   [3] § 39.   [4] I. i.
[5] 'Illud quidem apud omnes bonos extra controversiam est si quid imperent juri aut divinis praeceptis contrarium, non esse faciendum quod jubent.' I. iv. § 1.
[6] I. iv. §§ 8 and 10.   [7] I. iv. § 13.

the primitive condition of the human race; that it is, in addition, conformable to Natural Law; and that the system of private property is a pure convention, only guaranteed by the tacit consent of the community[1]. Several isolated phrases and sentiments of a contrary tendency, however, are to be found. Despite the expression of his conviction of the certainty of Nature's Law, Grotius seems to have felt that it might be wiser to confine his authorisation of resistance to cases where the positive law was attacked. Yet his influence was in the main democratic. It is significant, for example, that when the Civil Wars broke out in England, though the sympathies of Grotius were with the king[2], his authority was adduced in one of the earliest vindications of the right of resistance[3], and that he figures among the teachers of rebellion in the *Holy Commonwealth* of Baxter[4].

But before the exiles and refugees were to return to their homes and put in practice the lessons they had learned, a steadily increasing number of their countrymen were being led by misgovernment to the adoption of similar principles.

[1] I. i. § 10, and II. ii.
[2] In December, 1642, he wrote to his brother, 'Regi Angliae opto prosperiora, tum quia rex est, tum quia bonus rex.' *Grotii epistolae*, 946.
[3] *Jus Populi*, 17, T. P. vol. 12.
[4] 466–70, T. P. vol. 1720.

CHAPTER III

The Growth of English Democracy during the first forty Years of the Seventeenth Century

I

A<small>T</small> the accession of James political thinking still retained what may be called an Elizabethan character[1]. Of the three men who meditated most seriously about the deeper principles of politics, Bacon, Lord Brooke and Raleigh, not one ventured beyond the bounds of conservative constitutionalism.

Bacon's Essays on 'Seditions and Troubles' and on the 'True Greatness of Kingdoms and Estates' proclaim noble principles; but those on King and Nobility set forth a very comprehensive scheme of absolutism. In the *Advancement of Learning* he assures James that if he were to live for a thousand years, he should never be tempted to disagree with the philosophy of the *True Law of Free Monarchies*[2]. Speaking on the Essex Trial he remarked that, though subjects were given cause of discontent by princes, they ought not to enter on any undutiful act, much less rebellion[3]. Again, though ready to grant that a republic might be 'a better policy' than a kingdom, the change from the latter to the former was not to be thought of[4]. Yet Bacon believed in the organic unity of king and people. His desire was to see 'the civil state purged and restored by good and wholesome laws

---

[1] [On the general evolution of English Political thought see G. P. Gooch, *Political Thought from Bacon to Halifax; Social and Political Ideas of the Sixteenth and Seventeenth Centuries*, ed. by F. J. C. Hearnshaw. H. J. L.]

[2] Book 2, xxi. 8.

[3] *Occasional Works*, II. 227.

[4] *ib.* I. 85, cp. IV. 177.

made every third or fourth year in Parliaments assembled, devising remedies as fast as time breedeth mischiefs[1].'

Lord Brooke, in a similar way, never ventures beyond a strictly constitutional position. Monarchy is of course the best form of government[2], but the 'overracked unity' of Spain is not good. Its sway should not extend to soul as well as body[3]. For that indeed is no true Monarchy which makes Kings more than men, men less than beasts[3]. Democracy, on the other hand, is a name of contempt with Lord Brooke.

> How can the democratical content,
> Where that blind multitude chief master is ?[4]

It debases men's minds and manners and 'eclipses all the arts of civility[5].' And the danger of popular inundations is never old[6].

Much the same ideas meet us in Raleigh. Monarchy is the best regiment, as it resembles the sovereign government of God[7]. A commonwealth, on the contrary, is the government by the common and baser sort without respect of the other orders. The truly Free or Popular State is the government of 'the choice sort of the People,' who in another work[8] are defined to be the Members of Parliament. But Raleigh was an admirer of Holland and Venice[9], and the *History of the World* was called in by the king as being 'too saucy in censuring princes[10].'

---

[1] *Occasional Works*, III. 105. For the mass of the people, however, Bacon's contempt was undisguised. See the remarkable passage in his speech on deer-stealing, V. 88.

[2] *Works*, ed. Grosart, I. 'Treatise of Monarchy,' stanza 15.

[3] Stanza 209.   [4] Stanza 610.   [5] Stanza 612.

[6] *Life of Philip Sidney*, vol. IV. 56.

[7] 'The Prince, or Maxims of State,' in *Works*, vol. VIII.

[8] 'The Prerogative of Parliaments,' in *ib*. vol. VIII.

[9] VIII. 296, 356, 374, etc.

[10] Chamberlain to Carleton, *Court of James I*, I. 291. The reference is probably to the Preface, *Works*, II. 27–30.

There were, however, as we have seen, elements of discord. That the new king's views of the relations of Sovereign and People were of a kind little calculated to let sleeping dogs lie had already been proved by the *True Law of Free Monarchies* and the *Basilicon Doron*. And some of his earliest utterances proved that he had not departed from them[1]. Though sympathy with the Dutch was a national sentiment, the king used to maintain that they were rebels, being engaged in resistance to their lawful king[2]. He even declared that it was unfit for a subject to speak disrespectfully of any 'anointed king,' 'though at hostility with us[3].' Not content with writing books himself, he caused a work of suitable tendency to be composed for the benefit of the young, and gave special instructions to the Lord Mayor to circulate it[4]. When Parliament met, the king explained his theory of kingship, and took occasion to describe the Puritans as 'ever discontented with the present government, and impatient to suffer any superiority, which maketh the sect unable to be suffered in any well-governed commonwealth[5].' The Session itself was filled with petty squabbles, and at its close the Commons took occasion to present a counter manifesto, asserting that the king had been misinformed and that their privileges were not of royal grant. They were actuated, they said, by no Brownist spirit, and had even committed to the Tower the author of a petition which spoke disrespectfully of Bishops[6]. To this the king replied that,

[1] He struck a medal to commemorate his accession with 'Caesar Caesarum' under his effigy. *Scaligerana*, II. 540.
[2] Wicquefort's *Ambassadeurs*, 455, 6, ed. 1677.
[3] Wilkins' *Concilia*, IV. 405.
[4] Overall's *City Remembrancia*, 32.
[5] *Parl. Hist.* I. 982.
[6] *Parl. Hist.* I. 1030–43. 'Puritans were still very unpopular.' Manningham's *Diary*, 110, 156, etc. C. S. Cp. Bradshaw's *English Puritanism*, Introduction. 'The odious and vile name of Puritans.' Ed. 1605.

though he could not accuse them of disloyalty, he hoped they would use their liberties with greater modesty.

From Parliament James had heard political principles that shocked him by their audacity; but he was now joined by two notable allies. The Universities declared that to petition for changes, however small, was the mark of a rebellious spirit[1]. The same note was sounded by the clergy. 'In all state alterations,' complained Fuller, 'be they never so bad, the pulpit will be of the same wood with the Council-board[2].' Originating in the royal will and bound to the Sovereign by oaths and statutes, the Establishment might have been expected to exalt the king at the expense of the people[3]; but its teaching exceeded all expectations. The Homilies had taught that the King's power was from God alone; that, as it was a perilous thing to commit to subjects the judgment which prince was godly and his government good and which was otherwise, as though the foot should judge of the head, it was in no case lawful to resist, wicked though he might be[4]. The Canons of 1606[5] repeated the chief articles of this creed with an emphasis that caused them to be regarded by later generations as the fountain-head of the doctrine of absolutism[6]. Thus, a few years after the death of Elizabeth, the nation was divided into two camps, the King, the Church, and the Universities on one side, Parliament and the Puritans on the other.

At this moment began the championship of the Opposition creed by Coke. Hitherto Parliament had opposed the claims of

---

[1] Gardiner, I. 150, 1.   [2] *Church Hist.* IV. 153.

[3] This is very strikingly and almost cynically put by Jeremy Taylor, *Works*, VII. 23.

[4] Homily on Wilful Rebellion.

[5] Especially Book I. Canons 2 and 28, Overall's *Convocation Book*, 3, 51, A.-C. L.

[6] Welwood's *Memoirs*, 32–4, ed. 1820.

the king by assertions of its own, appealing to common knowledge for their truth; but the antagonist who now confronted
James was still more formidable. The true ruler of the kingdom
was not the king but the Law, to which the king was subject;
and what the Law declared was not a matter of assertion but a
matter of fact. Though Coke's claim logically implied not only
the rule of the Law but the rule of the lawyers, it was an immense
support to the popular party that the position they had assumed
was in the main conservative. Hot as was the indignation of
Bacon and the king at the attitude of Coke, they joined him in
denouncing the unblushing assertion of absolutist principles put
forward at this time by Dr Cowell[1]. But while the king desired
the offender to go unpunished, Parliament was anxious to record
its disapproval of the tenets by making a signal example of the
author[2]. The gulf was revealed anew in the question of Proclamations. Though the king admitted that the assent of Parliament was necessary to legislation, he was of opinion that by
Proclamation he could compensate himself for this impotence.
The Judges, on the other hand, declared that he could do no
more than admonish his subjects to keep the law that was already
in existence.

Irritated by repeated thwartings of his will and criticism of
his conduct, and exasperated by the failure of the negotiations
concerning what was called the 'Great Contract,' the king, after
suffering the Parliament for seven years, could bear with it no
longer, and pronounced its dissolution in 1611. 'Not for all the
treasure in the world,' said Bacon on behalf of his master, 'will
he quit any point of his just sovereignty, but will leave it sacred

---

[1] Cecil's Message, Debates of 1610, 22–4, C. S.
[2] ''Tis thought they will go very near to hang him.' Winwood's *State
Papers*, II. 125.

and inviolate to his posterity[1].' The claims of the king now became more extravagant than before. 'No foreign king or state,'
said Judge Whitelocke, 'could or did set on as the king of
England did[2].' 'The most religious,' wrote another critic gently,
'could wish that his Highness would be more sparing in using
the name of God and in comparing the Deity with the prince's
sovereignty[3].' On one occasion the king compared himself to a
mirror which might be defiled by the eyes of certain beholders[4].
In the new Parliament this theory of government was more
sharply opposed. So little was the hectoring speech of Neile to
the taste of the Commons that they refused to grant supplies
prior to the discussion of grievances, and at this elementary
demand for justice the king dissolved Parliament after a session
of two months, in which no Bill had been added to the Statute
Book. Excuses were shortly found for depriving Chief Justice
Coke of his post[5].

It was at this time that Bacon, in a New Year's letter to the
king, drew the following picture: 'I many times do revolve in
my mind the great happiness which God hath accumulated on
you. Your people military and obedient; fit for war, used to
peace. Your Church enlightened with good preachers, as heaven
with stars. Your judges learned and learning from you; just, and
just by your example. Your nobility in a right distance between
Crown and People; no oppressors of the People, no overshadowers

---

[1] *Works,* v. 25.   [2] Whitelocke's *Liber Famelicus,* 42, C. S.
[3] Nichols' *Progresses of James I,* ii. 286.
[4] *Parl. Hist.* i. 1149, 50.
[5] The king's method is well illustrated by his behaviour when the city
desired Whitelocke, an old enemy of James, as its Recorder. 'The aldermen
desired to know his pleasure, whether he would not give them leave to have
a free election. He answered Aye; but still pressed his commendations,
which he expected they should regard.' Whitelocke's *Liber Famelicus,* 66,
67, C. S.

of the Crown. Your servants in awe of your wisdom, in hope
of your goodness; the fields growing from desert to garden; the
City grown from wood to brick. Your merchants embracing the
whole compass of the earth. Lastly your excellent issue entaileth
these blessings and favours of God to descend to all posterity[1].'
But what the great Chancellor saw was seen by nobody else.

The foreign policy of the king was next to contribute its share
to the exasperation already aroused by his conduct towards Parliament, towards the Bench, and towards the religious sentiments
of the people. Since the death of Cecil, the Spanish ambassador
had seemed to occupy the place of Foreign Minister, and had
shaped the king's course in a direction profoundly distasteful to
the convictions of his subjects. The only foreign policy which
the people understood was opposition to the Catholic powers and
above all to Spain. When, therefore, the life of the last great
Elizabethan was sacrificed to the pleasure of the Spanish Court,
and when negotiations were undertaken for a definite alliance
and even the project of a marriage was mooted, the indignation
of the people knew no bounds. But more was to follow. When
events on the Continent soon after led up to the commencement
of a religious war, the strongest Protestant people in the world
saw their king not only refuse to go to the rescue of the champion
of their faith, who chanced to be his own son-in-law, but remain
in alliance with Spain. The Elector and his wife became the
heroes of the country, and when they were disrespectfully mentioned by Floyd, Parliament was so enraged that it took the law
into its own hands[2]. So high now rose the tide of national feeling
that Parliament declared itself ready to grant as much money as
would be needed to roll back the advancing tide of Romanism.

[1] *Works,* VI. 452, 3.
[2] *Parl. Hist.* I. 1250–62.

The king, however, had 'taken upon himself to be a mediator[1].'
Had he frankly taken the Commons into his confidence, explained
to them his own very reasonable policy, and asked their assistance
in its execution, the story of the latter years of his reign might
have been different.

Disappointed of effecting their object abroad, the Commons
fell upon the domestic abuses that had risen in rank growth.
Though no Act was placed on the Statute Book, some very plain
speaking was heard on the subject of Monopolies, and the right
of impeachment was revived. A heavy stroke was also aimed at
judicial corruption. But in the crowning event of the session, the
discussion of the right of freedom of speech, the king's brute
force again triumphed. The Protestation[2] was torn from the
Journals, Parliament was dissolved, and the leaders of the Opposition imprisoned. The words of the king's letter to the Speaker
seem to have been chosen expressly to insult the Commons.
'Certain fiery and popular spirits' had dared to debate and argue
publicly on matters 'far beyond their reach and capacity.' The
Speaker was therefore to acquaint them with the king's pleasure
that none should 'presume to meddle with anything concerning
our government mysteries of State[3].' The battle, however, was
only beginning. The problem of obedience was openly and boldly
discussed. Tillières, the French ambassador, told his Government
that none of the usual forerunners of civil war was absent[4]. From
an Oxford pulpit the doctrines of resistance on behalf of religion
were heard, and, though every copy of Pareus that could be
procured was burnt, the discussion continued[5]. In some of the

---

[1] *England and Germany in 1619*, 82, C. S.   [2] *Parl. Hist.* I. 1361.
[3] *Parl. Hist.* I. 1326, 7; cp. Bacon's draft of a Proclamation, *Works*, VII.
156, 7.   [4] In Raumer's *Briefe aus Paris*, Letters 64 and 65.
[5] There is a full account in the Letters of Vossius, 33, 4, ed. 1699. Cp.
Mullinger's *University of Cambridge*, II. 567.

earliest sermons of Sanderson the dangerous mood of the people
was noticed: 'We are discontented with our blessings; take care
God does not have to teach us to use and value them better[1].'
The servility of dramatists like Beaumont and Fletcher was
purely conventional, and did not reflect the sentiment of the
playgoers. It was not surprising that reverence for the kingly
office diminished with the waning of reverence for the king. In
the last year of his life, an English sovereign was for the first
time introduced on the stage in an indignant satire, to which
the public crowded every night till its representation was forbidden[2]. But there were other ways of expressing opinion. Proclamation followed proclamation against the sale of 'Seditious
and Puritan books[3],' and there was 'much talk of libels and
dangerous writings[4].'

Two points are borne in upon us by the study of the reign of
James I with overwhelming force. In the first place, if it had
been the intention of the king to alienate every class of the
community and to outrage the sentiment of every group of his
subjects, it would not have been necessary to act differently from
the way in which he acted. It is equally impossible not to feel
that after every fresh violation of a principle or a sentiment, the
evil effect could have been in large measure removed by abstain-
ing from acting in a similar way in future. The memory of the
people was so short, in other words, their loyalty was so ingrained

[1] Fifth Sermon ad Populum, *Works*, ed. 1854, IV. 193, 201, etc.
[2] Middleton's *Game of Chess*; Ward's *History of Dramatic Literature*, II.
93–102.   [3] Rymer, XVII. 616, etc.
[4] *Court and Times of James I*, II. 355. It was at this time that Ralph
Brownrigg, Fellow of Pembroke, invited several of his friends to his rooms
and asked them 'May the king, for breaking fundamental laws, be opposed?'
He was suspended from all his Degrees in consequence. Cooper's *Annals of
Cambridge*, III. 118, 19.

that, to use a homely expression, it was never too late to mend. Changes in the balance of power were rendered inevitable by the growth of wealth and intelligence and by the decline of the influence of the old nobility; but it was largely due to the king that the transition took the form of revolution instead of evolution. 'In the Parliaments of Elizabeth,' said Bacon naively, 'when she demanded anything, it was seldom denied[1].' By generous conduct, the king could at any moment have cancelled the accumulated store of discontent and hostility. It was only the rule of his successor that could make the intolerable vexations of the reign of James I seem light[2].

The new king soon learned that the contests which had filled his father's reign had not been buried in his grave. In the episode of Montagu the nation found in combination what it hated most, an Anglo-Catholic theology, an absolutist political philosophy, and the approbation of both by the sovereign. So hot was the indignation that even Laud, slow as he was to discover signs of the times, noted in his Diary his sense of coming danger[3]. 'Under the name of Puritans,' cried Pym wrathfully, 'he collecteth the greatest part of the king's true subjects[4].' Twenty years earlier, Parliament had expressly disowned the name[5], which indeed was rarely mentioned without abuse and contempt[6]. The tide had been flowing fast.

The Commons now flew at still higher game, and under the leadership of Phelips[7] so frightened the king that he thought it

[1] *Works*, v. 176.   [2] D'Ewes' *Autobiography*, I. 264, 5.
[3] *Works*, III. 180.
[4] Pym's Report, Debates of 1625, 179–86, C. S.
[5] *Parl. Hist.* I. 1039. 'We come not in any Puritan spirit.'
[6] Manningham's *Diary*, 156 and *passim*, C. S. Cp. Overbury's *Characters*, *A Puritan*.
[7] His theoretical attitude towards the prerogative, however, was strictly moderate. Debates of 1625, 81, 2, C. S.

necessary to dissolve Parliament to save Buckingham from impeachment. He then dismissed the keen-sighted Williams for his criticisms of the schemes of the royal favourite and of the high-handed dealings of the Crown itself. But the inevitable could but be delayed. Even though the chiefs of the Opposition were pricked as sheriffs, the new Parliament did not want for leaders. The fatuity of the king's behaviour almost passes belief. Instead of allowing the impeachment of Buckingham to proceed in the usual way, Charles shewed by his continual interference that he was directly or indirectly responsible for all that the favourite had done. Undaunted by having to face two foes instead of one, the Parliament, through the mouth of Eliot, threw to the winds the doctrine that ministers were responsible to the king alone. The importance of the pronouncement was not unnoticed. 'Since Henry VI,' wrote an anonymous correspondent to Charles, 'these discoursings have never been suffered, as being the certain symptoms of subsequent rebellions, civil wars and dethroning of kings[1].' Yet Eliot was by no means a revolutionary, and it is significant that a work of the leader of the Opposition only a few years before the Civil War should be censured by a friend as one in which Monarchy was 'too much extolled[2].'

That the existing embodiment of the monarchical idea, however, was regarded with increasingly critical eyes is proved by casual expressions of opinion preserved in the State Papers. The new professor of History at Cambridge, Dorislaus, in lecturing on Tacitus, selected for attention 'such dangerous passages and so applicable to the exasperation of these villainous times,' that Bishop Wren persuaded the Heads of Houses to censure the

---

[1] *Cabala*, ed. 1691, 255, 6. Cp. the similar utterance of Cotton, Edwards' *Founders of the British Museum*, I. 102, 3.

[2] Forster's *Eliot*, II. 653–81. Cp. his Petition from the Tower, *Parl. Hist.* II. 209–11.

audacious pedagogue[1]. Without the cloak of Tacitus, Gill, one of Milton's instructors, declared that the king had but wit enough to be a shopkeeper, and to ask ' What do you lack[2]?' The course of actual politics reflected the same tendency. Wentworth found that he had in vain devoted his magnificent abilities to the reconciliation of king and Commons, and it was left to less squeamish men to force through the Petition of Right. But even when, impatient of the constant appeal to the law[3], he was, in the pregnant words of Fuller, 'gained by the Court from the country[4],' the accession of strength to the royal cause was rather apparent than real. A few weeks later, the king's position was rendered still more perilous by the murder of Buckingham[5]. The bulwark being washed away, the waves beat full on the throne itself. In the following session, further blows were struck by the refusal of the House to adjourn at the king's order, and by Eliot's resolutions against the religious and fiscal policy of the Crown[6].

With Eliot in prison and Parliament dissolved, England seemed to have entered on a period of comparative calm. It was not, however, of a kind to inspire satisfaction or confidence. 'All men are so overawed,' wrote Dury to Roe, 'that they dare not say their soul is their own[7].' We learn from a letter of Selden that discussions of public affairs had to be carried on under the shelter of anagrams[8]. Above all, Separatists had begun to make their appearance[9].

---

[1] C. S. P. 1627, 8, 470.   [2] C. S. P. 1628, 9, 319.
[3] See a very striking letter, *Letters*, I. 201.   [4] *Worthies*, II. 365.
[5] Speaking of the Puritans, Wren described Felton as 'their head,' and added 'they hold it lawful to kill any man that opposes their party.' *Court and Times of Charles I*, I. 410.   [6] *Parl. Hist.* II. 487–92.
[7] C. S. P. 1633, 4, 453.   [8] C. S. P. 1634, 5, 185.
[9] Traske, the Christian Jew, had quickly found himself at the head of a very numerous following. *Court and Times of James I*, II. 65.

II

The Baptists would never have been distinguished from other religious bodies of the Reformation merely by their preference for adult baptism[1]. Their connection, however, with the Peasant Revolt and the tragedy of Munster drew attention to a phase of the movement which was far from being typical of its real nature. Inasmuch as Baptist tenets maintain the divine institution of magistrates, the outbreak of 1536 must be traced to the oppression which goaded men to madness. Such was one line of defence[2]. That the story of Munster as told by the historians was suspicious was another[3]. To disown all connection was a third[4]. The charge of descent from these fanatics, however, was naturally often brought against the sect when it grew to formidable dimensions in England[5]. The source from which the English Baptists in chief measure sprang was in reality widely different. Early in the seventeenth century, Smyth and Helwisse seceded from the Church of England refugees in Amsterdam, and adopted the opinions of Menno, who, in addition to antipædobaptism, had

[1] [On the political theories of the Baptists, especially during the Interregnum, cp. L. F. Brown, *Baptists and Fifth Monarchy Men.* H. J. L.]

[2] Cf. Underhill, Preface to *Tracts on Liberty of Conscience,* 80, Hanserd Knollys Soc.

[3] Baillie, *Dissuasive vindicated against Cotton and Tombes,* T. P. vol. 234, charges Tombes with being the first of his sect to defend the memory of the 'tragedians of Munster,' 73, 4. But a Presbyterian, Saltmarsh, was soon after to profess his suspicion of an account 'from the pen of an enemy.' *Smoke in the Temple,* T. P. vol. 316.

[4] *Tracts on Liberty of Conscience,* 101.

[5] Baillie traced their origin to Munzer and David George. *Anabaptism the true fountain of Independency,* etc. ch. 1, *Origin of the Anabaptists,* T. P. vol. 369. Cp. D'Ewes' *Autobiography,* II. 64, 5. Accounts of the Antinomians of the Reformation were composed or translated to serve as missiles against the movement. *Harl. Misc.* VIII. 258–74; *Munster's Siege; Translations of the histories of Guy du Brez and Spanheim,* T. P. vols. 2137 and 362.

taught that no Christian might swear or carry arms or wage war, and that magistrates should be obeyed in all things not contrary to the mind of God. With these principles he led off the moderate party after the great conference of continental Anabaptists in Westphalia in 1536, and since then had had no relations with the Antinomians[1].

When Helwisse, therefore, founded his Church in London in 1611[2], he introduced not the anarchic or communist but the moderate or Mennonite Anabaptism. In common with every other non-conforming body, the Baptists denied the authority of magistrates in matters of religion; but in all other ways their political orthodoxy was unimpeachable. In the first declaration of their position we learn that it is 'a fearful sin to speak evil of them that are in dignity, or to despise government[3].' In the first plea for liberty of conscience, the contention that its concession would not interfere with the interests of peace and order occupies a prominent place in the argument[4]. A few years later, in an address to the king, the petitioners describe themselves as 'loyal subjects, not for fear only but for conscience' sake[5].' Of a similar

---

[1] Barclay's *Inner Life*, 68–92. Cp. Dorner's *Person of Christ*, iv. 152–6. The third form assumed by Anabaptism, that, namely, which combined the communism of the one party with the moral and political orthodoxy of the other, was the least widely spread. Though its adherents were called with some reason the best of the Protestants, and though they won the sympathies of the poorer classes in Central Europe (Loserth's *Mährische Wiedertäufer*, 223, 4), nothing seems to have been known of them by the English Baptists. It was customary for critics to give a large number of subdivisions: Pagitt's *Heresiography*, 1–65. Brereton, visiting Amsterdam in 1635, said he found 30 sections: *Travels*, 65, C. S. But this was merely part of the siege machinery.

[2] Crosby, I. 269–76.

[3] *Baptist Confessions of Faith*, 1611, § 24, Hanserd Knollys Soc.

[4] Busher's *Religious Peace*, 1614, in *Tracts on Liberty of Conscience*, 24, etc.   [5] Supplication to his Majesty, *ib.* 231.

character are all manifestoes and petitions emanating from the society until the outbreak of the War. Yet, in troubled times, every separatist is an incarnate protest and a menace.

A much more important movement, however, was in progress. Soon after the secession of the Baptists, a far-reaching change commenced in the fortunes of the Dutch settlements. With the embarkation of a portion of Robinson's congregation in the *Mayflower* in 1620, the scene begins to shift from the United Provinces to the New World. In his famous farewell, their pastor urged the emigrants not to stop short at the point they had reached under his ministrations. 'If God reveal anything to you by other instruments of His, be as ready to receive it as ever you were to receive truth through me. The Calvinists stick fast where they were left by that great man of God, who yet saw not all things. I beseech you to remember it,—'tis an article of your church covenant,—that ye be ready to receive whatever truth shall be made known unto you[1].' The rigid nature of Robinson's doctrinal opinions renders it almost certain that he had in his mind not so much any developments in theology as the ordering of individual and social life[2]. It is true that he indignantly denied the insinuation that his religious opinions involved any change in the existing order, and declared that, in his opinion, all forms were 'capable of Christ's government[3]'; but none the less did his teaching point to a democratic system. 'In this holy fellowship, every one

[1] Neal's *Puritans*, II. 110, 111. [On the political theories of the New England Puritans cp. H. L. Osgood, 'The Political Ideas of the Puritans,' in *Political Science Quarterly*, vol. VI.; and C. Borgeaud, *The Rise of Democracy*. W. Walker's *Creeds and Platforms of Congregationalism* is useful for its discussion of the church covenants in New England. H. J. L.]

[2] Dexter, 400–10.

[3] 'Justification of Separation from the English Church,' *Works*, II. 17. Cp. Bradshaw's *English Puritanism*, 32–5; and *A Protestation of the King's Supremacy*, ed. 1605, 4.

is made a king, a priest, a prophet, not only to himself but to the whole body....Not only the eye cannot say to the hand, I have no need of thee; but not the head unto the feet, the meanest members, I have no need of you[1].' Two interpretations of the Independent idea, however, co-existed; for Independency rested on a two-fold basis, the independence of each congregation and the sovereignty of its members. The latter principle could never be anything but democratic. But the first might give rise to a certain exclusiveness if the number of members was small, and might issue, on the larger area of constructive politics, in aristocratic and theocratic preferences. The difference had already become visible, the earlier teachers pressing for a government in which the real power should remain in the hands of the pastors and elders, the latter contending for a genuinely congregational control. The Independents had lived as exiles in a foreign country; it was now to be seen what fruit the principles on which the movement rested would bear when they formed a State as well as a Church.

With the parting words of Robinson still ringing in their ears, the Pilgrim Fathers covenanted and combined themselves into a civil body politic, for their better ordering and preservation[2]. The Act was duly drawn up and signed by all. It is characteristic that among the signatories of the first political document inspired by Independency should be servants and common sailors. The Governor and Council were chosen by the votes of all, and were subject to the popular assembly composed of the male colonists of full age. When the population increased and was spread over a wide tract of country, the assembly was replaced for the ordinary business of legislation by a meeting of delegates. The

---

[1] Robinson's *Works*, II. 139.
[2] Poore's *Fundamental Constitutions of the United States*, 931.

democratic Church had grown into a democratic State. And although New Plymouth remained a separate community till towards the end of the century, its influence over subsequently founded colonies was very great.

In the same year a trading Company, incorporated by Royal Charter, took up its position on the shores of Massachusetts Bay. Its members were to have the power to nominate their officers and to draw up such laws as should be in accordance with the laws of England. The Company was further declared to have the aim of promoting the spread of the reformed religion[1]. In a few years, however, by the admission of new members, the character of the settlement became changed. Many of the new comers, regarding it as a refuge rather than a commercial enterprise, devoted themselves to the work of colonisation. Among these the original members gradually disappeared; the Company grew into a colony and the Charter into a Constitution[2].

The emigrants, unlike those of the *Mayflower*, were nominal and in many cases sincere members of the Established Church. 'They esteemed it an honour to call the English Church their dear mother[3]'; but when they reached their new homes, partly owing to the difficulty of reproducing the ecclesiastical machinery, and partly to the example of their neighbours at New Plymouth, their churchmanship was discarded. Yet, though the form of Anglicanism was deserted, many of its principles were retained. With the Puritan conviction of the sufficiency of Scripture they combined the Anglican distaste for unauthorised interpretation. The religious life of the community in consequence crystallised into a system of which Rutherford remarked that it

[1] Poore, 921–31; cp. Cushman's *Lawfulness of Removing*; Young's *Chronicles*.
[2] Poore, 932–42.   [3] Hutchinson's *Massachusetts*, I. App. I.

only needed to give a little more power to synods in order to become Presbyterianism[1].

That Massachusetts was not to become a paradise of freedom was shewn in a second way. At the first General Assembly held in 1630, the colonists voted away part of their power by providing that the Governor should be elected by the Council, and that laws were to be made by the Governor and Council alone. Next year, the franchise was curtailed by making membership of some recognised Church a qualification[2]. Shortly after, it was enacted that any one speaking against the Council or the magistrate should be banished[3]. The principal reason why the colony was less democratic than might have been expected was that, though the civil government was in theory separate from the ecclesiastical, it was in reality strictly subordinate. By their ability and moral influence the ministers had acquired a supremacy in the state which they used in part to counteract the growth of democratic ideas. By far the most illustrious was John Cotton, and 'the ecclesiastic constitution of the country,' as Mather remarks, 'was that on which he employed his peculiar cares[4].' With Calvin's theology he had imbibed his political conservatism. It was considered that it would 'derogate from the sufficiency and perfection of the Saints if God had not instituted a form of Civil Government[5].' 'Democracy,' he wrote to Lord Say, 'I do not

---

[1] Dexter, 412–14. Cp. Fuller: 'Synods they account useful and in some cases necessary; yet so that their power is but official, not authoritative,' VI. 278. The Boston Ministers drew up a scheme which, they flattered themselves, would conciliate the Independents and Presbyterians in England. Waddington's *Independents*, II. 506–8.

[2] *Records of Massachusetts*, I. 79–87.   [3] *ib.* 212, 13.

[4] Cotton Mather's *Magnalia*, I. 252–86, ed. 1853.

[5] John Eliot's *Christian Commonwealth*, Massach. Hist. Soc. 3rd Series, vol. 9, 134.

conceive God ever did ordain as a fit government, either for Church or Commonwealth. If the People be governors, who shall be governed? As for Monarchy and Aristocracy, they are both clearly approved and directed in Scripture, yet so as referreth the sovereignty to Himself and setteth up theocracy in both as the best form of government in the Commonwealth as in the Church[1].' The vital principle of true Independency, the separation of Church and State, is missing. 'That is a civil law whatsoever concerneth the good of the city,' wrote Cotton in answer to Roger Williams; 'now religion is the best good of the city, and therefore laws concerning religion are truly civil laws[2].' Liberty of Conscience was to be saved by the distinction between fundamentals and circumstantials[3]; but the dominant party found it impossible to regard members of other religious bodies as entitled to rights and privileges[4]. It was therefore, said Cotton, a sin to call him and his fellows Brownists[5]; and indeed no self-respecting controversialist did so. 'They are not Brownists,' wrote Cheynell, 'they admit the magistrate to be head in the Church.... I do not know why men should cry out they are greater enemies to the State than the Papists[6].' Sometimes even the name of Independent was scouted. 'We are much charged,' said Hugh Peters, 'with what we own not, namely Independency; whereas we know no churches more looking to sister churches for help[7].'

---

[1] Hutchinson's *Massachusetts*, 1. App. No. 3, 497.

[2] *Bloody Tenet Washed*, 151, T. P. vol. 387.

[3] Cotton's *Reply to the Reasons against Persecution*, 19–30, in Hanserd Knollys ed. of the *Bloody Tenet*.

[4] Johnson's *Wonder Working Providence*, Pt. 1. T. P. vol. 969.

[5] Baillie's *Dissuasive Vindicated*, 9, T. P. vol. 234. The information was derived from Roger Williams who had heard Cotton say it.

[6] Cheynell's *Rise of Socinianism*, 62–70, T. P. vol. 103.

[7] Dexter, 413.

And Cotton plainly declared, 'We are wrongly called Independents[1].'

It thus happened that the colony of Massachusetts became a theocracy modelled on and imitating with considerable success the republic of Geneva. Making every allowance for the fact that Lechford held a brief against New England[2], the picture that he draws may be taken to contain at least a large portion of truth. The great democratic principles of manhood suffrage and the popular election of magistrates were nominally recognised, but in practice they were sadly mutilated. Nobody could become a freeman of the colony nor exercise the franchise if he was not a church-member; and this limitation, which might have been nothing more than a formality, was oppressive from the fact that the majority were excluded by it[3]. Writers frequently advocated liberal and illiberal opinions in the same breath. 'If I were a king,' said Ward, 'I would honour them who would take me by the head and teach me to king it better when they saw me unkinging myself and the kingdom'; but when it was suggested that greater facilities should be afforded to the community to express its will, he 'could rather stand amazed than reply[4].' People began to complain that they were ruled like slaves, and Lechford became convinced that some change was imminent[5].

Almost from the first there had been signs of opposition. The direct election of the Governor, which had been abolished in 1631, was restored in the following year, and, shortly after, the

---

[1] *Congregational Churches Cleared*, 11, T. P. vol. 426. Cp. Owen's *True Nature of a Gospel Church and its Government, Works*, vol. 20.

[2] 'It is false and fraudulent,' said Cotton; 'his plain dealing is not true.' *Way of Congregational Churches Cleared*, 71, 2, T. P. vol. 426.

[3] *Plain Dealing*, ed. 1867, 58, 9.

[4] Ward's *Simple Cobbler of Agawam*, ed. 1843, 12, 58.

[5] *Plain Dealing*, 89, 90, 129–31.

legislative power of which the Governor and Council had become possessed was removed[1]. In 1641 the enactment of the 'Body of Liberties' marked the highest point in the influence of the demo-crats. But the concession of certain instalments of such legislation was unable to conciliate a large number of colonists to whom the system as a whole became increasingly distasteful. Of this party Hooker, who had been expelled from the Church of England and had spent several years in Amsterdam[2], was the spokesman, and under his leadership the malcontents of certain settlements on the banks of the Connecticut united into an independent federation. The 'Fundamental Orders of Connecticut[3]' include the sovereignty of the general assembly of citizens and the an-nual election of officers. No property qualification was demanded and, except in the case of the Governor, no religious test was imposed. The connection of the first written constitution of modern democracy with Independency is confirmed by the expression of precisely similar principles in Hooker's books and sermons[4].

Connecticut was more democratic and less theocratic than Massachusetts. Nevertheless between Cotton and Hooker the difference was not very great. Mather records that the 'Pillar of Connecticut' was in the habit of declaring that the elders must have a Church within a Church, if they desired to preserve its peace, since the discussion of important matters before the whole body would break any Church in pieces[5]. Thus the Connecticut migration represents merely the more democratic, as Newhaven the more theocratic aspect of the system which appears in its

---

[1] *Records*, I. 95, 117.   [2] Waddington, II. 291–7.   [3] Poore, 249–52.
[4] Above all, in the *Survey of the Sum of Church Discipline*, T. P. vol. 440. It is paying him too high a compliment, however, to call him, with Fiske, the Founder of American Democracy. *Beginnings of New England*, 127, 8.
[5] *Magnalia*, I. 349. Cp. *Survey*, Preface, where his view of Independency is presented in a few vigorous strokes.

normal shape in Massachusetts. If democracy, however, in its ultimate meaning, be held to imply not only a government in which the preponderant share of power resides in the people, but a society based on the principles of political and religious freedom, Rhode Island beyond any other of the American colonies is entitled to be called democratic.

Roger Williams crossed to America in 1631 in company with one of the numerous reinforcements which went to join the colonists of Massachusetts[1]. On landing he discovered that the religious and, to some extent, the political principles which he found prevailing were by no means to his satisfaction[2]. When a vacancy occurred in the ministry at Boston, Williams was invited to fill it, but declined on the ground that the congregation was an unseparated people[3]. He became the pastor of Salem; but it was only to urge his congregation to separate from the churches of the colony[4]. He next passed to an attack on the Charter, but on a warning from the Court undertook to desist. He broke his promise, and the Court determined to closely scrutinise his opinions. He had been teaching that the king's Patent was no title to the land, which still belonged to the natives, and that the oath of fidelity which had been imposed as a condition of office was to be resisted[5]. He was thereupon again summoned before the Court and banished. The formal act of expulsion attributed the step to 'new and dangerous opinions against the authority of magistrates[6]'; but Cotton declares that it was due exclusively to his attitude towards the oath and his 'violent and tumultuous carriage against the Patent[7].' He was banished because his attitude

[1] Knowles' *Life of Williams.*
[2] Cotton's *Reply to Mr Williams' Examination,* 2, T. P. vol. 387.
[3] Dexter's *As to Roger Williams,* 5.   [4] Mather's *Magnalia,* II. 495-9.
[5] Cotton's *Reply to Mr Williams,* 24, 5.
[6] *Records,* I. 160.   [7] *Reply,* 27-9.

to the civil and ecclesiastical polity of the colony was altogether revolutionary. The Patent was 'the life of the colony,' and the Court simply acted on the principle of self-preservation[1]. From the moment of his arrival, Williams had been regarded as a young man of great promise but of hastily formed convictions. Governor Bradford had described him as having 'many precious parts, but very unsettled in judgment[2]'; and Mather recorded the general impression of the colony that he had at this time 'less light than fire[3].' In a word, he was very young, and his notions were very crude. As far as they concerned the Church they were purely Brownist, if indeed they did not deserve the name, which Fuller had applied to Brown, of Donatist[4].

The little body that had followed their pastor from Salem to Providence undertook to obey all laws made by a majority of their number, providing that the laws should deal exclusively with civil matters[5]. Shortly after, a scheme of government according to which the executive should reside in a Court of Five, and the legislative power in the General Assembly of the community, was passed into law by a plebiscite. The principle of liberty of conscience was also affirmed[6]. A second wave of emigrants quickly reached Narragansett Bay and named the place of settlement which, with the advice of Williams, they had chosen, Rhode Island. The General Assembly at once proceeded to declare that the government should be 'Democratic or Popular'; that is, it should be in the power of the freemen 'to make laws by which

---

[1] Mather. This is admirably put by Palfrey, *History of New England*, I. 412–20.

[2] Dexter, 7, 8.   [3] *Magnalia*, II. 495.

[4] Wild rumours reached England. Baillie wrote 'Mr Williams will have every man serve God by himself alone, without any church at all.' *Journals*, II. 191.

[5] Williams, *Works*, VI. 5.   [6] *Rhode Island Records*, I. 27–31.

they should be regulated and to depute members to see them faithfully executed[1].' Two years later, the contemner of Patents sailed to England and brought back with him a Charter which incorporated the various settlements and gave them power to 'rule themselves as they should find most suitable to their condition[2].' It was therefore once more declared that 'the form of government established in Providence Plantations is democratical; that is to say, a government held by free consent of all or the greater part of the free inhabitants[3].' A series of Acts and Orders was then adopted, forming a Declaration of the Rights of Man[4]. Five years later slavery was abolished within the territory[5].

By this time the founder of the colony was maturing his ecclesiastical theory. While still residing in Massachusetts, Williams had sent a copy of one of the earliest Baptist pleas for liberty of conscience to Cotton, with a request for his opinion upon it[6]. The reply, though given privately, was published by Williams with a lengthy refutation. Cotton had distinguished between fundamentals and circumstantials, and disclaimed persecution for 'conscience rightly informed.' 'But if the heretic persisted in his errors after admonition, it would not be out of conscience[7].' In opposition to this teaching Williams maintained that error would receive its own punishment, and that the blind Pharisee, resisting the doctrine of Christianity, might be as good a subject and as peaceful and profitable to the civil state as any[8]. Whatever the points which were considered fundamental, the souls of thousands who did not accept them were 'bound up in the bundle of eternal life.' The civil sword would make a nation of hypocrites but not

---

[1] *Records,* I. 112.   [2] Poore, 1594, 5.   [3] *Records,* I. 156.
[4] I. 157–208.   [5] I. 243.
[6] The story is told in Cotton's *Bloody Tenet Washed,* 1, 2, T. P. vol. 387.
[7] The Hanserd Knollys edition of the *Bloody Tenet,* Cotton's reply to the tract sent to him, 19–30.   [8] 94–6.

a single Christian[1]. In a word, freedom of thought might not only be granted with safety but could not be withheld without danger. The sovereignty, the original and the foundation of civil power, lay in the people, and the people might create what form of government seemed to them most meet for their civil condition[2]. But even the people's power was but natural and civil, and they could not give the magistrate religious jurisdiction, because they did not possess it themselves[3]. The Prelatists, Presbyterians and Independents all struggled to 'sit down under the shadow of that arm of flesh.' The Separatists alone could make a fair plea for the purity of Christ, in whose cause Barrow and Greenwood and Penry had been hanged[4].

The rough experience of life could hardly fail to compel the governor of a colony to modify some of his opinions; and, but for his robust faith in liberty, the difficulties which arose might almost have tempted him to desert them. The year after his arrival, Williams became convinced that his followers must be 'compact in a civil way,' and felt that the young men ought to obey what was determined by the householders[5]. In 1638 one of the settlers forbidding his wife to attend the pastor's ministrations so frequently was disfranchised on the ground that he had broken his oath to respect liberty of conscience[6]. In 1640 occurred a more important interruption of the government. A certain Gorton arrived in Providence and was kindly received, but soon began to issue 'envenomed reproaches against the rulers and Churches, and denials of all order[7].' Being thus confronted with antinomianism, Williams lamented to Winthrop that Gorton was 'denying all visible and external order in the depth of Familism[8].' Encouraged

[1] 107.   [2] 214.   [3] 341.   [4] 300, 425.
[5] Letter to Winthrop, *Works*, VI. 80.   [6] *Records*, I. 16.
[7] Mather's *Magnalia*, II. 594.   [8] *Works*, VI. 141.

to vigorous measures by the reply, Williams imprisoned the incendiary. Three years later an opportunity arose for him to explain his position in regard to toleration. A number of colonists had published a declaration to the effect that it was 'blood-guiltiness' and contrary to the rule of the Gospel to execute judgment on transgressors. On this Williams declared that all he had ever pleaded for was that, on board a ship carrying men of different creeds, none should be forced to come to the ship's prayers nor detained from their own. 'But I never denied that the commander should command the ship's course and that justice, peace and sobriety should be kept. And if any refused to obey the common laws and orders, mutinied or preached there should be no commanders nor officers because all were equal in Christ, I say I never denied but that such transgressors might be resisted, judged and punished according to their deserts[1].' When, a few months later, a member of the colony became convinced that his 'conscience ought not to yield subjection to any human order among men,' Williams gave practical expression to his recent declaration of principle[2].

The sorest trial was still to come. In 1656 the colonies agreed to exclude all 'Quakers, Ranters and notorious heretics,' and invited the Providence Plantations to do the same. The General Assembly rejoined that freedom of conscience was the principal ground of their charter, and was prized by them as the greatest happiness men could possess in the world. The Massachusetts Commissioners replied that the doctrines tended to 'the very absolute cutting down and overturning of civil government among men[3].' The inhabitants of Providence and Rhode Island thereupon wrote to England for advice. When the Commissioners arrived, Williams told them that they had a people who would

---

[1] Knowles, 278–80.   [2] Dexter, 93–6.   [3] *Records*, I. 377.

not join in their government, and asked what course should be taken with them. 'Do they live peaceably among you?' was the answer. And when Williams replied that they did, the Commissioners retorted: 'If they can govern themselves they have no need of your government[1].' We seem to miss something of the old spirit in the dialogue, and the impression is confirmed by the subsequent development of the story. Three Quakers met Williams in formal conflict to defend themselves against the charges which he had brought against them. His opponents were Sabellians, Socinians, Jews, Papists, Manichees and Indians in one breath[2]. The true character of their teaching was completely missed, and it was only the outlying extravagances that were noted. Certain of their number had appeared in different places without clothes, and for Williams this is the kernel of the entire movement[3]. Next to their antinomianism their doctrine of political separation meets with the severest rebuke. They owned no magistrates but such as were godly in their own dark sense, exclaimed Williams with indignation, forgetting that it was his own special doctrine of pollution transferred from Church to State. That women should preach now seems to him 'unnatural[4].' The venerable founder of the movement is described as a 'filthy sow[5].'

If such words uttered in the heat of controversy embodied the mature thought of Roger Williams, we could not regard him as one of the most liberal minds of the century. But he was of excitable and passionate temperament, and his opinions are to be sought rather in the history of the colony than in hasty expressions. Rhode Island remained the home of liberty that it had been from its foundation. Had any change taken place in Williams'

[1] *Works*, vol. v. 'George Fox digged out of his burrows,' Introduction.
[2] 'George Fox digged out,' etc., v. 167.
[3] 13, 59–61, 242, etc.   [4] 134.   [5] 501.

innermost thought, the Charter of the Restoration would not have enacted that none should be called in question for opinions or for conduct which did not actually disturb the civil peace of the colony[1]. When the Royal Commissioners arrived in 1665, they reported that the colony admitted 'all religions, even Quakers[2].'

The relations between Williams and the mother country throw a little additional light on the nature of his political opinions. Williams cared no more for the political than for the ecclesiastical system of the land of his birth. His intimate friends in England were drawn from the most ardent Republicans, and he was on excellent terms with the Protector. He recommended a royalist lady of his acquaintance to 'read over impartially Mr Milton's answer to the king's book[3].' When Vane and the Protector quarrelled, his sympathies were with the former, because the *Healing Question* contained a form of government more to his taste than the iron rule which it was intended to replace[4]. And when the Republicans had no place to hide their heads, Rhode Island sheltered Goffe and Whalley and preserved their lives[5].

'We have drunk of the cup of as great liberties,' wrote Williams to Vane, 'as any people we can hear of under heaven[6].' Despite the modifications which the pressure of experience compelled the founder of the colony of Rhode Island to make, he remained faithful to the ideals which he had formed in his early manhood, and by the fearless application of his principles he secured for his followers 'as great liberties as any people under heaven.'

---

[1] Poore, 1596–1603 ; Charter of 1663.   [2] *Records*, II. 127.
[3] *Letters*.   [4] 373.
[5] Arnold's *Rhode Island*, I. 413, 14.   [6] *Records*, I. 285–7.

III

The influence of the American colonies worked like a leaven in the mother country. The relations between the settlers and their well-wishers at home were of the closest. Glowing accounts of their piety and prosperity were brought back by visitors, and invitations sent over to 'come and see the work of the Lord[1].' In return, the reforming party looked on New England as sacred ground. 'I could not but wonder at God's holy providence,' wrote D'Ewes in his diary in 1634, 'that put it into the hearts of so many godly persons to hazard themselves to go to New England, there to plant one of the most absolutely holy, orthodox and well-governed churches in Christendom[2].' As the horizon darkened at home, it was to America that ever-increasing numbers turned their steps. Anglican divines lamented that their country-men 'flew out of England as out of Babylon[3].' An agent of Laud wrote to his employer in 1634 from Suffolk that he had found a party of 600 about to start. The praise the pilgrims won seemed to him the chief inducement, he added, 'even bankrupts being able to earn a reputation for holiness by flight[4].' The affectionate relations may be further illustrated in the following remarkable passage from a sermon delivered in 1640. 'How have they always listened after our welfare! How do they (I mean the multitudes of well-affected persons there) talk of New England with delight! And when a New England man returns thither, how is he looked after, entertained, the ground he walks on beloved for his sake and the house held better where he is! How are his words listened

---

[1] C. S. P. *America*, I. 123, 154; Winslow's *Good News from New England*; Young's *Chronicles*, etc.

[2] *Autob.* II. 112–14.

[3] Sanderson's 8th Sermon ad Aulam, 1638, *Works*, I. 215.

[4] C. S. P. 1633–4, 450.

to, laid up and related when he is gone! Neither is any love or kindness too much for such a man[1].'

New England models became the more alluring by contrast with the condition of things at home. The king had been emboldened by the fact that, since Coke had ceased to speak for the law, the judges had taken their stand on the side of prerogative. So long as the popular feeling could speak through the mouth of the law, no very revolutionary change was to be apprehended; but when the purely conservative attitude was exchanged for one in which the necessity was recognised of supplementing the system of laws, the gate was thrown open to unlimited change. The first writ of ship-money met with little opposition; but the second and third, in conjunction with the legal pronouncements to which they gave rise, stirred the country to its depths. Things that might not be done by the 'rule of law' might be done by the 'rule of government.' The burden was small, it may be said, and the country was rich enough to pay it; and had it been an isolated imposition, it might have been less vigorously resisted. 'But all the wheels of the prerogative,' in the words of Whitelocke, 'were set in motion to provide money'; and the parallel crusade against the religious sentiments of the mass of the nation was in full swing.

Since Laud had become Bishop of London his influence had been predominant, but as Archbishop it became uncontested. The Court of High Commission was frequently engaged with charges of 'keeping conventicles and holding erroneous opinions[2],' Laud being 'always observed,' according to the testimony of

---

[1] Hooke's *New England's Tears for Old England's Fears*, 16–21, T. P. vol. 208.

[2] *Cases in Star Chamber and High Comm.* Vicars' Case is typical, 198–238; cp. 181–6, 316–21, etc. C. S.

Fuller, 'to concur with the severest sentence[1].' Heresy and schism were not to him as to Hales 'theological scarecrows[2].' The visitation which he proceeded to institute sowed the seeds of disaffection broadcast. Even his old friend, Judge Whitelocke, remarked that, good man as he was, Laud would set the nation on fire if he proceeded in the way he was in[3]. His colleague of York proved an apt pupil. 'Everywhere,' ran his report on the Province of York to Laud, 'I found ministers chopping, changing, altering, omitting, adding[4].' Such was his zeal for conformity that, on discovering that the Dutch workmen employed in draining the fens were worshipping in the manner to which they had been accustomed, he pulled down their chapel, dismissed their minister and compelled them to attend the neighbouring churches.

'If the presses were open to us,' exclaimed the mutilated Bastwick of Laud, 'we would scatter his kingdom about his ears[5].' There were three main reasons at this time for the disapproval of the Church of England by the mass of the nation. The head and front of its offending were that it was Anglo-Catholic. The majority of Protestants of the sixteenth and seventeenth centuries refused to believe that there could be any middle course between Protestantism and Romanism. But though there was little ground for their distrust of the Anglican body, though the king had refused even to discuss the possibilities of conversion while in Spain[6], and Laud had shewn in the controversy with Fisher how groundless were the fears of both friend and foe, it is easy to understand how such a distrust arose[7]. Though but one dignitary

---

[1] *Church Hist.* VI. 299.   [2] Hales, *Works*, I. 114.
[3] Whitelocke's *Memorials*, April 13, 1640.
[4] C. S. P. 1633–4, 443, 4.   [5] Wallington's *Diary*, I. 91, 2.
[6] *Spanish Marriage Treaty*, 209, 10, C. S.
[7] Cp. Coleridge, *Table Talk*, June 10, 1830.

of the English Church joined the Roman Communion[1], conversions among the nobility were by no means unknown[2]. Moreover, the testimonies to the continued strength and activity of Romanism are too numerous to neglect. Catholic visitors and envoys were amazed to find such a prosperous community of the faithful[3]. Another evidence of vitality was found in the series of plots, real or imaginary, that were discovered by zealous Protestants[4]. For this reason any supposed approximation on the part of professing Protestants created a panic. Though Montagu's famous book contained a most vigorous attack on Romanism[5] and was placed on the *Index*[6], the fact that the author felt himself unable to affirm that the Pope was Antichrist and that he was in frequent conclave with Panzani and Con was sufficient to create the belief that he was himself a secret convert[7].

The dominant tendency of the Church seemed dangerous to many whose loyalty was beyond question. Not only London citizens[8] and country gentlemen[9], but even certain of the clergy[10] looked on with pain and suspicion. The opinion of a vast number of thoughtful churchmen was expressed by D'Ewes. 'I can honour a virtuous Papist,' he wrote in his *Autobiography*; 'but for men to

[1] Fuller's *Worthies*, III, 532, Goodman, Bishop of Gloucester.

[2] Butler's *English Catholics*, IV. 29–88.

[3] Père Cyprien's account of the Capucin mission, *Court and Times of Charles I*, II. 310, 343, etc.; Bentivoglio's *Relazione*, Opere, I. 203–17; cp. the judgment of the Venetian friend of May, *Long Parliament*, 16, 17, ed. 1843, and Sarpi's *Lettere*, II. 13.

[4] Useful summaries are to be found in Foulis' *Popish Treasons*, 675–726, ed. 1671, and Ware's *Foxes and Firebrands*, ed. 1683, 173–89.

[5] *Appello Caesarem*, Pt. II. ed. 1625.   [6] Reusch's *Index*, II. 120.

[7] The conversion of sons was taken to shew the teaching on which they were nourished. Cosin's *Corresp.* I. 285, Surtees Society.

[8] Wallington's *Diary*, vol. I. *passim*.

[9] Yonge's *Diary*, C. S.; cp. Mrs Hutchinson's *Memoirs*.

[10] Rous' *Diary*, C. S., presents an interesting picture of gradual alienation

call themselves Protestants, to inveigh against Popery in word only and to project the ruin of truth, to maintain the most gross errors of the Romish synagogue, to cause God's day to be profaned, his service to be poisoned by idolatry, his faithful ministers to be censured, suspended, reviled, deprived—this my soul abhors[1].'

The foreign policy of the Crown increased the suspicion which was felt of the soundness of the Protestantism of those in high places. While England stood aside, the Swedes stepped into their place as the champions of the Protestant interest. The career of Gustavus was followed with breathless interest, and when the news of his death arrived, the English were unwilling to credit it[2]. So strong was the enthusiasm for the Palatine family that it was said that the Puritans had prayed that the king might have no children, in order that his nephews might succeed to the throne[3]. So deep had been the distrust that one of the charges in the impeachment of Buckingham was that of intending to use English ships against the Huguenots[4].

No less distasteful to the nation was the political teaching of the Church. Laud forbade the printing of part of Spelman's *Glossary*, though a personal friend, because he was scandalised by the remarks upon Magna Charta[5]. The doctrine of absolutism had indeed grown to be uncontested. 'How shall we distinguish when God hath not distinguished?' asked Bramhall[6]; and Heylyn

---

[1] D'Ewes' *Autob.* II. 112–14. The promotion of a Protestant was so rare that it was hailed as a national event. When Preston received the mastership of Emmanuel College, 'the news ran swiftly all through the kingdom; good men were glad honest men were not abhorred as they had been.' Ball's *Life of Preston*, 88, 1628, ed. 1883. It was, however, an isolated example. Strafford demeaned himself by jeering at the names of certain of the Puritan leaders. *Letters*, I. 344.   [2] C. S. P. 1631–3, 338.
[3] Heylyn's *Laud*, 209.   [4] *Impeachment of Buckingham*, 139–302, C. S.
[5] Aubrey's *Lives*, II. 539.
[6] 'Serpent-Salve,' *Works*, A.-C. L. III. 352.

wrote that the King of England had always been accounted an absolute monarch[1]. In an authoritative exposition of Anglican notions, Thorndike declared that Christianity obliged superior and inferior to maintain the relations in which they found themselves[2]. Even Fuller, a representative of what may be called the Broad Church party, declared that none might 'search the reasons of kings' actions but such as stood on an equal basis with them[3],' and abruptly ended his discussion of 'the King' with the words, 'But I must either stay or fall. My sight fails me, dazzled with the lustre of majesty[4].' So much did the divinity of kings become part of the mental equipment of the Church that even a man of cool temper like Williams lived silent some time after the execution of Charles, 'only lifting up his head sometimes to ask what had become of the king's triers, looking for some remarkable judgment of God to come down upon them[5].'

A third ground of the unpopularity of the Church was the conduct of the clergy. Without suggesting that the general level of character was unusually low, there can be no doubt that the

---

[1] 'Stumbling-block of Disobedience and Rebellion, proving the kingly power neither coordinate with nor subordinate to any other on earth.' *Tracts*, ed. 1681, 715–32.

[2] *Laws of the Church*, ch. 23, *Works*, A.-C. L. IV. 868–71.

[3] *Holy and Profane State*, 193, ed. 1840.   [4] *ib.* 284.

[5] Hacket's *Life of Williams*, II. 226; cf. Plume's *Life of Hacket*, 68. These doctrines were of course not shared by all churchmen. Hales, for instance, speaks severely of the clergy 'giving rules for government,' *Works*, II. 102. The rigidity with which the tenets were held varied. Yet even Ussher could write, 'Though the representatives of the Commons bear the show of a little democracy among us and the Lords of an aristocracy, yet our government is a free monarchy, because the supreme authority rests neither in the one nor the other but solely in the king.' *Power of the Prince*, *Works*, XI. 277, 8. It need hardly be pointed out that the purpose of this chapter is not to pronounce judgment on Church or Monarchy, but to shew how they appeared to a large part of the people.

laxity of life which was widely prevalent made a deep impression on a generation which, whatever its faults, took its religion seriously. It may well be that the picture exhibited in White's *Centuries* is exaggerated[1]. But confirmations reach us from witnesses of different parties. Baxter's account of the Church in Shropshire may serve as an instance. Preaching was unknown, and the ignorance and moral laxity of the ministry extreme. His father was called a Puritan and a Precisian because he read the Bible and reproved drunkenness. As he grew to manhood, he made the acquaintance of certain non-conformists from whose holy lives he derived great benefit. 'And when I understood that these were the people that were persecuted by the Church, I thought those that troubled such men could not be the genuine followers of the Lord[2].' Thinking to strengthen his case, the author of *The Sufferings of the Clergy* complains that they were treated 'with all possible contempt and insolence[3].' That a part of their unpopularity may be explained by the precisianist notions of the Puritans in respect to the *Book of Sports* and the erection of Maypoles is undoubted; but the apostasy of the people from the Church at this time can be no more explained by caprice than the apostasy of the people from the Crown.

The same policy that had transformed England into a camp of revolt was put in practice beyond its borders. Since Balmerino's Trial, popular feeling in Scotland had been rapidly growing hostile to the Court, and when Laud determined to substitute a real for a nominal Anglican government, the outrage on the national and religious sentiment evoked passionate indignation. The dispute which had arisen seemed to turn only on the adoption of the Book of Common Prayer; but it opened up the whole question

[1] Neal's *Puritans*, III. 28–34.   [2] *Life*, 1–13.
[3] Walker's *Sufferings of the Clergy*.

of the validity of the king's assumption of an absolute authority in ecclesiastical affairs. In other words, it involved the discussion of the grounds and limits of obedience[1]. The nation bound itself by a covenant to defend its most cherished possession, and when the king shewed that he was not to be frightened, proceeded to give practical demonstration of its principles by arms. The king was defeated and the necessity of covering his defeat led to the summoning of Parliament. It came to be generally recognised that the vigorous opposition of the Scots was the first open step in the king's downfall. 'A Scotch mist,' as Fuller remarked, 'was often enough to wet a man to the skin[2].' The invaders had declared that the cause of Scotland was no less the cause of England[3]; and England began to hold the same opinion. 'In 1639,' wrote Mrs Hutchinson, 'even the most obscure woods began to be penetrated with flashes[4].'

[1] It was characteristic that some Scots now proposed to print in Amsterdam the *De Jure Regni* in Latin, French and English. Laud to Strafford, *Works,* VII. 544.

[2] *Worthies,* II. 543.   [3] *Treaty of Ripon,* 70, 71, C. S.

[4] *Memoirs.*

CHAPTER IV

The Birth of Republicanism

THE Royalist picture of the period immediately preceding the outbreak of the quarrel is well known. 'Peace, wealth and a model king,' wrote Clarendon[1], 'could but enable, not compel us, to be happy. There was a strange absence of understanding in most and a strange perverseness of understanding in the rest; every man more troubled and perplexed at what they called the violation of one law than delighted with the observation of all the rest of the charter.' 'Every man,' relates Sir Philip Warwick, 'sat quiet under his own vine, and the fountains of justice ran clear and current[2].' According to Isaac Walton the nation was 'sick of being well[3].'

The explanation of the outbreak itself is of a corresponding character. 'It arose,' said Bishop Hall in a sermon before the king, 'from men who took pleasure in the embroiling of states[4].' 'Nothing less than a general combination and universal apostasy in the whole nation from their religion and allegiance,' declared the great Royalist historian, 'could in so short a time have produced such a total and prodigious alteration and confusion over the whole kingdom[5].' On the meeting of Parliament the members, we learn from Sir John Bramston[6], acted as they did 'some out of malice and revenge, others to shew they had parts[7].'

---

[1] *History of the Rebellion*, I. 162, 3.   [2] *Memoirs*, 62.

[3] *Life of Sanderson*; cp. Lloyd's *Memoirs*, Preface; and Bates' *Elenchus*, 17–19.

[4] Hall's *Works*, V. 504; cp. Walker's *Historical Discourses*, 260, ed. 1705; and Cowley's *Works*, ed. 1707, 626–8.

[5] Clarendon, *History*, I. 1.   [6] *Autobiography*, 73, C. S.

[7] Contemporary Royalist judgments naturally mistook the nature of the crisis. 'The mutinies of the base multitude,' wrote Conway to Laud, 'are

I

In so far as this reading of history declares that the great revolt was not due to deep-rooted causes, it is childish; but in its testimony to the outward suddenness of the crisis itself, it is substantially correct. 'The people,' Strafford had recently written, 'are in great quietness and, if I be not much mistaken, well satisfied, if not delighted, with his Majesty's gracious government and protection[1].' Sir Henry Wotton had declared in 1638, 'We know not what a rebel is, nor treason. The names themselves are antiquated with the things[2].' Through the forty years of Stuart rule, despite the discontent evoked by the conduct of the king, no voice was raised against the more important privileges of the Monarchy, much less against the Monarchy itself; and even during the progress of the struggle, the growth of an anti-monarchic sentiment is curiously slow. 'Monarchy,' declared the Speaker of the Short Parliament, 'is of all sorts of government the most excellent. And I hope there are not any of this nation of anti-monarchic dispositions themselves or friends to such as are so. If there be, I wish no greater honour to Parliament than to discover them and to assist your Majesty to suppress them[3].' 'I hold there are not three men in all the king's dominions, except Papists and Anabaptists,' wrote Henry Parker, 'who hold it lawful to depose or by any force to violate the person of kings, how ill soever they act[4].' A member was indignantly denounced

not to be feared;...'tis a turnip cut like a death's head.' Prynne's *Laud*, 183, ed. 1644. Strafford, however, no longer permitted himself any illusions. Whitaker's *Radcliffe*, 204. [1] *Letters*, II. 93.

[2] *Reliquiae*, 451, ed. 1685. It was afterwards reported that portents had been frequent. The Cam was observed to turn blood-red. Cooper's *Annals*, III. 303; cp. instances in Kingston's *Civil War in Hertfordshire*, 179.

[3] *Parl. Hist.* II. 538.

[4] *Discourse concerning the Puritans*, 43, T. P. vol. 204; cp. *Canterburians'*

by the Speaker for daring to attribute intentions to the House
of deposing kings by Parliament[1]. Even Calibut Downing, who
in the very month the Long Parliament met told the Artillery
that 'the estates might go very far before they could be counted
rebels,' and that circumstances might occasionally justify offen-
sive as well as defensive resistance[2], added that he was confident
that the king would extricate the country from its troubles[3].
What it was desired to destroy was the Church, not the Monarchy. It is hardly too much to say that two-thirds of the speeches
and pamphlets—and 'the very streets were strewn with them[4]'
between the meeting of Parliament and the breach with the king
in 1642—deal with the question of the Church. 'Let religion
be our primum quaerite,' said Rudyerd, 'for all things are but
etceteras to it[5].' The majority deal with it in the same spirit. It
had become proverbial to say, 'when anything was spoiled,' 'the
Bishop's foot hath been in it[6].' Yet the most active opponents
of the Church explain that No Bishop does not imply No King[7].
It is along the line of democratic constitutionalism that we must
first seek for the great transformation of political thought that
was coming over the country.

The members of the new Parliament set out with the resolution to transfer the general direction of Government from the
King to the House of Commons[8]. The Star Chamber, the High

Self-Conviction, 14, T. P. vol. 168. But divines were no longer allowed to
preach the doctrines of divine right with impunity; Nalson, I. 367, 673.
[1] D'Ewes' *Diary*, Dec. 4, 1641, *Harl. MSS.* 162, f. 212.
[2] *Sermon to the Artillery*, 12, 37, 8, etc. T. P. vol. 157.
[3] *Discursive Conjecture*, 42, 3, etc. T. P. vol. 206.
[4] *Clergy's Complaint*, T. P. vol. 84.   [5] *Speech*, T. P. vol. 196.
[6] *Smectymnuus' Answer*, 103, T. P. vol. 101.
[7] Lord Brooke's *Discourse on Episcopacy*, T. P. vol. 177, is typical.
[8] Certain members entertained a very exalted opinion of its wisdom.
Grimston's *Speech*, T. P. vol. 200, is typical.

Commission, the Courts of the Marches, the Court of Wards, the Forest Courts, in a word all the jurisdictions that had given the Tudors and Stuarts their exceptional position, were swept away. The attack on Strafford, too, was in accordance with the wishes of the whole Parliament; but when the impeachment was unable to compass its design, the line of cleavage made itself for the first time clearly felt. The substitution of a charge of treason against the nation for that of treason against the king constitutes the beginning of the formation of the creed that the nation, speaking through its elected representatives, may do what it considers essential for its safety and well-being. Though more than 50 members felt themselves unable to assent to the Attainder, the whole House consented to a Bill perhaps more revolutionary in character[1]. In the urgent need of money, Parliament had proceeded to borrow on the security of the customs. But if a dissolution were to take place, the money would go to the king; and therefore, in the confusion following the discovery of the Army Plot, the House resolved to accept dissolution at no hands but its own.

Soon after came the news of the Irish massacre, and the panic lent strength to the forward party. Pym introduced a motion which made the assistance of the king in Ireland conditional on the dismissal of his evil counsellors. The proposal was rejected by the House; but when it was presented a few days later with different wording, it passed by a considerable majority. Spurred on by the two Army Plots and the Scotch Incident, Parliament thus struck at the executive itself. The majority of the House now threw off the mask of conventional deference, and appealed to the nation against the king. The Grand Remonstrance was a victory for the party of Pym; and a few days later was enunciated

[1] Cp. Salvetti's Remarks, *Corresp.* XI. 77, b, *Addit. MSS.* 27,962; and *Life and Times of Sir Julius Caesar*, 69.

the complementary claim of the Lower House to override the Upper, in consideration of its nature and constitution. It was moved for a Committee 'to review what bills we had passed and the Lords rejected, and the reasons why.' Among the instructions to the Committee was that to urge on the Lords that the Commons were 'representatives of the whole kingdom,' but the Lords only 'particular persons,' 'coming to Parliament in a particular capacity[1].'

The Commons were preparing to impeach the Queen herself, when they were frustrated by the attempt on the Five Members. The reply of the House was a demand for the control of the Militia; and its rejection was followed by the refusal to open the gates of Hull. As if this were not a sufficient declaration of war, a scheme of government was submitted to the king in which the crown was reduced to the place which it holds in the Constitution to-day. For what the Petitioners describe as 'our humble desires,' and what Vicars called 'a most submissive petition[2],' really reduced the kingship to a shadow. As in the Constitution of 1791, there runs through the 'Nineteen Propositions' a perpetual undertone of distrust. Parliament was to have the sole choice of Ministers[3], the sole regulation of policy, domestic and foreign, the sole management of the Militia; to superintend the education of the royal children; to remodel the Church; to have a veto on the appointment of Peers; to undertake the custody of forts and castles. It is impossible not to feel that Charles was right when he declared that the new departure not merely weakened but practically set aside the king's sovereignty altogether[4]. The

---

[1] *Commons' Journals*, II. 330.
[2] Vicars' *Parliamentary Chronicle*, II. 87.   [3] Gardiner's *Documents*.
[4] *Parl. Hist.* II. 1330–45; cp. *Eikon Basilike*, ch. 11; and Hobbes, *Behemoth*, Dialogue 2. There is a very witty contemporary satire in the *Rump Songs*, I. 17–19.

Florentine ambassador wrote home that the Commons not only distrusted the king but rejected the monarchical principle[1]. To say this, however, does not imply that Charles was not responsible for bringing things to such a pass[2].

The position is illustrated by a pamphlet[3] published a month later by Henry Parker, who was becoming a recognised spokesman of the Parliament. Monarchy has lost all sanctity and romance for the writer. God is no more the author of one form of government than of another. All power is originally in the people, and God only confirms that form which is selected by common consent. Since the office of King was instituted to preserve the commonalty, it is absurd to imagine that any nation would give itself absolutely into the hands of an individual. The Charter of Nature entitles the subjects of all countries to safety, and the community, by virtue of its paramount interest, may justly seize power and use it for its own preservation. It may judge of public necessity without the king, who has 'no negative voice,' though it does not claim this power as ordinary. When a question arises between King and Commonwealth, it cannot fall under the examination of any inferior judicature, 'for that is furnished only with rules of particular justice, which rules being too narrow for so capacious a subject, we must refer to those that the original laws of Nature hold out to us[4].' The justification of this is to be found in the fact that, whereas the sting of monarchy is the danger of bondage[5], no age furnishes a story of a Parliament freely elected exercising any tyranny.

---

[1] '— per dire meglio, non volere più sottomettersi al governo monarchico, stimando troppo il democratico.' Salvetti, *Corresp.* x. 110.

[2] Sanford's *Studies*, 491–3.

[3] *Observations on some of His Majesty's late Answers*, T. P. vol. 153.

[4] *Observator defended*, 2 Aug. 42, T. P. vol. 114.

[5] 1–46.

The full bearing of this remarkable pamphlet and of the position which was now reached was at once recognised by the Royalists. The nation, said Bramhall, was governed by certain far-fetched conclusions drawn by empirics from the law of Nature and Nations. What was this Charter of Nature? Whatever it was, it might be limited by positive laws, which, in their turn, had a directive, not a coercive power over the king, his title being not election but conquest. The government should conceal from the promiscuous multitude its own strength; but now the incendiaries were magnifying the power of the People and breaking open the Cabinet of State. This license to censure and oppose the sovereign was destructive to all societies[1]. Bramhall's vigorous book really seizes all the points of the coming controversy. He recognises that a great battle is about to be fought, and that the enemy will rely equally on historical and philosophical weapons, on the Laws of England and on the Laws of Nature. Salmasius said later that he had foreseen the republic from the very origin of the conflict. But Salmasius wrote when all was over[2], while Bramhall's insight was prophetic.

'Both sides,' wrote the aged Sir Thomas Roe at this moment, 'are so confident in their cause that nothing can decide the quarrel but blood[3].' After the first campaign, however, the peace party in Parliament had been growing steadily. Many who had calmly contemplated a short struggle felt indisposed to commit themselves to a long one. Many, too, felt that, if the combat continued,

[1] 'Serpent-Salve against the Observator,' *Works*, A.-C. L. III. 302–421.
[2] Writing from Leyden, in April, 1649, of the King's death, he says, 'La nouvelle m'a troublé, mais ne m'a point surpris. Dès le commencement, il m'a esté aisé de juger qu'ils ont eu le dessein de se faire République.' Carte's *Original Letters*, I. 255, 6. Cp. Alice Thornton's *Autobiog.* 16–18, Surtees Soc.
[3] Webb's *Civil War in Hereford*, App. II. 356.

institutions that they reverenced and desired to retain might be endangered. To others again the growth of the sects, not less in numbers than in violence, seemed perilous if not to order at any rate to culture[1]. A still greater number, seeing the fortunes of war so equally divided, were anxious not to commit themselves irrevocably to either side. Of the latter class Bulstrode Whitelocke is typical. 'In all the great transactions of the time,' he explains, 'I would never appear to be entirely of any faction or party, but followed the dictates of my own reason and conscience[2].' The Commons were now willing to forgo their demand of judicial and administrative influence, but continued to press their claim of military control and the abolition of Episcopacy. It fell to White-locke to journey to Oxford to receive the king's answers. Charles, however, had a suspicion that the envoy was not wholly pleased with the terms of the party he represented, and began by flattering him. 'I wish, Mr Whitelocke,' he said pleasantly, 'others had been of your judgment, and then, I believe, we had had an happy end of our difference before now,' and begged him to give him his advice. Though protesting he had no power to do so, White-locke complied, taking the precaution, however, of disguising his

---

[1] The Adamists and Familists frightened people greatly. T. P. vols. 164, 168. It was in vain that it was urged that neither the tenets nor the con-duct of the Separatists provided cause for alarm. Second part of *Vox Populi*, T. P. vol. 124. It was suggested, for instance, that knowledge was useless and harmful. 'The sufficiency of the spirit's teaching without humane learning,' by How, the cobbler, is a remarkable exposition of this tenet and might well frighten all to whom learning was dear. T. P. vol. 25. It was the fear of culture suffering that drove Dering to join the Royalists. *Speeches*, 116, etc. T. P. vol. 197. There was a Royalist song,

> 'And so it be but new,
> Yet the Roundhead cries 'tis true,
> Because it contradicts the old.'

Political Ballads of the Commonwealth, 16, Percy Soc.

[2] *Memorials*, i. 194.

handwriting. 'What I did,' writes the astute diarist, 'was in compassion to our bleeding, distressed country[1].' The chief reason in reality was his indisposition to take an irretrievable step.

While nearly every prominent man took sides, a certain number found this either difficult or impossible or unnecessary. A few demanded time to think the matter over[2]. Not merely free lances like Sir Kenelm Digby determined to avoid it altogether, but men like Sir John Coke who had hitherto busied themselves in affairs[3]. In one case, the inhabitants of an entire county pledged themselves to remain neutral[4]. Many quietly changed with the times[5]. In describing the dissolution of the Monasteries, Fuller parenthetically remarks, 'I should think many of this age have wished for some such private place to retire to[6].' That this sentiment of neutrality was common to the greater mass of the working classes is obvious from the simultaneous appearance of the clubmen in different parts of the country[7].

The confusion that reigned in many minds is illustrated by Philip Hunton's *Treatise on Monarchy*[8]. Nobody may reject the commands of authority as unlawful, 'unless there be an open unlawfulness on the face of the act commanded.' But misgivings follow close upon this concession. No form of government can be

---

[1] I. 331–7.

[2] A very interesting and probably typical case is described in Whitacre's *Diary*, f. 4, *Addit. MSS.* 31,116. Cp. Reresby's *Memoirs*, 15.

[3] See the remarkable statement in Hist. MSS. Comm. 12*th Report*, II. 283, Coke to his father.

[4] The document in Phillips' *Civil War in the Marches*, II. 44, 5.

[5] Hollond's *Discourses of the Navy*, 110; Elrington's *Ussher*, 115, for Ussher's Chaplain, Dr Bernard, etc.

[6] Bk. VI.

[7] Their banner concisely exhibited their attitude: 'If you take our cattle, we will give you battle.' Warburton's *Rupert*, III. 118.

[8] T. P. vol. 103, 1643.

imagined without some inconveniences which admit of no remedy. That of limited monarchy is exposed to a fatal disease for which no salve can be prescribed, namely, the impossibility of constituting a judge to determine the last controversy, the sovereign's transgressing his fundamental limits[1]. Passing to a discussion of the English Monarchy, the same vagueness is everywhere apparent. Hunton writes of the existing constitution much as Burke was later to speak. 'Of the architecture of this government I am so great an admirer that whatever more than human wisdom contrived it, whether done at once or by degrees found out and perfected, I conceive it unparalleled for exactness of true policy in the whole world[2].' But may the two Estates resist the Monarchy? Against the person of the sovereign force may under no pretence be used; for he is irrevocably invested with the sovereignty which sets his person above all lawful power and force[3]. It is justified, however, by the necessity of securing the privileges of the people and the laws and frame of government[4]. These extraordinary confusions naturally gave the absolutists an easy triumph[5]; but none the less is the pamphlet of importance in representing the uncertain character of the thought at this moment.

II

Despite the forces which made for compromise, the War Party retained its ascendancy and invited the aid of Scotland. But the assistance of the Scots involved the domination of Presbyterian ideas.

The Elizabethan Presbyterians had been Conformists, and correspond closely to a large section of the Presbyterian party of

[1] pp. 17, 28.   [2] 43, 4.   [3] 50.   [4] 78.
[5] Filmer's 'Anarchy of Limited or Mixed Monarchy,' *Works*, ed. 1679, 258–307, contains an annihilating criticism.

the seventeenth century. 'Almost all those who were later called Presbyterians,' says Baxter, 'were before Conformists'; and he adds that they had taken many things as lawful in case of necessity, though they longed to have that necessity removed[1]. Of a widely different character, as we have seen, was the system which had grown up in Scotland. When the ministers were exhorted, by the king's request, to 'possess the people with loyal affections to the king,' they answered that their consciences 'could bear them witness how they endeavoured themselves thereto, neither had they ever had a thought to the contrary[2].' Yet the sovereignty of the people and the right of deposition were principles, as Heylyn bitterly lamented, which no true Scot would dare to question, unless he would be thought to betray his country[3]. These were the men who had inherited the teaching of Knox and Buchanan, who were nourished on the Commentaries of Pareus[4], who had combated every effort of James to introduce Anglicanism, who had attacked the doctrines of *The Law of Free Monarchies*. Even the gentle singer of Hawthornden declared that every prince should study Buchanan and Mariana, for his own and the public good[5]. In the manifestoes produced by the struggles of 1639–40, it was explained that the expedition was not to perform any disloyal act against the king, but to remove his evil counsellors[6]. Yet in the following year, if Montrose was speaking truly, there were 'some few upon courses for changing

[1] *Life*, 33, 4. Cp. Newcome's *Diary*, Chetham Society, *passim*; the differences from the Church are almost imperceptible.
[2] Noble's *Proceedings of the Kirk*, 1637, 8, 41, Bannatyne Club.
[3] *History of Presbyterianism*, ed. 1672, 168.
[4] Baillie's *Journals*, 1. 464.
[5] Masson's *Drummond*, 238–40.
[6] 'Lawfulness of an expedition into England,' *Treaty of Ripon*, 72–7, C. S. Cp. the prayers and other protestations of loyalty in C. S. P. 1640, 649–51.

G   7

the form of government. There is one motion for deposing the king, and there is another for setting up a dictator[1].' As the Scotch royalists lamented, 'no bounty could oblige subjects when the trumpet of rebellion sounded from the pulpits[2].'

It is in the works of Rutherford that we find the fullest exposition of the political thought of the Northern Presbyterians. Regarded at first as the spokesman of the left wing[3], with the march of events he came to be looked on as the representative of the entire party. The Bishop of Dunkeld tells us that 'every one had in his hand Rutherford's new book, *Lex Rex*, stuffed with questions that in the time of peace would have been judged damnable treason, but were now so idolised that, whereas in the beginning Buchanan was looked on as an oracle, he was now slighted as not anti-monarchical enough[4].' And indeed there is no hesitation in Rutherford. All jurisdiction of man over man is artificial and positive[5]. The form of government is determined by considerations of expediency. Aristocracy is as near to Nature as Monarchy; but if the latter is chosen, 'the people should measure out by ounce weights so much royal power and no more, on condition they may take it to themselves again if the conditions be violated[6].' In becoming a party to a contract the king remains strictly the servant of the people. To choose a king is the same thing as to make a king. If the people are the cause, the king is the effect. The king is subordinate, not coördinate[7]. Family constitutes no claim to the throne, for the origin of monarchy was elective. In like manner, Parliament can no more resist the people than can the king. Its power, too, is fiduciary, and,

---

[1] Napier's *Montrose*, 163, 4.   [2] Somerville's *Somervilles*, II. 191.
[3] Balfour's 'Annals,' *Works*, III. 410, 413.
[4] Guthry's *Memoirs*, 139.   [5] *Lex Rex*, 3, 91, T. P. vol. II.
[6] *Lex Rex*, 9.   [7] 377.

if it abuse it, the people can annul its acts[1]. The cause of the people in all countries is the same, and it is the duty of one country to go to the aid of another[2]. To freedom there are, however, limits. That the people, as a collective entity, should have their way is not to say that the component parts may do and think as they will[3].

In the early years of the crisis, the English Presbyterians had been lost in the ranks of the king's opponents[4]. Their position in 1643 is exhaustively stated in that work which was widely recognised as the quintessence of political wisdom[5], and which, according to Baxter, exercised immense influence on minds that were wavering[6]. Prynne's *Sovereign Power of Parliaments* commences by declaring that, dangerous as the paradox might seem, the Parliament was above the king and could enforce his assent to bills necessary for the common weal and safety of his subjects[7]. Most justly, by the Law of Nature and Nations, might measures directed to their destruction be resisted by the people and the agents be imprisoned; for the king was but the kingdom's public servant[8]. In such cases war was neither treason nor rebellion; for when the nobility joined with the Commons in defence of their

---

[1] *Lex Rex*, 152.   [2] 378–84; cp. 454–67.
[3] For the more popular government of Independents and others in Church matters Rutherford expresses his contempt, *Due Rights of Presbyteries*, 28, T. P. vol. 41. His name is pilloried among the Forcers of Conscience in Milton's famous sonnet; and his *Disputation against Pretended Liberty of Conscience*, T. P. vol. 567, deserves the punishment.
[4] They were singled out, however, for vigorous censure, as early as 1641, by Sir T. Aston, T. P. vol. 163.
[5] Voetius to Prynne, 'Non video quid ultra desiderari potest. Debet tractatus ille Latine et Gallice existere ut reformatis theologis et politicis in Europa legi potest' (*sic*). Vicars' *Parl. Chronicle*, III. 203.
[6] *Life*, 41.
[7] Ed. 1643, Part I. 33, 112; and Part II. 65–79.
[8] Part II. 16, 39; and Part IV. 14–36.

ancient liberties, they could not be called rebels[1]. This argued
no distaste for Monarchy, for the author had always been and
would always be an honourer and defender of kings and kingship[2]. To prove that evil monarchs alone suffered from the application of the theory, Prynne reminded his readers of the cases
of Mary Stuart and Philip II[3].

The exposition of the Presbyterian philosophy was closely followed by the League and Covenant. The proposals were little
short of revolutionary; but the subscribers were to endeavour
with their estates and lives to preserve and defend the king's person and authority, 'that the world may bear witness with our
consciences to our loyalty and that we have no thought nor intention to diminish his Majesty's just power and greatness[4].' The
Westminster Confession, in like manner, inculcated obedience to
'the power which God hath ordained[5].' But this reading of their
conduct was not generally accepted. Early in 1644 appeared a
royalist call of alarm. In his *Stumbling-block of Disobedience*[6],
Heylyn traced the new philosophy to its origin in the Reformation. When Elizabeth asked the Scotch Commissioners the
reason of their deposition of the queen, they replied with a quotation from Calvin. 'This will shew on whose authority the
Presbyterians build their damnable doctrine, not only of dis-
turbing and restraining the power of princes, but also of deposing
them whenever they shall please to pretend cause for it[7].' But
the scholars had gone far beyond their master, and their teaching
had borne fruit. The 'darling doctrine of the time' was that the
king, being but a creature of the people's making, could be un-
made as easily as made. The principles and aims of the Scotch

---

[1] *Sovereign Power of Parliaments*, Part III. 10, 115.
[2] Part IV. Preface.   [3] Appendix, 100–207.   [4] Art. 3.
[5] Ch. xx.   [6] *Tracts*, ed. 1681.   [7] 643.

and English opponents of the king, however, were so different
that it was impossible for the Presbyterians to remain long at the
helm. The opposition began with an attack on their theocratic
tendencies by the Erastians.

The 'Glory of England,' as he was called by Grotius, the
man of whom Howell wrote 'Quod Seldenus nescit, nemo scit[1],'
had played a distinguished part as the champion of popular rights
for twenty years preceding the meeting of the Long Parliament.
But though sympathising with the objects of the forward party
in the House, he disapproved of the methods they pursued[2]. Selden's energies were therefore devoted to resisting the new ecclesiastical pretensions that were arising. 'He was not over loving of
any, and least of all of Presbyterian, clergymen,' records Fuller[3].
Though Whitelocke's famous picture[4] is to a large extent a libel
on the learning of certain members of the Westminster Assembly,
it represents with complete accuracy the spirit in which Selden
moved amongst them. 'Mr Selden,' said the wits, 'visits them
to see wild asses fight, as the Persians used to do[5].' The hatred
with which he was regarded is mirrored in the pages of Baillie's
Journals. The Erastian party under the leadership of Selden was
stronger than that of the Independents, and was likely to do more

[1] *Letters*, ed. Jacobs, 660.
[2] 'How wicked soever were the actions which were every day done,'
writes Clarendon, 'I was confident that he had not given his consent to
them, but would have hindered them if he could consistently with his own
safety, to which he was always enough indulgent.' Clarendon's *Life*, I. 35,
6. [On Selden see Professor Hazeltine's article in *Harvard Law Review*,
vol. XXIV. 1910–11, p. 105; and the Introduction by D. Ogg to his reprint of Selden's preface to *Fleta*. There is now an excellent edition of the
Table Talk by S. H. Reynolds. H. J. L.]
[3] *Church Hist.* VI. 286.
[4] Aug. 12, 1643, I. 209.
[5] *Harl. Misc.* V. 99; Birkenhead's *Assembly Man*.

harm than all the sectaries of England. It was composed of lawyers, worldly profane men, 'extraordinarily affrighted to come
under the yoke of ecclesiastical discipline.' The good D'Ewes
found him 'so much more learned than pious' that he 'never
attained unto great entireness with him[1].' Even when they were
at last induced to consent to the erection of Presbyteries and
Synods throughout the land, they gave the ecclesiastical courts so
little power that the assembly was in great doubt as to whether
it would be worth while to erect them at all[2].

'Religion,' declared Selden, 'was no more to be left to the
clergy than the law to the Chancellor[3].' Convocation, in respect
to Parliament, is as a Court-leet, where they have power to make
by-laws, as they call them ; as that a man shall put so many cows
or sheep on the common[4].' 'The Minister when he is made
should be materia prima, apt for any form the state will put upon
him ; but of himself he can do nothing[5].' But the state is to take
over the settlement of theological questions merely to ensure
liberty. ''Tis a vain thing to talk of an heretic ; for a man can
think no otherwise than he does think. In the primitive times,
there were many opinions. One of these being embraced by some
prince and received into his kingdom, the rest were condemned
as heresies ; and his religion, which was but one of the several
opinions, is first said to be orthodox and then to have continued
from the time of the Apostles[6].' It was blasphemy to affirm that
the Holy Ghost was president of the General Councils ; the truth
was that 'the odd man was the Holy Ghost[7].' The questioning
spirit which breathes through every utterance in his *Table Talk*

[1] D'Ewes, *Autobiog.* I. 256.
[2] Baillie, II. 265–336.   [3] *Table Talk*, Religion.
[4] Convocation.   [5] Minister.
[6] Opinion.   [7] Council.

found its last illustration on his deathbed. If Aubrey is to be trusted, Hobbes came to visit Selden and found a minister at the door. 'What, will you that have wrote like a man now die like a woman?' said the philosopher of Malmesbury. And Aubrey relates that the minister was not allowed to enter[1].

Despite his opposition to the theory of Natural Right[2], Selden's political philosophy is distinctly democratic. 'A king is a thing men have made for their own sakes, for quietness' sake. Just as in a family one man is appointed to buy the meat; if every man should buy, or if there were many buyers, they would never agree[3].' Yet the title means different things in different places. 'Kings are all individual, this or that king, there is no species of kings. A king that claims privileges in his own country because they have them in another is just as a cook that claims fees in one Lord's house because they are allowed in another. If the master of the house will yield them, well and good. Prerogative is something that can be told what it is, not something that has no name[4].' For the people as a whole are the true sovereigns. 'The knights and burgesses sit for themselves and others. What is the reason? Because the room will not hold all[5].' What is the relation between these two sovereigns? May subjects take up arms against the prince? 'Conceive it thus. Here lies a shilling between us; tenpence is yours, twopence is mine. By agreement, I am as much king of my twopence as you of your tenpence. If you therefore go about to take away my twopence, I will defend it, for there you and I are equal, both princes.... To know what obedience is due to the prince, you must look into the contract

---

[1] Aubrey's *Lives*, ii. 532.
[2] *Table Talk*, Law of Nature; cp. his *De Jure Naturali*, ed. 1665, especially Lib. i. c. 8, 98, 9.
[3] *Table Talk*, King.   [4] King, Prerogative.
[5] House of Commons.

betwixt him and his people. When the contract is broken, the decision is by arms[1].' Nevertheless, the utmost hesitation should be observed. 'Pretending religion and the law of God is to set all things loose[2]. There is not anything in the world more abused than this sentence, *Salus populi suprema lex*. For we apply it as if we ought to forsake the known law when it may be most for the advantage of the people. It means no such thing[3].'

Under the three-fold influence of the constitutionalism derived from his legal training, the distrust of ecclesiastical influence which he imbibed in the course of his experience, and the critical bent of his mind, Selden ranks as one of the truest lovers of liberty of his time. Drawing his friends throughout life from men of all parties[4], few looked past party cries more than he. It is characteristic that he should have written in the beginning of every book which he added to his library, περὶ παντὸς τὴν ἐλευθερίαν[5].

III

Powerful as was the Erastian opposition to Presbyterian ideals, the secular spirit alone was not strong enough in the seventeenth century to undermine their ascendancy in England. A deadlier foe was the widespread determination to achieve a more complete political self-government, and to obtain freedom of thought and action in religious matters. But the anarchy involved in religious individualism seemed to the Presbyterians to threaten their dominion even more than episcopacy, and the increasing terror of

---

[1] *Table Talk*, War.   [2] Religion and Conscience.
[3] People.
[4] Suckling's *Session of the Poets*; Burnet's *Life of Hale*; Wordsworth's *Ecclesiastical Biography*, IV. 540; Whitelocke's *Embassy*, II. 478, 467, 8; Clarendon's *Life*, I. 35–7.
[5] Wood's *Athenae*, III. 368.

it gradually led them to sever their connection with the popular party and to work for a compromise with the king. In 1645, the very year in which Presbyterianism was proclaimed the state religion, the ascendancy of the Presbyterians came to an end.

The growth of radical sentiments had been making steady progress. Revolutionary and republican utterances had been throughout these years comparatively rare. In January, 1642, Heenvliet, the Dutch ambassador, was told by the queen that the citizens of London no longer raised their hats to herself and her husband, and that some cried out that he would not be the first king the people had deposed[1]. It was natural that Henry Marten, with his scanty reverence for established conventionalities and his keen independence of thought[2], should have been the first to express the feeling that was soon to find general acceptance. About the time of the Root and Branch bill, in the course of a conversation with Hyde, Marten remarked that in his opinion one man was not wise enough to govern all;—'the first word I ever heard man speak to that purpose' adds Clarendon[3]. In his answer to the Declaration of both Houses in May, 1642, the king declared that he must have inquiry made into the statement of Marten that 'the happiness of the kingdom did not depend on his majesty or any of the royal branches of that root[4].' Calamy

[1] Van Prinsterer's *Archives de la maison d'Orange*, III. 501.
[2] Aubrey's *Lives*, II. 434–7; Wood's *Athenae*, III. 1237–43. D'Ewes speaks of him as a 'violent' or a 'fiery' spirit. *Reports*, 1047 b, 1144 b, etc.
[3] *Life*, I. 92, ed. 1827. There was a tradition, and it is accepted by Ranke, II. 278, that in the debate on the king's journey to Scotland in August, 1641, when the proposal had been made that a deputy or *custos regni* should be appointed or that the royal functions should be entrusted to the Prince of Wales or the Elector Palatine, a voice cried that there was no longer need to observe monarchical forms, since the king, by absenting himself against the will of Parliament, had virtually abdicated. But the story receives no confirmation from the State Papers. C. S. P. 1641–3, xv.
[4] Clarendon, *History*, v. 280.

was credited with saying in 1643 that he hoped to see the Church and king pulled down[1], and L'Estrange quotes a letter of the same year calling for the punishment of 'great delinquents[2].' We learn on the same authority that a minister was in the habit of praying 'If thou wilt not bless us with a king, bless us without one[3].' It was noticed with alarm that Mariana's *De Rege* was 'everywhere[4].' Blake, too, may without doubt be counted as a republican at this early period[5]. The sentiment, however, gained ground but slowly. In defending a libel against the Court at this time, Marten dropped the words, 'Better one family be destroyed than many.' 'Who?' cried a chorus of voices. 'The king and his children,' was the reply, which was followed by removal to the Tower[6]. Though the detention was short, his offence was regarded as sufficiently grave to warrant his exclusion for over two years.

In 1644 the House was becoming less sensitive. Parliament, wrote Salvetti in June, had sent a leading member to Scotland to suggest that the countries should unite to depose Charles and transform the government into a republic, and several members had applied to the Venetian ambassador for an account of the constitution of the republic[7]. A month later, he wrote that there was a strong determination in both nations to depose the king[8]. The Prince Palatine was now invited to England, and Salvetti considered it could only be for the purpose of crowning him[9]. A few months later it was thought more probable that one

---

[1] Dugdale's *Diary*, 96.
[2] L'Estrange's *Dissenters' Sayings*, 68, ed. 1681.　　　[3] *ib.* 67.
[4] Twysden's *Government of England*, 18, C. S.
[5] Clarendon, *History*, xv. 57.
[6] *Commons' Journals*, Sept. 9, 1643.
[7] Salvetti, *Corresp.* x. 282 b. Sabran, the French ambassador, wrote home that the notion of a Republic was widely spread. In Raumer's *Briefe aus Paris*, Letter 71.
[8] Salvetti, x. 291.　　　　　　　[9] *ib.* 319 b.

of the young princes would be substituted[1]. The reverence for royalty, too, was departing. Harry Marten dressed up George Wither in the king's clothes, and the latter proceeded to perform 'a thousand apish and ridiculous actions[2].' The position is illustrated in the pages of a tract by Henry Parker, 'published by authority' in the autumn of this year[3]. In his most recent work the author had contended that, but for the fear of bondage, Monarchy was 'the most exquisite of all forms of government.' He now maintained that Monarchy and Aristocracy are 'derivative forms and are a dependence on Democracy,' which is the most natural. The origin of royalty is painted in far from flattering colours, and Barclay is introduced to testify that, according to the teaching of the most violent assertor of absolutism, the people may depose their king 'when he has a partial interest[4].' The Propositions of Uxbridge proved that all respect for the king and constitution of the country had disappeared. The peace party, in their desire to slacken the pace, consulted Whitelocke as to the feasibility of checking the rising influence of Cromwell by impeachment on the ground of being an incendiary. The cautious lawyer, however, gave it as his opinion that it would be unsafe to attack a man of such influence and ability[5].

The year 1645 marks the turning-point in the growth of Republicanism. In this year the Self-Denying Ordinance and the New Model transferred power from the hands of the Peace

[1] Salvetti, x. 418, and xi. 4, 4 a.
[2] Wood's *Athenae*, iii. 1237-43; cp. an instance at the same period, in Symonds' *Diary*, 67, C. S.
[3] *Jus Populi*, T. P. vol. 12.
[4] 60-7, cp. the 'Power of the Laws of a Kingdom over a misled King,' a tract of the same period, dealing with the question of deposition in a very outspoken way. *Harl. Misc.* iv. 563-6.
[5] *Memorials*, i. 346, 7.

to that of the War Party, and the king and his cause were in consequence crushed. It brought, also, the new elections. Marten returned to his seat, and several future republicans and regicides entered the House for the first time, among them Sydney and Blake, Ireton and Ludlow, Hutchinson and Skippon. Above all, the sects that had sprung forth like a harvest of armed men from the soil threw themselves into opposition to the Presbyterians.

At the basis of the creed of every religious body of the time, except the Presbyterians, lay the Millenarian idea. The abilities and the high position of Joseph Mede had given currency to Millenarian notions as far back as the twenties[1], but not till the outbreak of the crisis in 1640 did the doctrine cease to be the property of Professors. It then appeared in an extravagant form in a tract by a lady[2], and in the following year was championed by Archer in a lengthy pamphlet[3]. Foreign works, too, now begin to appear in an English dress[4]. So popular did the teaching become that Bishop Hall thought it necessary to compose a refutation[5]. But the idea was too much in harmony with the age to yield to argument, and its spread was rapid[6].

To the Millenarian substratum was quickly added an Antinomian superstructure. About 1643 Antinomians[7] began to increase rapidly and to cause the Westminster Assembly grave anxiety[8]. Their critics derived them from the Anabaptists of Munster and Henry Nicholas[9], and credited them with the intention to kill

---

[1] Fuller considers Mede the first. *Worthies*, I. 519.
[2] T. P. vol. 172, The Lady Eleanor's Appeal.
[3] T. P. vol. 180.   [4] T. P. vol. 90, etc.
[5] *Works*, vol. VIII. The Revelation Unrevealed.
[6] Cp. Joseph Lister's *Autob.* 50, 1.
[7] The title, however, was disowned in Saltmarsh's *Free Grace*, Preface, T. P. vol. 1152.
[8] Lightfoot's *Works*, XIII. 9; and Gillespie's *Works*, II. 10.
[9] Rutherford's *Spiritual Antichrist*, Preface, T. P. vol. 415.

'as Antichrists' all who were not of their own following[1]. As a
matter of fact the names of their spokesmen, except for a dis-
respectful reference by Saltmarsh to the king in 1643[2], do not
meet us in connection with politics at all, while their teaching
in relation to political questions is undefined[3]. And yet there was
danger lurking behind the quietism. 'We are not under the Law,'
said Saltmarsh, their earliest spokesman, 'but under Grace. Who
shall say anything to the charge of God's sheep? Who shall condemn[4]?' In America, it was remembered, this teaching had borne
fruit in the career of Mrs Hutchinson and had thrown Massachusetts into a panic[5].

With the Antinomians were commonly connected the 'Anabaptists,' and Baillie, on reaching London in 1643, found the
latter advancing only less rapidly than the former[6]. Two years
later they were described as the most numerous of the sects[7]. The
character of the movement was undergoing a corresponding
change. In the sect that had so often declared itself to be quiet
and law-abiding no alteration was observed at the meeting of the
Long Parliament[8]. In 1641, however, Lord Brooke had testified
to the existence of a radical wing[9], and Baillie was soon after

[1] Rutherford's *Secrets of Antinomianism*, 239, T. P. vol. 415.
[2] *C. J.* Aug. 16, 1643.
[3] The fullest expression is in Saltmarsh's *Sparkles of Glory*, 135–40, T.
P. vol. 1114. Their hostility was confined to outward forms of worship.
Dell's *Forms the pillar of Antichrist*, T. P. vol. 883. They held the doctrine
of the Inner Light with all the intensity of the Quakers. Dell's *Voice from
the Temple*, T. P. vol. 945.
[4] *Free Grace*, 128, T. P. vol. 1152. The Millenarian element is prominent in Dell's *Christ held forth by the Word*, T. P. vol. 1170.
[5] The whole American movement is most fully described in Welde, *Rise
of the Antinomians of New England*, T. P. vol. 33.
[6] *Journals*, II. 117.   [7] *ib.* II. 327; and Baxter, *Life*, 50.
[8] *Discovery of 29 Sects*, T. P. vol. 168.
[9] *Discourse on Episcopacy*, 99, 100, T. P. vol. 177.

offended by their 'insolencies intolerable[1].' In 1645 charges of a more definite character are met with. ' In all the sects, especially the Anabaptists,' wrote Baillie, 'there is a declared averseness from all obedience to the present magistrates and laws, and frequent motions to have the very fundamentals of government new modelled. They do no more dissemble their detestation of monarchy[2].' Fuller, too, credited them with declaring that a king could not make a good law if he were not perfectly regenerate[3]. But these charges prove rather that such notions were prevalent in the army than that they were to be found pre-eminently among those who rejected infant baptism[4].

Most important of the religious bodies that ranged themselves in opposition to Presbyterianism was that of the Independents. About the middle of the thirties, Independency or Brownism began to grow rapidly, and to attract attention as a possible danger. 'If I hate any,' wrote Howell in 1636, ''tis those that trouble the sweet peace of our Church. I could be content to see an Anabaptist go to hell on a Brownist's back[5].' No less than thirty distinct attacks were made on 'the Brownists' in the three years before the meeting of the Westminster Assembly[6], and, though the term is of course generic, we may infer that of the heretics against whom the shafts were directed a part were Congregation-

---

[1] *Journals*, II. 140, 157, 215–18.

[2] *Anabaptism*, 59, T. P. vol. 369.

[3] *Church Hist.* VI. 180.

[4] 'Anabaptist' was a generic title. Cp. Selden's *Table Talk*, Conscience; Cheynell's *Rise of Socinianism*, 55, T. P. vol. 103. Cotton Mather even describes Goodwin and Owen as Anabaptists. *Magnalia*, II. 534. This view is confirmed by the testimony of Edwards, a year after Naseby, that multitudes of the sectaries were deserting the 'Anabaptists' and were turning 'Seekers and Libertines.' *Gangraena*, II. 13, 14.

[5] *Letters*, ed. Jacob, 337.

[6] Dexter's *Bibliography*.

alists[1]. In the House of Peers, during a discussion on the Liturgy, Lord Say had urged the Archbishop to conciliate the growing movement on the ground that they differed from the Church in no fundamental doctrine; but Laud replied that their opinions were widely different from those of the Church. Was it not a fundamental whether the Church was or was not a true Church? Many of them, too, were tainted with heresy[2]. There is, however, no charge of political heterodoxy in Laud's attack, and in the first of the lists of heretics that were to become so common the Brownist is denounced rather as a fool than a knave[3].

The return of the Five Ministers from Holland and the appearance of their Apology marks a turning-point in the history of Independency in England. The movement had hitherto counted but few adherents[4], and was spoken of with contempt[5], chiefly because it numbered the poor and ignorant in its ranks[6]. Some of the ablest divines in the country, discreet, learned and godly men, as Baxter admits[7], had now declared themselves Independents, had become members of the Westminster Assembly[8], and had issued an appeal for toleration. They insulted the dignity of magistrates by pleading for toleration, said Edwards, a tenet which they had learnt from Roger Williams[9]. Yet the authors

---

[1] 'There are many reverend and learned Independent Ministers,' wrote Cheynell in 1643, 'and they are all put down as Brownists.' *Rise of Socinianism*, 65, T. P. vol. 103. But the names were interchangeable in controversy. *Anatomy of Independency*, 15–32, T. P. vol. 50, etc.

[2] *Works*, VI. 129–41, Answer to Lord Say.

[3] *Discovery of 29 Sects in London*, 3, T. P. vol. 168.

[4] 'Indeed they are but a few people,' said their defender, Catherine Chidley, in 1641. *Justification of the Independents*, Dis. 2, 3, T. P. vol. 174.

[5] Parker's *Contra Replicant*, 9, T. P. vol. 87, etc.

[6] T. P. vols. 164, 84, etc.   [7] *Life*, 140.

[8] 'Very few; but prime men,' wrote Baillie, II. 336.

[9] *Gangraena*, I. 20, T. P. vol. 323.

stated that they prayed publicly for kings and all in authority[1]. In the thunderbolt that was soon after launched by Baillie, the fear that the movement was beginning to inspire becomes apparent. Some members, he said, like the grossest Anabaptists, denied the lawfulness of any magistrate at all. They would abolish all existing laws and hinder any more from being made[2]; and the author set himself to establish this conclusion in a separate work[3].

The difficulty of distinguishing the Independent position from that of other bodies was now becoming insuperable. Where, asked the first part of the *Gangraena*, where is an Independent Church that is merely Independent? Independency was the mother of all sects, and every error took sanctuary in her. Those who were once merely Independents or Brownists at most, into what errors had they fallen! And their activity and their vices were beyond all doubt; men of an hundred eyes and hands out-acting and out-working all the Presbyterians, having their agents everywhere; and their members were libertines or needy men[4].

In response to Edwards' attack, the leader of the Independents came forward. John Goodwin, while still a clergyman of the English Church, had more than once come under the notice of Laud for ecclesiastical and doctrinal eccentricities[5], and his scruples had led him to throw up the appointments which his learning had won for him in Cambridge University[6]. On the outbreak of the war he joined the side of Parliament, and published a justification of his action. His theory was still fairly orthodox. The people were not opposing the king, but 'defending his royal

[1] 23, 4, T. P. vol. 80. It is significant that neither here nor in the *Antapologia*, T. P. vol. 1, does Edwards refer to any political heresies.
[2] *Dissuasive*, 124–96, T. P. vol. 317.
[3] *Anabaptism the true Fountain of Independency, Brownism*, etc.
[4] 16–185.   [5] *Works*, v. 333, 356.
[6] Calamy's *Ejected Ministers*, 1. 239.

person, honour and estate, endangered by his accursed retinue.'
To this they were urged by the manifest law of God and by the
light of nature[1]. It was the duty of subjects to examine the commands of their superiors; and if the clergy had preached this
doctrine instead of the contrary, kings would have had a better
record in history[2]. But 'as for offering violence to the person of the
king or trying to take away his life,' he adds, 'I never travelled
with any desires or thoughts that way. It is a just prerogative of
the person of kings in what case soever to be secure from the
violence of men, and their lives to be as consecrated corn, meet to
be reaped and gathered only by the hand of God[3].' A development
of political thought is to be found in the notable championship
of Lilburne against equally unfounded accusations[4]. Goodwin
was very far from being a Calvinist, and in the second volume
of the *Gangraena* he is told that in a few years he will prove 'as
arch an heretic as England ever bred[5].' He is further accused of
making all the heretics saints and faithful servants of God[6]. In
the third volume, he has become 'a monotonous sectary, a com-
pound of Socinianism, Arminianism, Libertinism, Antinomianism,
Independency, Popery and Scepticism[7].'

In these indictments there is little which definitely connects
the Independent divines with radical opinions. Several of the
London congregations declared that they disapproved of no form
of civil government, but freely acknowledged that a kingly govern-

---

[1] *Lawfulness and Necessity of the War*, T. P. vol. 123.
[2] *Anti-Cavalierisme*, 18, etc. T. P. vol. 123.
[3] *Lawfulness*, etc. 10, 11.
[4] *Cretensis*, 48, T. P. vol. 328.
[5] 44, T. P. vol. 338. Baillie writes, 'Goodwin is said to be a Socinian.'
At any rate, some of his followers were. Cp. Wallace's *Anti-trinitarians*, III.
372–89.
[6] *Gangraena*, 36.   [7] 114, etc. T. P. vol. 368.

ment was allowed by God and 'a good accommodation to men[1].'
Needham, then a Royalist, advised the king to ally with the Independents, on the ground that their principles led them to admit
rather of monarchy than of any other government[2]. There is,
indeed, reason to believe that the march of their thought merely
kept pace with that of the Independents among the Army leaders.
The tone of a pamphlet by Cook, the most theological of laymen,
is studiously moderate[3]. The chief object of the movement is
still to attain complete religious freedom. With this, he argues,
politics would assume a new phase. 'Such liberty will wonderfully endear all conscientious men to the magistrate, King and
Parliament, and gain the hearts of the People.' But though the
author held it 'very uncivil not to yield to a civil government,'
a warning note is struck by the question, What is an argument
from authority to a wise man[4]?

A more radical element was introduced among the Independent
divines by the appearance of the 'Vicar General of the Independents of Old and New England[5],' Hugh Peters. After owing his
early training to Hooker in Rotterdam, and familiarising himself
for several years with New England methods[6], he returned and
became a chaplain in the New Model Army[7]. In a short time

---

[1] Neal, III. 121. The charge that the Independents were concocting a
plot to murder the king in the autumn of this year, 1647, was of course
merely an attempt to blacken their character. *Independent Plot discovered*,
T. P. vol. 419.

[2] *Case of the Kingdom stated*, 2–4, T. P. vol. 1948.

[3] *What the Independents would have*, T. P. vol. 405.

[4] 8–14.

[5] *Gangraena*, II. 61.

[6] It is illustrative of his secular character that his memory in the New
World was chiefly associated with his activity in connection with the
fisheries. Winthrop's *Journal*, I. 209–11. Cp. 'Peters Pattern,' a 'funeral
sermon' of some pretensions to wit. *Harl. Misc.* VI. 181, 2.

[7] This connection between American Independency and the English

he raised himself to a position of great influence, and it was said of him that, as sure as Peter kept the keys of heaven, Peters kept the keys of the consciences of the Grandees, opening and shutting them at pleasure[1]. The suggestions contained in one of his earliest pamphlets shew no little moderation of thought[2]; but he seems to have been nevertheless of a rough and almost brutal nature[3]. There was a report that he had once suggested that the records of the country should be burned. If we may believe Warwick, he worried Laud all the way from his prison to the scaffold[4]; and, if Lilburne is to be trusted, Peters declared, in the course of conversation in Newgate, that Law was the sword and what it gave, and that there was no government in the world but what the sword maintained[5]. Although, then, the Independents as a body had developed no precise political philosophy, the teaching of certain of its members had prepared the soil for the reception of seed scattered by other hands[6].

The final defeat of the king opened the flood-gates of radicalism that was stored up in the newly grown religious bodies. It was immediately after Naseby that Baxter visited the camp, and 'understood the state of the army much better than ever before.' He found a state of things, he adds, 'he had never dreamt of.' The revolutionary spirit was abroad. 'I heard the plotting heads

revolution is interestingly noticed in the *Kingdom's Division Anatomised*, T. P. vol. 545.

[1] Walker's *History of Independency*, Pt. II. 180.
[2] 'Word for the Army,' *Harl. Misc.* v. 607–13.
[3] Cp. Heath's *Chronicle*, 197.
[4] *Memoirs*, 181. Clarendon tells the story that Peters told Hotham and his son, to whom he was sent as chaplain, that they would not be executed, and thereby encouraged them to reveal matters on the strength of which they were put to death. VIII. 282, 3.
[5] *Discourse between Lilburne and Peters*, 5, T. P. vol. 556.
[6] Cp. Goodwin's *Innocency Triumphing*, 97, T. P. vol. 24.

very hot on that which intimated the intention to subvert Church and State. A few proud hot-headed sectaries had got into the highest places, and by their very heat and activity bore down the rest and carried them along.' The life of the new chaplain of Whalley's regiment was a daily contention. 'I found many honest men of ignorance and weak judgments seduced into a disputing vein, to talking for Church democracy or State democracy.' But Baxter under-estimated the strength of the new ideas, for he thought that with a few more Presbyterian ministers 'the whole plot might have been broken down, and King, Parliament and Religion preserved[1].'

The same revolution is reflected in the pages of Thomas Edwards. In the first volume of the *Gangraena*, appearing in February 1646, but written no doubt earlier, the heresies catalogued are almost purely theological. But for the passing remark[2] that the Civil Government had been 'blasphemed,' we do not hear of any political offences. In the second volume, on the other hand, published in May of the same year, among the 'new errors,' the second runs that 'monarchical government is unlawful and that it cannot be said to what use kings serve except to debauch and vex the people[3].' It had been further related to the author that Walwyn the Leveller had declared it sin to pray for the king, and had expressed his surprise at the simplicity in the hearts of the people that they should suffer themselves to be governed by a single person, since with such a government the kingdom could not be safe[4]. The third volume appeared in the autumn, and it is significant that its explicit intention is to deal primarily

---

[1] *Life*, 50–3.   [2] 39.   [3] 3.
[4] 26–8. Cp. Salvetti, *Corresp.* xi. 165, 266 b. 'Every day the people grow more tired of the King and Monarchy. England is already a republic, for everything is done in the name of the State.'

with the errors in connection with Civil Magistracy and Government[1]. That all places should be filled by direct election, that the king and Parliament are the mere creatures of the people and may be deposed at pleasure, that men of the present age should regard themselves as absolutely free from what their forefathers yielded to, that the land should be divided into equal shares: such were some of the tenets of the people's new creed. Fairfax's chaplain told his congregation that, as the people owned the power, they ought not to part from it[2]. Peters had remarked in conversation what a stir there was about the king, as if they could not live without one[3]. The lawyers themselves had been affected[4]. Worse than all, the Levellers had arisen, and the political heresies of Lilburne were too numerous to be noticed in the present work, and deserved to have a special volume devoted to them[5].

[1] *Gangraena*, 1. [2] 63.
[3] 121. Cp. Clarendon, *State Papers*, 11. App. 39; and Rushworth, VII. 768, 9; and Dalrymple's *Memorials*, 11. 166, 7.
[4] L'Estrange's *Dissenters' Sayings*, 67. [5] 153.

CHAPTER V

The Political Opinions of the Army

I

WHO were the Levellers[1], and what did they teach? In respect to no party of the time is our information so abundant, and of none are the judgments of contemporaries so conflicting. The name, which is of itself answerable for not a little misunderstanding, appears to owe its currency either to Charles I or to Cromwell[2]. Ultra-Royalists, as a matter of course, took the designation literally. "'Twas their devilish intention,' writes Heath, 'to abrogate and abolish the laws, to invade all property, and by a wild parity to lay all things in common[3]!' Even Clarendon affected to believe that they preached equality of estates[4]. Among the Presbyterians great confusion of opinion prevailed. To Edwards, John Lilburne resembled John of Leyden 'as if he had been spit out of his mouth[5].' Prynne credited them with a desire for 'the total abrogation of the laws[6].' On the other

---

[1] [The best book on the Levellers is T. C. Pease's *The Leveller Movement*, which slightly modifies the account here given. On the notion of fundamental law C. H. McIlwain's *High Court of Parliament* is of great importance. There is also material of importance in W. Rothschild's *Der Gedanke der geschriebenen Verfassung in der englischen Revolution*. Professor Pease's criticism of Rothschild, *op. cit.* 193, is, however, justified. He points out also that Lilburne had a direct influence on Hone and the Radicals of the early nineteenth century. *ib.* 362. H. J. L.]

[2] 'The Leveller,' *Harl. Misc.* IV. 549; Baxter's *Life*, 61. It first appears in a Letter in the Clarendon MSS. Gardiner's *Civil War*, III. 380.

[3] *Chronicle*, ed. 1676, 131; and cp. 233.

[4] *Hist.* X. 122, 140.

[5] *Gangraena*, vol. 3, 262, T. P. vol. 368.

[6] *Seasonable Vindication*, 9, T. P. vol. 488.

hand, Baxter dismissed with contempt the notion that they 'wanted to level all men[1].' Clement Walker regarded them as 'the truest asserters of liberty, the most constant to their principles of any in the army[2].' Sedgwick, the well-known preacher, considered that they were men 'justly sensible of the miscarriage of all that had gone before,' and only mistaken in applying the remedy[3]. Among the Independents, the same variety of judgments meets us. For Cromwell, the party took its rise in avarice and secured in consequence the support of all poor and all bad men, but of no others[4]. Phillips, on the other hand, admits that their endeavour was to 'obtain such an equal, righteous distribution of Government to all degrees of the people that it should not be in the power of the highest to oppress their inferiors, nor the meanest be out of capacity to arrive at the greatest office and dignity of the State[5].' Finally, the Levellers themselves, throughout their numberless manifestoes, tell a tale which is at least perfectly consistent. They are styled Levellers 'unjustly[6]'; they are Levellers only so far as they are against any kind of tyranny[7]; 'equal justice to be impartially distributed to all, this is the levelling aimed at[8].'

The defeat of Presbyterianism meant the triumph of toleration and republicanism. Of these two principles, the first alone formed part of the original demand of the more powerful section of the Independents. Its practice and profession was the very *raison*

---

[1] *Life*, 61.
[2] *History of Independency*, ed. 1648, Part II. 138. Cp. 129, 168, 197, 201, 248, etc.
[3] *Leaves of the Tree of Life*, 45–7, T. P. vol. 460.
[4] Speech II. Carlyle, IV. 23.
[5] Continuation of Baker's *Chronicle*, ed. 1696, 591.
[6] *Manifesto from Prince, Overton*, etc. T. P. 550.
[7] *Second Part of England's New Chains*, 5–9, T. P. vol. 548.
[8] *The Commoner's Liberty*, 4, T. P. vol. 463.

d'être of the party, for by serving as a beacon to attract all sectaries it had secured its victory. Republicanism was only definitely admitted when every compromise had been attempted. Its acceptance was the result of circumstances, not of intentions, and it is to this hesitation that the origin of the Levellers is to be attributed.

When the defeat of the king became a certainty, the abolition of monarchy began to be discussed in the ranks. Baxter, coming to the army two days after Naseby, found that 'a great part of the mischief was caused by distribution of the pamphlets of Overton and Lilburne and others, against the King and the Ministry and for Liberty of Conscience; and the soldiers in their quarters had such books to read when they had none to contradict them[1].'

John Lilburne, whose name now first appears in connection with a new party, was by this time a well-known figure. He had been one of the nonconformist victims of the Star Chamber[2]. He had undergone exile in Holland and had stood in the pillory before the meeting of the Long Parliament[3]. When the war broke out he entered the army, rose to the rank of Lieutenant-Colonel, and was taken captive. At the trial, he refused to plead to the indictment, and sturdily maintained that he had not taken arms against the king[4]. On this occasion he received eloquent testimonies of the regard in which he was held by the Parliamentarians[5]. Up to this time, his opposition to the Government had sprung mainly from his religious principles. He stood sentinel night and day, he informed the world, to defend Sion against

---

[1] *Life*, 53.　　　　　　　　　　[2] *State Trials*, III. 1315.

[3] Rushworth, II. 466. The sentence was quashed and Lilburne awarded reparation at the instigation of the Long Parliament. II. 134. Cp. Wallington's *Diary*, I. 137.

[4] *Special Passages*, Dec. 6–13, 1642, T. P. vol. 130.　　[5] Rushworth, V. 3.

her enemies[1]. But by a transition which anticipated that which was to take place generally, Lilburne now became convinced that political no less than religious freedom was hampered by the existing order; and the trend of his political thought was influenced, as that of his religious principles had been, by his personal experiences. His attack on Manchester having caused his committal by the Lords, he was led to insist on the sovereignty of the Commons[2]. On being imprisoned by the Lower House itself for his attack on the king, he was induced by considerations of self-defence to attribute sovereignty to the nation at large. Hence it arose that at the very moment when, by the victory of the Parliament over the king and of the Independents over the Presbyterians, the time seemed ripe for new political ideas, Lilburne had reached a number of conclusions which could not fail to be peculiarly acceptable.

These conclusions were first set forth in the pamphlets that he issued during his imprisonment in Newgate in the summer and autumn of 1645[3]. To maintain that Parliament was more considerable than the body whom they served was to say that an ambassador had more authority than the prince by whom he was sent[4]. Was it likely that when the people chose it they would give it an unlimited power? Monopolies of preaching and publishing, again, interfered, no less than the claims of Parliament, with the sovereignty of the nation. By their means lies were dispersed and declarations of the rights of the people suppressed as seditions[5].

[1] *Answer to Nine Arguments*, 43, T. P. vol. 25.
[2] *Letter to his friends in London*, T. P. vol. 84.
[3] He is recognised as a dangerous speculator by Prynne in July. *Discovery of New Lights*, 7, 17, 29, 34, T. P. vol. 261.
[4] *England's Misery and Remedy*, 4 and 1, T. P. vol. 302.
[5] *England's Birthright justified against arbitrary usurpation, royal or parliamentary, or under what vizor soever*, 6–10, T. P. vol. 304. The title is itself typical of the position Lilburne had but lately reached.

Such were the ideas which spread like a conflagration through the army when the fighting was over and soldiers had leisure to reflect. While the Parliament burned their petitions, imprisoned their authors, and dispersed their meetings, the propaganda of the little group in Southwark took root in the camp.

The soil was prepared in several ways. The Congregationalist notions that prevailed not only familiarised the mind with the operation of democratic principles, but taught the individual to consider himself as in a special sense the instrument of some great purpose of God[1]. The fact, again, that the troops were militia inspired the citizen-soldiers with the feeling that, since they had saved the nation from a great peril, they must secure it from being endangered in the future. In the third place, the favour with which the growth of radical notions was regarded by many of the officers was scarcely concealed. With some it was a welcome of conviction, with others a welcome of interest. A prolonged struggle with Parliament was obviously at hand, and any danger from the new propaganda seemed a long way off. The studied coldness of the welcome that was extended to Baxter[2] need not be entirely explained by ecclesiastical differences.

The effect of Lilburne's teaching soon passed beyond the camp fires. The first instalment of the *Gangraena* describes him as the darling of the sectaries, and laments the popularity of his pamphlets[3]. About this time an address was presented to Parliament the title of which proves how aptly the lesson had been learned and how many outside the army had learned it. It is characteristic that the first anti-monarchical manifesto should be professedly connected with the name of the chief Leveller. The *Remonstrance*

---

[1] Cp. John Hodgson's *Memoirs*, 89, ed. 1806, for an account of the spirit in which he entered on the war.

[2] *Life*, 52.   [3] 39–96.

*of many thousands of citizens and other freeborn people to their own
House of Commons occasioned through the illegal imprisonment of that
famous and worthy sufferer for his country's freedom, John Lilburne,
calling their Commissioners in Parliament to account how they in
this session have discharged their duties to the Universality of the People,
their sovereign Lord, from whom their power and strength is derived
and by whose favour it is continued*, demands not only the election
of a new Parliament but the abolition of Monarchy and the
peers[1]. In the third volume of the *Gangraena* the name of Lilburne has become terrible for Edwards. One sectary was accustomed to pray, 'O Lord, cast down and confound all monarchs,
and lift up and advance thy servant, John Lilburne[2].'

Lilburne's imprisonments are of importance through the manifestoes they inevitably produce[3]. When the Lords bade him kneel,
he refused to do so; peers were encroachers and usurpers and had
never been entrusted with power by the Parliament[4]. The Abbots
and Bishops had been ejected, and the Lords had no more right
to sit than they[5]. Interesting developments have also occurred in
the attitude to monarchy. Hitherto it has been rather against
monarchy as incompatible with popular sovereignty that the
darts of the Levellers have been aimed. We now learn that, since
it is an instinct of Nature that there is a God, it is rational we
should not make gods unto ourselves. But certain monsters of
the devil's lineage assume to themselves the very sovereignty,
style and office of God. And these monsters are commonly called

[1] *Parl. Hist.* III. 493.   [2] p. 116.
[3] During the early years of the movement his thought is always a little
way in advance of the other Leveller spokesmen. In the autumn of 1646
Overton is still content with the notion of a king with purely executive
power. *Arrow against all Tyrants*, 2, T. P. vol. 356.
[4] *Anatomy of the Lords' Tyranny*, 4, 5, T. P. vol. 362.
[5] *Regal Tyranny discovered*, 43–5, T. P. vol. 370.

Kings[1]. A final point of importance in this pamphlet in the development of Lilburne's constructive politics is his conviction that the Commons were tampering with the public money on the pretext of personal losses[2]. That the representatives of the people were dishonest was another reason why their power should be reduced by stricter supervision and shorter service. Further experience of Newgate impelled the prisoner to issue an account of his sufferings[3]. The Commons retorted by a still stricter imprisonment[4], and Lilburne's impatience becomes desperation. He protested his resolution to maintain his civil liberties 'with the last drop of his heart's blood[5].' By its injudicious treatment of the most popular man in England, Parliament was arraying against itself a force which only awaited an opportunity to sweep it away.

The opportunity was created by Parliament itself, and sooner than Lilburne could have ventured to hope. In the spring of 1647 it passed a series of votes for the disbandment of the army and the dispatch of a small force for the reduction of Ireland. A few regiments alone were to be maintained in England under the command of Fairfax, and were to have no officer above a Colonel. In addition, the soldiers were to receive but a small portion of their pay and inadequate securities for their arrears. But in a series of petitions and meetings it became clear that, although a few of the higher officers were ready to go and others took no very decided position, the soldiers themselves would never obey. The leaders were in part unfeignedly desirous of remaining on friendly terms with Parliament, and in part too

---

[1] *Regal Tyranny*, pp. 9–11. [2] *ib.* p. 108.
[3] *Oppressed Man's Oppressions*, 3–13, T. P. vol. 373.
[4] *Commons' Journals*, v. 437, 8.
[5] *Resolved Man's Resolutions*, 21, T. P. vol. 387.

timid openly to manifest their disapprobation of its conduct. Concerted action had begun even before the mission of Cromwell and Fleetwood to London; and when on their return it was ordered that, as Parliament was considering the grievances of the army, the officers should see that no further meetings were held, it was too late for the order to be carried out. Two 'agitators' had been already chosen from each regiment, had met as the representative Council of the Army, had constructed a policy and had communicated their opinions to their leaders[1]. Correspondence was to be held with the soldiers and well-affected, who were to choose two legislators in every county[2]. Pamphlets were to be issued to undeceive the people; disaffected persons were to be secured; punishment was to be called for on all offenders[3]. The whole scheme had been conceived and put in execution by the representatives of the Levellers. In thus expressing the mind of the soldiers while the officers stood aside, the Levellers had risen to the command of the army[4].

Their triumph reached its height when, despite the attempts at mediation, Parliament fixed the date and place of disbanding for the several regiments, and the officers themselves came over to the position that had been taken up by the soldiers. Cromwell's negotiations with the Parliament had been undertaken with entire sincerity and were brought to a close only when he recognised the futility of proceeding with them[5]. For the time, at

---

[1] Agitators to Skippon, Cary's *Memorials of the Civil War*, I. 201–5.

[2] A copy of the letter is printed in Hist. MSS. Comm. 13*th Report*, Portland MSS. I. 432, 3.   [3] *Clarke Papers*, I. 22–4.

[4] Cp. Fairfax's *Short Memorial*: 'The power I once had was usurped by the Agitators....From this time I gave my consent to nothing that was done'; *Maseres Tracts*, 444–50; and *The Character of an Agitator*, T. P. vol. 414.

[5] Despite the absurd story Burnet heard from Harbottle Grimston, *Own Time*, I. 77.

least, he was in thorough accord with the radicals. The army governed all, as a correspondent wrote to Clarendon, and the Agitators governed the army[1]. The general rendezvous that had been urged by the soldiers was held at Newmarket and repeated at Triploe Heath. A statement of the grievances of the entire army was subscribed by both officers and soldiers. They declared that they would disband when a Council, composed of the officers and two representatives of each regiment, should agree that sufficient satisfaction had been obtained[2]. The definite proposals contained in the Declaration of the Army issued a few days later includes nothing with which the Levelling party were not in agreement[3].

These halcyon days of concord were brought to an end by two causes. In the first place, the leaders of the army commenced negotiations with the king; in the second, further elaboration of the political philosophies of the two parties disclosed fundamental disagreements.

A month after the great rendezvous, Lilburne wrote from prison to say that several members of the army had told him that the officers were likely to desert the soldiers. He felt that the people had leaned too much on Cromwell[4]. The Agitators now proceeded to demand an immediate march on the capital. Cromwell and Ireton vehemently opposed the suggestion, declaring that it was necessary that the army should make a declaration of its political intentions and principles. The *Heads of Proposals* were therefore drawn up and offered to Parliament as a basis of settlement for the kingdom. Before the document was published,

[1] Cal. Clar. S. P. I. 397 ; cp. 'A la mode,' a popular song of this date, in *Political Ballads of the Commonwealth*, 58, Percy Society.

[2] Rushworth, VI. 510–12.

[3] *ib.* 505–8.

[4] *Jonah's Cry out of the Whale's Belly*, 3–9, T. P. vol. 400.

however, two of the articles had been modified in conference between Ireton and Sir John Berkeley, in the hope that the king would be able to accept them. In a long interview between several of the army leaders and the king, several further alterations were introduced, and sentiments of cordiality began to be entertained. Reports of these secret interviews stole abroad, and it was rumoured that the officers were playing fast and loose with the interests of the army[1]. The report spread that Cromwell and Ireton were about to restore the king to his rights, and the Royalists were already congratulating themselves[2]. So strong was the resentment that Oliver begged Berkeley to visit him less frequently, 'the suspicion of him being so great that he was afraid to lie down in his own quarters[3].' The king's flatteries, said Wildman, proved like poisoned arrows, infecting the blood in the veins of Cromwell and Ireton[4]. They had been promised earldoms[5]. They had even knelt to the king and kissed his hand.

The suspicion that had arisen from the private conferences of the leaders seemed to be confirmed by their public conduct. For when the question of a new treaty with Charles came before the House in September, Cromwell and Ireton opposed Marten's motion that no more addresses should be sent to the king. To crown all, the meetings of officers and men had been discontinued. So great was the dissatisfaction felt at the conduct of the leaders that several regiments determined to revive the scheme

[1] Cp. Ashburnham's *Narrative*, II. 97.
[2] See a remarkable letter in Hoskins' *Charles II in the Channel Islands*, II. 168.
[3] Berkeley, *Maseres Tracts*. The king's agents, in their turn, did not escape suspicion. Lady Fanshawe's *Memoirs*, 66.
[4] *Putney Projects*, 10, 11, T. P. vol. 421.
[5] Holles' *Memoirs*, 254.

which had been previously so successful. Representatives were elected, under the old name of Agents and Agitators, and their purpose was declared to be that of seeking to remove misunderstandings. The Agents at once proceeded to present a statement of their position, *The Case of the Army*, and, a few days later, *The Agreement of the People*.

The Agreement of the People sets forth the political philosophy of the Levellers or radicals both without and within the army. The exordium states that the purpose of the authors of the proposals is to prevent the occurrence of another war or a relapse into slavery. The present Parliament is to terminate in a year's time, and its successors are to be biennial. A redistribution of seats in proportion to population is to be undertaken. The authority of all future Parliaments is to be inferior only to that of those who chose them, and is to extend to whatever is not reserved by the Instrument. Such matters are freedom of religion, freedom from impressment, the equality of all before the law. 'These things we declare,' conclude the authors, 'to be our native rights, and we are therefore resolved to maintain them with our utmost possibilities against all oppression whatsoever, compelled thereto not only by the examples of our ancestors, but also by our own woful experience, who, having earned and long expected the establishment of these certain rules of government, are yet made to depend for the settlement of our peace and freedom upon him that intended our bondage[1].' *The Case of the Army*, after recalling the history of the past few months, added a number of particular demands. Monopolies were to be abolished and all trade was to remain free; no man should be forced to testify against himself in court; a Committee should undertake a codification of the laws; all usurped privileges, such as common lands now enclosed,

[1] Rushworth, VIII. 859, 60.

were to be restored to the poor; sinecures were to be abolished[1]. These documents were presented to the House of Commons, and declared by it to be destructive of the authority of Parliament and of the very foundation of government[2].

What welcome was accorded to them by the army chiefs? The discovery of Clarke's reports of the debates at Putney enables us accurately to measure the extent of the differences between the two parties in the army. The suspicions that had been rankling in the breasts of the soldiers were expressed, and Cromwell and Ireton attempted to prove that they had been misrepresented. Sexby[3] retorted that the misery of the army arose from its attempt to satisfy all men, and that the proposals of the army should have been carried out. By neglecting this, the credit of the leaders had been blasted. To this Cromwell rejoined that he had done nothing but with the approbation of the Council, and Ireton declared his intention to persevere in his attempts at a compromise[4].

It was now suggested that, before the proposals could be discussed, the public engagements of the army should be considered[5]. The general question of the nature of engagements was hereby opened. Rainborough, whose views were closely allied to those of the Leveller spokesmen, stated his opinion that, since all the good laws that were now enjoyed were once innovations, the army should without delay proceed to secure the liberties of the People. In the same strain, Wildman disowned the principle that, when persons had made an engagement, they must 'sit down and suffer under it,' however unjust it might be. The

[1] 18, 19, T. P. vol. 411.   [2] Rushworth, VIII. 867.
[3] The Levellers were represented by seven men, of whom Sexby and Mildmay were the most notable. See their portraits in Clarendon, XIV. 48, 9; XV. 133.
[4] *Clarke Papers,* I. 227–35.   [5] *ib.* 236–44.

G

principle was most dangerous and was directly in contradiction with their earlier declarations, which stated that they stood on principles of right and freedom and the laws of nature and nations. In such a case as the present, a short delay might lead to the loss of the kingdom[1].

On the following day, leave was obtained to read the *Agreement of the People*, and the Council proceeded at once to the discussion of the first clause. The *Heads of Proposals* had advocated more equal electoral districts; but the demand that seats should be distributed according to the number of the inhabitants implied the adoption of universal suffrage. After Ireton's attack on the proposal, Pettus summarised the radical position by remarking, 'We judge that all inhabitants who have not lost their birthright should have an equal voice in elections.' Rainborough added that no man was bound to a government under which he had not put himself. For a vote it was not necessary to possess property; that reason which God had given to all was sufficient qualification. A retort of Ireton that they under-valued the importance and sacredness of property evoked an indignant disavowal of anarchy, and Pettus asked whether it was just that a leaseholder who paid £100 a year should have no vote, and whether if they were framing a Constitution they would exclude all who did not possess a 40s. freehold. Sexby added indignantly that even the poor had a birthright[2]. Would it not be unjust if they had fought all this time for nothing? They should have been told

---

[1] *Clarke Papers*, I. 264–71.

[2] As early as 1640 it had been moved by D'Ewes that 'the poor man ought to have a voice and that it was the birthright of the subjects of England.' D'Ewes' *Reports*, Harl. MSS. vol. 162, 9. In the following spring, he descended to details and proposed that all 'non-vagrants' should vote, 377 b. The proposal recurs but seldom. It was, however, one of Petty's numerous projects. Fitzmaurice's *Life of Petty*, 279.

before they engaged, for, indeed, they had taken up arms on that very ground. To Ireton's remark that their proposals, except in the question of the franchise, were very much the same, Wildman retorted that the manifestoes of the officers were fundamentally different from the programme under discussion. The *Heads of Proposals* had admitted the institutions of Monarchy and a House of Lords, and had even given them joint control of the militia; they had not only restored the king to his personal rights, but had allowed him a negative voice. Instead of 'laying the foundations of freedom for all manner of people,' as was done by the *Agreement*, the foundation of slavery was riveted more strongly than before[1].

In the Committee that was appointed to consider the *Agreement*, the *Heads of Proposals* were practically reaffirmed; but a qualification was introduced as a result of the representations of the radicals. The franchise was extended to all freeborn Englishmen who had served the Parliament in the last war or had lent money, plate or horses, and, after further discussion, to all who were not servants or beggars. The remainder of the debates dealt with the concessions to the king and the House of Lords in the *Heads of Proposals*. The radicals affirmed that, since the king's coronation oath disowned a legislative power, such power was an usurpation, and by granting the Lords a suspensive veto and the king a negative one, the usurpation was confirmed. It was in vain that Ireton reminded them that by his scheme certain fundamentals would have been recognised and accepted by the king before his negative voice was restored to him, and that this in effect amounted to a recognition on his part of the sole right of a Parliament to make laws in matters of national importance[2].

[1] *Clarke Papers*, I. 204, 356.   [2] *ib.* I. 386–90.

The result of the Putney meetings was very disappointing. The sole achievement of the radicals was to have forced their plan of manhood suffrage through the Council; yet even this was of no value[1], for Ireton and Cromwell remained invincibly hostile to its adoption. The opinion of the army leaders that the radical programme 'tended very much to anarchy' remained unchanged. The opinion of the Agitators was still that in the proposals of the officers 'the king's corrupt interest was so intermixed that in a short time, if he should so come in, he would be in a capacity to destroy the people[2].' The one hope that remained to the Levellers was that at the forthcoming rendezvous an imposing demonstration of their forces might lead the grandees to submit. But instead of the general meeting which they desired, it was arranged that a succession of meetings should be held. The radicals were therefore unable to offer an united front, and when two regiments arrived at Ware without orders, wearing on their hats copies of the *Agreement of the People* with the motto 'England's Freedom and Soldiers' Rights' in capital letters, Cromwell ordered the removal of the paper, and on refusal shot one of the mutineers at the head of his regiment[3]. The execution restored discipline, and the restoration of good relations between officers and men was effected by a Remonstrance drawn up in the name of Fairfax, doubtless by Ireton[4]. The General was made to declare that, if the divisions and discontents in the army were to continue, he would resign his post. The greater number of the men pro-

[1] This was forcibly put in the Letter of several Agitators to their respective regiments. T. P. vol. 414.

[2] *Clarke Papers*, I. 411, 441. Cp. Wildman's *Putney Projects, passim*, T. P. vol. 421.

[3] Rushworth, VIII. 875, 6.

[4] There were still dissentients, however. Bray's *Representation to the Nation*, T. P. vol. 422; *Call to the Soldiers of the Army*, T. P. vol. 412.

ceeded to sign an engagement to be bound by the decision of the
General Council in the prosecution of the objects that had been
set forth[1]. The General Council met several times during the
next two months at Windsor, whither the Parliamentary Commissioners came to arrange a number of details in reference to
the billeting, pay and partial disbandment of the army. The last
meeting of the Council, on January 8th, 1648, agreed with
unanimity upon a declaration to Parliament expressing their satisfaction at the recent vote for no further addresses to the king,
and promising their support in settling the kingdom without
him[2].

When the army leaders gave up the cause of the king in
January, 1648[3], the vast majority of the soldiers became convinced that they were honestly endeavouring to secure the common desires of the army, and that their differences should no
longer justify a division. As a result the Levellers became a
civilian party. With the diminution of the importance of the
party consequent on its ceasing to represent the entire radicalism
of the country went a deterioration of its tone[4]. It had sprung
into existence in response to a widely spread apprehension that
the victory of the people might be rendered fruitless. Its call had
found an echo in the ranks of the army, and by its admirable
organisation it had insisted that the leaders should hear what it
had to say. It had powerfully influenced their conduct, and had
introduced a radical element into their programme. When this
had been done, the soldiers felt that its *raison d'être* as a separate

[1] *Parl. Hist.* III. 795–8.
[2] *ib.* 831–4. Cp. Salvetti, XII. 22.
[3] It began to be rumoured abroad that the king was already executed.
D'Ormesson's *Journal*, I. 449.
[4] This was very vigorously set forth in the *Free Man's Plea for Freedom*,
T. P. vol. 443.

or potentially separate party had come to an end. The battle had
been fought and the victory, at least for the time, had fallen to
Ireton.

II

The most perverse notions have till very recently prevailed as
to the character and ability of Ireton. The worthy Burnet informs us that 'this Cassius hoped all concerned would become
irreconcilable to monarchy and would act as desperate men'; and
adds 'he stuck at nothing that might have turned England into
a Commonwealth[1].' Sir Philip Warwick reproduced the story
that the last words of the dying man were 'I will have more
blood[2]'; and his severity at Colchester was adduced as convincing
evidence of his sanguinary character[3]. Some writers of the time
remembering, in Whitelocke's words[4], that 'none could prevail
with Oliver so much nor order him so far,' declared that, had
not Ireton died, Cromwell would not have dared against the
opposition of so stout a republican to seize the reins of Government[5].

The *Clarke Papers*[6], illuminating as they are for every aspect
of the intellectual life of the army, are in no instance more
valuable than in the flood of light that they throw on the political

[1] *Own Time*, I. 84. Cp. Lloyd's *Memoirs*, 510.

[2] Warwick's *Memoirs*, 355. The same view of his character appears in
Evelyn's comments on his death, *Diary*, March 6, 1652, and in Wood's
notice, *Athenae*, III. 298–302.

[3] Sir James Turner's *Memoirs*, 60, etc.; but contrast the remarks on his
surprising humanity in the *Contemporary History of Ireland*, ed. Gilbert, III.
21, 2.

[4] *Memorials*, Dec. 8, 1651, III. 371.

[5] Mrs Hutchinson's *Memoirs*, 358; Clarendon, XIII. 178, etc.

[6] It is scarcely necessary to say how deeply every student of Ireton is
indebted to Mr Firth for his edition of the Papers and for his admirable
Introduction.

opinions of the long misunderstood Commissary General. Before their publication it was possible for historians to maintain that the insertion of a monarchical element in the *Heads of Proposals* by a convinced republican was a piece of outrageous political immorality[1]. But on learning that the opinions informally expressed by Ireton in the debates of the Council coincide with those of his proposals to the king, the evidence of his sincerity becomes complete. Possessed of a larger stock of legal knowledge than his fellow-officers, of a greater skill in putting ideas into shape, of a delivery more fluent, of opinions more definite and dogmatic than those of Oliver, Ireton was not only the penman of the army but the actual fashioner of its political opinions, in fact, as Lilburne said, 'its Alpha and Omega[2].' Those who were behind the scenes knew that 'Cromwell only shot the bolts that were hammered in Ireton's forge[3].' Read in their true light, therefore, the *Heads of Proposals* issued in August, 1647, become an authoritative exposition of the political opinions of Ireton. Despite all that had passed, the author is prepared for a fresh trial of government by King, Lords and Commons, with certain securities against the renewal of despotism. Biennial Parliaments are to sit from one hundred and twenty to two hundred and forty days, and the Members are to be elected by constituencies partitioned according to population and property. The Militia is to be controlled by Parliament for ten years, and the disaffected to be temporarily excluded from office. Recently created peers must receive permission from the Commons to take their seats. The civil power of the Church is to be abolished and the Covenant no longer to be imposed. The Royal Family is to be re-

---

[1] Godwin's *Commonwealth*, II. 377, etc.
[2] Lilburne's *Legal Fundamental Liberties*, 29.
[3] Ambrose Barnes' *Memoirs*, 114, Surtees Society.

stored to 'a condition of safety, honour and freedom, without further limitations to the exercise of the regal power than according to the particulars aforesaid[1].'

The outlines may be filled in from the speeches delivered in the following months before the General Council of officers. So long as Monarchy could be preserved, Ireton was anxious to preserve it. 'Ireton,' wrote his kinswoman, Mrs Hutchinson, 'was as faithful as his father-in-law, but was not so fully of the opinion (till he tried it and found to the contrary) but that the king might have been managed to comply with the public good of his people[2].' Although nobody whose theory transferred sovereignty so decisively to the Commons or the army can be strictly called a constitutionalist, Ireton may be described as the leader of the constitutional party in the army. When twitted by Sexby and Rainborough in the Council at Putney[3] for 'labouring to please the king,' he replied that he did not seek, and would not join with those who sought, the destruction of Parliament or king. He told Ashburnham that he would 'never give over the thought of serving the king, though there were but six men in the army to stand to him, and would dispute the king's interest to the uttermost of his life and fortune[4].' But indeed he was still further removed from the majority of his contemporaries by his whole intellectual attitude. The historical arguments on which they based their pleas and proposals had little meaning for Ireton. 'I think,' said he, in reply to Sexby in the great meeting at Putney, on October 29th[5], 'I think we ought to keep to that constitution that we have because it is the most fundamental we have, and because there is so much reason, jus-

---

[1] *Heads of Proposals*, Gardiner's *Documents*.   [2] *Memoirs*, 305.
[3] Oct. 28, 1647, *Clarke Papers*, I. 226–33.
[4] Ashburnham's *Narrative*, II. 97.   [5] C. P. I. 230–363.

tice and prudence in it as I dare confidently to undertake that there are many more evils that will follow in case you do alter than there can in the standing of it.'

The philosophical argument of his antagonists is rejected. The whole theory of natural rights is attacked with a vigour scarcely less than the great onslaught a century and a half later in the *Reflections on the Revolution in France*. In discussing the clause dealing with the franchise, Ireton was led to explain his theory of property. The Law of God did not give man property, nor did the Law of Nature; property was of human institution. Sexby thereupon cried out that the soldiers had ventured their lives to recover their birthrights, but if the Commissary General were right, they had none. Ireton replied that he had penetrated his meaning. Other birthright than permission to live in England and the use of air, the freedom of the highways and the fundamental part of the Constitution there was none. If merely on the pretence of birthright they were to maintain that the constitution should not stand in their way, it was the same as seizing upon anything a man called his own. 'Supposing no civil law and no civil constitution,'—Ireton means, supposing the Civil Law could at any moment be overridden by an appeal to the Law of Nature or to birthrights,—'no property, no foundation for any man to enjoy anything would be left.' He points out that the kernel of the theory of Natural Rights is ultra-individualism. 'When I heard of men's laying aside all engagements for some wild notion of what in every man's conception is just or unjust, I tremble at the boundless and endless consequences of it.' The sole foundation of rights is the law of the land. 'We are under a contract, under an agreement; and that agreement is that a man shall have the use of land that he hath received from his ancestors, with submission to that general authority which is agreed on among us. This I take to be the foundation of right for matter of land. For matter of goods, that which doth fence me from another's claim by the Law of Nature to take my goods, that which makes it mine really and civilly, is the Law.' From this aversion to the appeal to natural rights springs Ireton's theory of the franchise. 'I think it is clear,' Rainborough had said, 'that every man who is to live under a government ought first by his own consent to put himself under that government; and I do think the poorest man in England is not strictly bound to that government that he hath not had a voice to put himself under.' To this Ireton replied as we might anticipate. 'That by a man's being born here he should have a share in that power that shall dispose of all things here, I do not think it a sufficient ground.' A man should be subject to laws to which he had not assented; but he might obtain permission to leave the country if he was dissatisfied. If he had money, it was good in any other place.

The hard, unyielding dogmatism of the system is nevertheless tempered by the readiness to sacrifice the individual to the community. 'If all the people in the kingdom, or their representatives, should meet and give away my property, I would submit to it, rather than make a disturbance.' This is indeed a very partial modification; but his political conservatism itself is qualified by his respect for the logic of events. 'It is not to me so much as the vainest or lightest thing you can imagine whether there be a King in England or no. If God saw good to destroy not only kings and lords but all distinctions of degree, nay, if it go further, to destroy all property, so that there is no such thing left, so that there be nothing at all of the Civil Constitution left, if I see the hand of God in it, I shall quietly acquiesce, and shall not resist at all.' A year later, accordingly, he surrenders the framework of the old constitution, and so far yields to the clamours of the army radicals as to allow that the franchise should be extended to all who had directly assisted the army against the king in the recent struggle[1]. But his distaste for the popular individualism remains as great as ever. It is perhaps not wholly fanciful to find, in the clause of the *Agreement of the People* imposing penalties on disobedience to the ruling of the Representatives, a result of the advocacy to which he had listened of the right of independent action for all who did not expressly accept the government and laws[2].

In the debates which took place between the Council of Officers and the Levellers in connection with the attempt of the latter at reunion, the distrust of popular ideals appears more clearly than ever. 'Men as men,' said Ireton, 'are corrupt and will be so[3]'; and, like all who shared Hobbes' view of human nature and therefore of the primitive condition of mankind, he traces the origin of society uniquely to the necessity of securing order, and draws the inevitable inference. 'If I did look at liberty alone,' said he (and the use of the word in this restricted sense points to a certain narrowness of thought), 'I should mind no such thing as a Commonwealth; for then I am most free when I have nobody to mind me. But that which necessarily leads all men into civil agreements and contracts and to make commonwealths is the necessity of it to preserve peace.' For this reason the sphere of the magistrate is confined to no special department, but extends over the whole range of the life of the community. The Levellers, reinforced by several of the Independent ministers who had been invited to the discussion, insisted that his power should stop short of matters of religion. But to this contention Ireton offered the most strenuous opposition. There were

[1] *Agreement of the People*, Jan. 15, 1649, Art. 3, Gardiner's *Documents*.
[2] Art. 10.   [3] *Clarke Papers*, II. 176.

many things men might 'own and practise under pretence of religion that there might, nay, there ought to be restraint of them in.' Moreover, it was the practice in Jewish times to do so. 'The magistrates were commanded to beat down idols and groves and images of the land whither they went.' It was merely an excuse to contend that what was a rule under the Law was not a rule under the Gospel. 'What was sin before is sin still; what was the duty of a magistrate to restrain before remains his duty to restrain still[1].'

In a word, human nature would require strong government as long as it remained unchanged. ' I am confident that it is not the hand of men that will take away the power of monarchy in the earth,' said Ireton, comprehending under the term all forms of strong government[2]; 'if ever it be destroyed, it will be by the breaking forth of the power of God amongst men to make such forms needless.' But the most probable date for this event seemed to Ireton the Greek Kalends.

[1] *Clarke Papers*, II. 78–130.
[2] In Ireland 'his authority was so absolute that he was entirely submitted to in all civil as well as martial affairs.' Clarendon, *History*, XIII. 174.

CHAPTER VI

The Foundation of the Republic

I

IN Parliament, no less than in the army, there were men to whom the conduct of the military chiefs in 1647 was profoundly distasteful. The 'Commonwealth party' took its rise from the combination of those who entered Parliament in 1645 with the more radical members, such as Marten and Vane, who were already there. The support given by thirty-four voices in September, 1647, to Marten's proposal that no more addresses should be sent to the king marks the appearance of the party as a party, and no doubt accurately measures its strength[1]. But though, on that occasion, the army leaders voted with the majority, a somewhat similar motion received their support, as we saw, in January of the following year. At this time, wrote Mrs Hutchinson, Cromwell was incorruptibly faithful to his trust and the people's interest[2]. But the union was rather apparent than real, and the Lieutenant-General hastened to summon a conference of conciliation. The Commonwealthsmen declared that monarchy was 'neither good in itself nor for us.' The former opinion they proceeded to prove from the Book of Samuel, the latter by an appeal to history and reason. They had suffered infinite mischief and oppressions under it; their ancestors had indeed consented to be ruled by a Single Person, but with the proviso that he should govern according to law, which he bound himself by oath to perform. The present king had broken his oath and, having caused the effusion of a deluge of blood, had

[1] *Parl. Hist.* III. 781.　　　　[2] *Memoirs,* 304.

rendered it incumbent on Parliament to call him to account, and to proceed to the establishment of an equal Commonwealth founded on popular consent and providing for the rights and liberties of all men[1]. The response to this exposition of the political faith of the Commonwealthsmen, the first that they had ever vouchsafed, was reserved for the following day. Meeting Ludlow in the House, the Lieutenant-General told him that he was convinced of the desirableness of their plans, but could not as yet regard them as feasible[2].

For some weeks longer, Oliver continued his attempt to establish a closer *rapprochement* with the party. A letter written in February relates that he has 'bestowed two nights' oratory' on Vane, but without result. A few days later Vane is described as seeming changed; but the writer regards him as 'still coy at heart.' Even less successful was the interview with the leader of the party; and a report got abroad that Marten and Cromwell had 'parted much more enemies than they had met[3].' The Commonwealthsmen became convinced that the Lieutenant-General had only intended to cajole a party of which he needed the support for selfish purposes; and Cromwell had come to the conclusion that the Commonwealthsmen were 'a proud sort of people, only considerable in their own eyes[4].'

The strained relations of the Grandees and the Republicans were saved from snapping by the conduct of the Presbyterians, taking shape in the invasion of the Scots and the second Civil War. Since the final defeat of the king, the Presbyterians had set themselves to undo their own work. When the king in effect refused the Propositions of Newcastle, themselves a modification of those of Uxbridge, they gave up all attempts at coercion and

[1] Ludlow, *Memoirs*, I. 183–6.   [2] *ib.* I. 185, 6.
[3] *Hamilton Papers*, 149–56, C. S.   [4] Ludlow, I. 186.

fell back on the principle of re-establishing the royal authority
as it was in the summer of 1641, in return for a concession of
Presbyterianism for three years. Their conduct was mainly determined by two causes. The first, of course, was that only by
joining the king could they secure even the partial triumph of
Presbyterianism. Nobody believed that their sentiments were
changed. The king himself had recently declared that they were
enemies of monarchy[1], and this opinion was generally held. They
were equally masters of dissimulation, wrote Clarendon, in classi-
fying them with the Independents, and were equally unrestrained
by any examples or motion of conscience[2]. A severe indictment
was brought against them in Milton's first political treatise[3].
Bramhall had remarked that if the king would not grant them
Presbyterianism, they were for the people; and when the people
resisted their will they were for the king. To those who did not
realise that their policy was dominated by their ecclesiastical aim[4],
it was natural enough that they should seem, as they seemed at
different times to both Royalists and Independents, a 'crafty and
perfidious generation[5].' The saying afterwards became current
that the Presbyterians had brought the king to the block and the
Independents had cut off his head[6].

But the Presbyterians deserted their late companions, not only
because they differed from them in relation to Church government, but because the basis of their creed was far less democratic.
In every Presbyterian writer from Calvin downwards, while the
People are exalted, the Plebs are treated with scanty respect.

[1] *Letters to Henrietta Maria*, 73, C. S.   [2] *History*, x. 168.
[3] *Tenure of Kings and Magistrates*.
[4] Cp. Selden, *Table Talk*, Presbytery.
[5] *Nicholas Papers*, ii. 32. Cp. *The Scots' Apostasy* in the *Rump Songs*, 19–21;
and Fuller's *Worthies*, ii. 105, 6.
[6] Stephens' *Church of Scotland*, ii. 287.

'The popular government,' declared Baillie, 'bringeth in confusion, making the feet above the head[1].' Thus the action of the Independents in taking the Plebs into their counsels was opposed to the fundamental principles of the rival party. 'They have cast all the mysteries and secrets of government before the vulgar,' wrote Clement Walker in indignation, 'and taught the soldiery and the people to look into them and to ravel back all governments to the first principles of nature. They have made the people so curious that they will never find humility enough to submit to a civil rule[2].' The Presbyterians desired to retain at least the framework of the ancient constitution. Of this sentiment Prynne was the spokesman. His mind was filled with a worship of the laws of his country as ardent as that of Coke, and this cult led him into temporary association with men whose principles were utterly different. But exclusive homage to the past, though capable under special circumstances of providing inspiration, involves a limitation of outlook. He had authorised active opposition to an unjust ruler when the balance hung undecided; but when fortune had declared against the king, he interposed with a plea for legality. No Protestant kingdom had ever yet defiled its hands or stained the purity of the Reformed religion with the blood of its prince or king. No other machinery than that which was used to secure the well-being of the country in times of peace was to be called into requisition during a crisis. As soon as Presbyterianism had been declared the national religion, the greater number of the Presbyterians cared more for the defence of the framework of the Constitution than for the attainment of those objects which the Constitution had failed to secure.

The events of the summer of 1648 proved that Presbyterianism had not gained firm hold in England. That it was alien to the

[1] *Dissuasive*, 185. [2] *History of Independency*, ed. 1648, Part I. 48, 123.

English spirit was implicitly admitted by Baillie when he wrote that he expected much assistance to his arguments from the advance of the Scotch army[1], and frankly admitted by Henderson. 'I confess I could have wished,' said he on his deathbed, 'that a Presbyterian government could have been established in England; but I find the disposition of that kingdom so generally opposite that it is not to be expected. They are a people so naturally inclined to freedom that they can hardly be induced to embace any discipline that may abridge it[2].' 'Presbytery,' echoed Baxter, 'was but a stranger here[3]'; and Rutherford despaired of 'a reformation[4].'

The Presbyterian majority in Parliament still continued to negotiate with Charles[5]. Though Prynne had written hundreds of pages to prove that the deposition of a king and the election of another were authorised by reason and precedent, he now denied that the king could be deposed and that his son could be excluded from the succession. 'No ordinance you can make,' he told the dominant party, 'will be any legal bar against his return[6].' He also strove to get the king's proposals accepted[7]. But the result of the war was quickly seen. A monster petition, probably drawn up by Henry Marten, demanded the abolition of

[1] *Journals*, II. 121.   [2] *Death-bed Declaration*, 5, T. P. vol. 443.
[3] *Life*, Part II. 146. Cp. Forster's *Marten*, 267–83.
[4] *Letters*, ed. 1863, II. 313, 14.
[5] 'We only desired settlement,' said Hollis, 'without specifying any form.' *Memoirs*, 192–6.
[6] *Memento against the Execution of Charles I*, Somers Tracts, V. 174–83. Cp. the protest of the Scotch Commissioners, *Parl. Hist.* III. 1277, 8. The tidings of the execution, however, caused but little emotion in Scotland. Burton's *Scotland*, VI. 424–6.
[7] The speech appeared as a manifesto a month later, T. P. vol. 539. Attention was called to the change of attitude in *Prynne v. Prynne*, T. P. vol. 540.

the Monarchy and the House of Lords[1]. To Ludlow and many
others it seemed that the time had now come to determine
'whether the king should govern as a God or whether the people
should live under a government derived from their own consent[2].'
To this question the declaration of St Albans shewed that the
army returned the same answer as the minority of the Commons[3].
A month later the army replied to the resolution that the king's
concessions at Newport were ground for a future settlement by
the dispatch of Colonel Pride to Westminster. On January 4,
the Commons passed three great resolutions. The first declared
that the people were the original of all just power in the State;
the second that the Commons possessed the supreme power
as representatives of the people; the third, that whatever was
enacted by them should have the force of law, without needing
the consent either of the king or of the House of Peers. A month
later, the theory embodied in these resolutions became a fact.
Theoretically a republic since January 4, 1649, and visibly from
January 30, England was a republic in every sense from the
formal abolition of the Monarchy[4] and the House of Lords on
February 7[5].

II

'Even the crucifying of our blessed Saviour,' wrote Digby to
Ormond, 'did nothing equal this murder, his kingdom being
not of this world and he being judged by a lawful tribunal[6].'
A large number of persons, however, was now prepared for some
form of republican government, whether or not they approved

---

[1] *Parl. Hist.* III. 1005–11.   [2] Ludlow, I. 206, 7.
[3] Rushworth, VI. 564–70.
[4] The statues of the Kings were now thrown headlong from Inigo's
portico. Milman's *St Paul's*, 353.
[5] *Commons' Journals* under dates.   [6] Carte's *Ormond*, VI. 606.

of the execution of Charles I. The publications during the last month of the king's life witness to the prevalence of republican ideas. An anonymous author, in *Rectifying Principles of the Sovereignty of Kingdoms*, repeated the thrice-told tale, challenging the world to find him any other use of a king than in the welfare and safety of the people, and to deny that, this lost, a king was useless. 'We desire,' he concluded, 'that these premises may be accepted as absolute[1].' *The Army's Vindication* a few days later reveals even more remarkably the confidence of the impregnable theoretical position of the winning side. What form of government is best? asked the author, and replied that in his judgment monarchy was the worst[2]. 'Much land,' he continues, 'is unnecessarily detained from public use and profit to maintain an unuseful creature. What more absurd than for a people to be at such an expense to keep one of whom they have no need nor use at all, and can do much better without?' When abuses break forth in a State, they are less easily and thoroughly suppressed in a monarchy than in other governments. A king is useless because he hears only by other men's ears and sees only by other men's eyes. The ministers are usually corrupt and oppressors of the people, whereas in other governments places are not open for such men. For where the people choose their own magistrates, they must needs be good. A Republican Government is the best, being the mean between Monarchy and Anarchy. People are less sensible than beasts if they remain in bondage under Monarchy, when they are able to free themselves.

Every religious body, again, except the Presbyterians[3] and the

---

[1] T. P. vol. 537, 30, 1.

[2] T. P. vol. 538, 61. Cp. *Parliament justified*, by Three Students of Trinity, T. P. vol. 545.

[3] If Dorothy Osborne is to be trusted, Stephen Marshall was perhaps an

Anglicans, had now become friendly to republican principles. Though their manifestoes had told a tale of an exceptionally conservative character[1], the Baptists had no theoretic preference for Monarchy, and contemplated the execution of the royal victim without emotion. As a party they did not erect the fact into a theory; but the opinions of some of the more radical of their members were expressed by a pamphlet entitled *The Golden Rule of Justice advanced*. The author, Canne, had been pastor of the Baptist Church in Amsterdam, and on his return to England had founded Broadmead Chapel. He had already gained notoriety by his attack on the Church and on those who continued in communion with it[2], and during the war had aided in the spread of radical ideas. His latest work expressed the common form of the theory of the sovereignty of the people. St Paul had inculcated obedience lest the Christians might imagine they owed no duties to a heathen magistracy. Passing from the general to the particular, Canne asks why, since all agree that a tyrant may be assassinated, he may not be brought to trial. If the execution of a king after legal process was a novelty, it pointed not to depravity, but to a sense of justice and a love of fair dealing which were new[3].

Above all, the Independents had now assumed a definitely republican position. In the discussions on the proposals of the Levellers in the autumn of 1648, in which Goodwin and some of his fellow-ministers were called, the Independents found

exception. She describes a sermon of his to Temple. 'What do you think he told us? Why, if there were no kings nor queens, it would be no loss to God at all.' *Letters of Dorothy Osborne*, 190, 1.

[1] *Confessions of Faith*, 273, 287.

[2] *Necessity of Separation*, ed. Hanserd Knollys Society, especially 194, 273, 274.

[3] 20–36, T. P. vol. 543.

themselves fighting side by side with Lilburne and Wildman for complete exclusion of the magistrate from ecclesiastical matters[1]. A few weeks before the death of the king, Hugh Peters took advantage of a command to preach before the two Houses to declare that he had had a revelation how to free the nation from its Egyptian bondage. Monarchy, 'both here and in all other places,' was to be extirpated, and Charles himself was compared to Barabbas, whom the foolish citizens would have released[2]. The most obvious proof of the change which the political theory of certain members of the sect had undergone was the approval extended to the conduct of the regicides by its leader[3]. During the trial of the king, Goodwin issued his *Might and Right well met*, the most striking document in the development of the political theory of the Independents. Revolutionary conclusions are now stated as axioms. 'It is lawful for any man even by violence to wrest a sword out of the hand of a madman, though it be never so legally his;...for the lives and limbs of men are to be preferred before the exorbitant wills and humours of men under distemper.' It was absurd to protest that there was no mandate from the people for an act which was of sovereign necessity for their benefit. 'The army conforms to a law of far greater authority than any one, yea, than all the laws of the land put together, the law of Nature, of Necessity, and of love to their country and nation; which being the law of God written in the fleshly tables of men's hearts, hath a jurisdiction over all human constitutions.... Yea, many of the very laws of God themselves think it no disparagement to give place to their elder sister, the law of necessity,

---

[1] *Clarke Papers*, ii. 73–132.
[2] Echard, 652. Cp. Evelyn's *Diary*, Jan. 17, 1649.
[3] Though many of its members would willingly have crowned Gloucester. Welwood's *Memoirs*, 90.

and to surrender their authority into her hand, when she speaketh. For no law is of universal application or validity.' The lawfulness and goodness of an action was to be measured and judged by what was likely to follow from it[1].

Though Goodwin maintained that he had said nothing which was not implicit in the works of the Reformers, nay, in Prynne's *Sovereign Power*, there was some truth in the accusation that he was 'the first Protestant parson to approve regicide[2].' For the position which he had assumed was, indeed, a most extreme one. To set the laws of God and Nature above those of man was done by most of those who had taken sides against the king; but to subject the laws of God to the 'Law of Necessity' was a novelty in its frank cynicism. Beyond this it was impossible to go. Goodwin, who had before represented the more moderate wing of the party, had now reached a position indistinguishable from that of Hugh Peters, who repeated with fervour the Nunc Dimittis immediately after the king's head had fallen[3].

A far more powerful advocacy of the new government came from the greatest thinker and writer in the Independent ranks. Any examination of the sources of Milton's political opinions must begin with his classical studies. Aubrey remarks[4] that his republicanism arose from his 'being so conversant in Livy and the Roman authors, and the greatness he saw done by the Roman Commonwealth.' He may stand therefore as the chief of those whom Hobbes describes as having in their youth read the books 'written by famous men of the ancient Grecian and Roman Commonwealths, concerning their polity and their great actions, in which the popular government was extolled by the glorious

---

[1] 12–36, T. P. vol. 536.
[2] Goodwin's *Reply to Attacks*, I. T. P. vol. 540.
[3] Brooks' *Puritans*, III. 350–69.   [4] Aubrey's *Lives*, II. 447.

name of Liberty and Monarchy disgraced by the name of tyranny, and who thereby became in love with their forms of government[1].' In the whole spirit of his political thinking, in his conception of the State as an organism, in his sacrifice of the undistinguished multitude to the natural peers of mankind, he is classical. Of the influence of the Italian republics there is little explicit trace, though a letter to Diodati proves that he attentively studied their history[2]. It is with Macchiavelli that his acknowledged debt to modern thinkers begins. The great Florentine's love for ancient Rome may well have attracted Milton's notice; and he further gratefully recognised in him the author of the theory that the best government was mixed[3]. But though in the *Commonplace Book* we hear more of teachers than of events, the Aragonese formula of coronation, the note that Scotland was originally an elective kingdom, the testimony from Holinshed that the sovereign was not crowned until he had sworn to administer justice, seem to speak already of the *Tenure of Kings and Magistrates*[4].

The importance of the discovery of this work lies in the evidence it provides that Milton's earliest political views were merely those of liberal constitutionalism. But the writings which issued from his pen in the years between his return from Italy and the execution of the king seem to foreshadow the rejection of the potential tyranny involved in the monarchical idea. In one series of tracts he pleaded for intellectual and religious liberty, at first against the Church, and, after the fall of the Church, against the Presbyterians. In another, he claimed domestic liberty, in opposition to men of all parties, though supported, as he took

---

[1] *Behemoth*, Dialogue 1. The classical students were the fourth class of 'seducers' of the nation. Cp. *Leviathan*, ch. 29. The Tsar Nicholas I was of a similar opinion, denouncing the classics as the fosterers of revolt.

[2] *Prose Works*, ed. Bohn, III. 495.

[3] *Commonplace Book*, 41, C. S.

[4] *ib* 27-33.

pains to shew, by some of the Fathers of the Protestant Church. The books proved, not only that the dominant impulse of his life was the achievement of liberty, but that he was bold enough to pursue his way undaunted by the opinion of men. When Milton came forward as a political teacher he was already known as a 'libertine who would be tied by no obligation to God or Man[1].'

It is no longer possible to discover at what date the *Tenure of Kings and Magistrates* was begun. At any rate, the appearance of the pamphlet a fortnight after the king's execution announced that Milton had attached himself more closely to the Regicides than any other person in England. But although he declares that he would have been ready to have added his signature to the Death-Warrant, we do not find the detestation of monarchy that his later works were to contain. Men were born free, declares Milton, in the image and resemblance of God Himself; but wrong and violence entering in among them from Adam's sin, they agreed by common league to bind each other from mutual injury. One or more individuals were selected on account of their wisdom and virtue and entrusted with the administration of the affairs of the community, not as lords but as commissioners. The power remains fundamentally in the people and cannot be taken from them without a violation of their birthright. To say that kings are accountable to none but God overturns all law and government; for if they fear not God,—and most do not,—the people hold their lives and estates by the tenure of their grace and mercy. The people may therefore reject and depose them whenever they

[1] Walker's *Independency*, Part II. 199 ; *Gangraena*, I. 34 ; Baillie's *Dissuasive*, 116, etc. It need scarcely be said that the view of Milton's attitude towards public affairs so ably expressed in Mark Pattison's biography is untenable.

care to do so, by the right of freeborn men to be governed as seems to them best. If, however, it is the people's right to depose a good king, it is their duty to depose a tyrant. If the law of nature allows a man to defend himself even against the king in person, does not it justify much more the self-defence of a whole Commonwealth? If no Protestant nation has yet punished its ruler, it is not because the nation was Protestant but because the king did not deserve punishment. Honour, then, to those who have had courage to set a precedent, who have dared to teach the world that 'for the future no potentate, but to his sorrow, may presume to turn upside down whole kingdoms of men[1].'

There are several points to be noticed in this eloquent pamphlet. By his declaration of the original freedom of men and his acceptance of that variety of the social contract theory which retains for the people a power greater than they surrender, Milton belongs decisively to the liberal school of political thought. By his championship of the theory of Natural Rights, he separates himself from Ireton and what may be described as the positive school. By his adducing the teaching of leading Reformers, he connects his political theory with his Protestantism. By his historical illustrations, he desires to prove that the reason of mankind, whether or no expressed in laws, points in the same direction. And yet there is nothing to denote that he as yet preferred a Republic to any other form of government. He is still able to conceive a king who should not be a tyrant. Further events had to take place before Monarchy is rejected as necessarily incompatible with the liberty which Milton cherishes equally with life itself.

The King's Book had appeared at the same time as Milton's

---

[1] Cp. the magnificent passage at the end of c. 8 of the *Defensio Prima*, beginning 'Our ancestors, if they have any knowledge of our affairs, must needs rejoice over their posterity.'

earliest political pamphlet, and, rising on the crest of the great wave of reaction, appeared to the Council of State sufficiently formidable to demand an answer. The *Eikonoklastes*, accordingly, made its appearance in the autumn of the same year. The greater part of the work closely follows the king, 'or his household rhetorician[1],' chapter by chapter, through the events of the long struggle. Two developments, however, are to be discerned. In the first place, the character of the references to the monarch himself has changed. The glee with which the author traces the plagiarism from the *Arcadia* and rushes to inferences therefrom, the credulity with which he accepts the story of the king's murder of his father and of his connection with the Irish massacres, his unfeeling jeer at Charles' vain request for his chaplains: these and many other passages point to a bitterness that is new. Traces, accordingly, of a less sympathetic attitude towards monarchy in general become visible in this treatise. 'We learn from both sacred and profane history,' he remarks in introducing a discussion on Church government[2], 'that the kings of this world have both ever hated and instinctively feared the Church of God.' Kings though strong in legions are but weak in argument, 'since they have ever been accustomed from their cradle to use their will only as their right hand, their reason as their left[3].' The possibility of a monarch not being a knave or a fool is forgotten. Equally does a second point demand notice. When the *Tenure* was written, the author believed that the vast majority of the nation took what he regarded as the rational view of the relations of kings and subjects. But the tide was turning while Milton was writing his first book, and was running rapidly while he was engaged on his second. He learned that he had over-estimated the area in which wisdom was to be found, and that he had exaggerated the worth of the

[1] c. 4.   [2] c. 17.   [3] Preface.

mass of individuals who composed the nation; and the shadow of disenchantment falls darkly across the pages. The country of free men, each with his birthright, his instinct for freedom, his divine origin and model, has now faded away, and in its place we have an 'inconstant, irrational and hapless herd, begotten to servility,' enchanted with the device of the king at his prayers.

In the following year appeared Milton's *Defence of the English People against Salmasius*, the fruit of almost twelve months' hard work. His opinions have now reached the point where Monarchy itself meets with unqualified rejection. 'You liken a monarchy to the government of the world by one God! I pray you, answer me whether you think any can deserve to be invested with a power here on earth that shall resemble His power that governs the world, except such a person as doth infinitely excel all other men?' We find, in the second place, the fullest statement of his conception of the Law of Nature. His opponent having defended his case by an appeal to the teachings of this code, Milton grapples with the whole question[1]. It is easy to prove that nothing is more agreeable to the Law of Nature than that punishment should be inflicted on tyrants. For it is a principle imprinted on all men's minds to regard the good of all mankind. Since, then, it does not regard the private good of any particular person, even of a prince, no king can pretend any right to do mischief. Hereditary government is contrary to the Law of Nature; for nobody has a right to be king unless he excels all others in wisdom and courage. Those who reign without these qualifications have climbed to power by force or faction. Nature appoints that wise men should govern fools, not that the wicked should rule over the good; and those who take the government out of such men's hands act agreeably to the Law of Nature.

[1] c. 5, *passim*.

III

Among lesser literary champions of the Republic was John Cook, already famous as chief prosecutor of the king and honourably distinguished from his fellow lawyers by the readiness with which he accepted proposals for the reform of the law[1]. A few days after the execution of Charles appeared the speech which he had intended to deliver, should the prisoner have pleaded to the charge[2]. The work throws an interesting light on the mental attitude of the average regicide. By what law is the king condemned? Such is the crucial question. Without a moment's hesitation comes the reply, 'By the unanimous consent of all rational men in the world, written in every man's heart with the pen of a diamond in capital letters.' That there is no special statute empowering the people to judge and condemn a tyrant is irrelevant; such a law is no more necessary than one enacting that men should eat and drink. Nay, were there a law specially forbidding such conduct, it would be invalid; for the Law of Nature not only supplements the laws of men, but overrides them. The application of the rule to the particular case is as indisputable as the rule itself. The community had agreed to offer the king power for the preservation of society, and on his acceptance a mutual trust had been created. On the breach of this trust,

---

[1] *Vindication of Professors and Profession of the Law*, T. P. vol. 662, 6, 30, 70, 92, etc. [A special study is badly needed of the movement for law reform under the Commonwealth. Among the Thomason Tracts is a large collection of pamphlets on the subject, which was a favourite theme of the Levellers and the followers of Winstanley. An essay in F. A. Inderwick's *The Interregnum* hardly scratches the surface of the material. The main projects evolved will be found in C. H. Firth and R. S. Rait, *Acts and Ordinances of the Interregnum*. Upon these a pamphlet by an anonymous writer (Philostratus Philodemius) entitled *Seasonable Observations* (1654) is of high value. H. J. L.]   [2] T. P. vol. 542.

the penalty which was implicit in the very idea of a contract had been enforced[1].

The 'babbling and brazen-faced solicitor,' as he was designated by Sir Philip Warwick[2], proceeded to devote such leisure as his official duties in Ireland allowed him to the further illustration of these principles. The character of the new work is indicated in its title, *Monarchy no creature of God's making, proving by Scripture and Reason that Monarchical Government is against the mind of God, and that the execution of the late king was one of the fattest sacrifices Queen Justice ever had*[3]. Unlike its predecessor, it reveals a definitely anti-monarchical position. A good king is a contradiction in terms. One who appears so simply gives the people 'many good words and a few good acts in order to enslave them faster, like those we call good witches that seem to cure one that they may without suspicion bewitch many.' Cook solemnly announces the Divine disapprobation of monarchy. Parliament put an end to kingship, not out of any affection for change, nor merely for the ease of the people, but because God commanded it to be done[4]. No other variety of monarchy than absolutism is presumed possible, and, since God appoints only such government as is just and reasonable, He is no more the author of monarchy than of sin. If it be objected that kingdoms nevertheless exist, we must reply that, as in the case of evil, they are permitted 'for ends and reasons best known to His Divine Majesty.' The ground of the erroneous impression that God approves of it is to be found in the habit of 'snatching at the Scriptures,' reading here a verse and there a verse, instead of taking pains to know the whole mind of God. Presumably on the strength of his proficiency in this exalted science, the author

[1] 22–42. [2] *Memoirs*, 337.
[3] T. P. vol. 1238. [4] Preface.

recalls to the memory of his readers the wet summer of 1648, and declares that it testified to the Lord's exceeding displeasure with those who would have made peace with the king[1]. After such an unmistakeable proclamation of the Divine disapproval of the government of a Single Person, it is remarkable that Cook should express a directly contrary opinion. What abundance of good, he soliloquises, might one rare incomparable person do in a short time, when great councils can move but slowly. But he recollects himself almost immediately and adds that such a thought is but worldly wisdom, since the best of men are but men and there is no grace but may be counterfeit. Such power would corrupt the best man living[2]. That such a thought should have flashed across the mind of so resolute a republican helps us to understand the welcome that greeted the *coup d'état* of two years later.

The slip does not recur. When the question arises whether a nation may live happily under a mixed monarchy, the reply is in the negative. Monarchy and Liberty are incompatible. A people must be in total bondage or wholly free, if they would live in quiet. In the same way, a good king is no more possible than a mixed monarchy. An apprentice with a kind master may in a certain way be said to be free; but, to speak strictly, he remains a servant. Besides, the analogy is merely fanciful. Monarchs are nearly always monsters, born for the scourge of mankind. Do men gather grapes of thorns or figs of thistles[3]? A more reasonable spirit appears in the protest against the notion of 'many godly, honest hearts' that knowledge was less requisite in a commonwealth than in a monarchy; whereas learning was not only for a Court, but for the glory of all nations. Equally dangerous was the opinion that every honest man was fit to be

[1] 1–44.   [2] 51, 2.   [3] 129–131.

a magistrate or a minister. The discussion of legal reform re-affirms the positions of his earlier pamphlet. Doubtless many formalities and ceremonies deserved to be buried in the sepulchre of monarchy. The author hoped that his colleagues were not possessed with the pernicious principle that, if an inch of their prerogative was parted with, it would be their destruction. If the Commonwealth flourished it was no matter what became of their practices. The impression left by a study of Cook's works is that of weakness and crudity. His convictions, such as the supremacy of the Law of Nature, the impossibility of a mixed monarchy or a good king, are stated as axioms requiring no proof. He appeals to Scripture and scorns the 'puddles of history.' The attitude of mind is fundamentally subjective; the method purely abstract.

Of equal importance was Marchamont Needham. Commencing his journalist's life by editing a paper in the Parliamentary cause from 1643 to 1646, he had proceeded to devote his services for an equal period to the Royalists. His royalism was never more than skin-deep and his appearance as a republican was not long delayed, for in the spring of 1650 he issued his *Case of the Commonwealth, proving the equity, utility and necessity of submission to the present government against all the scruples and pretences of the opposite parties*[1]. The pamphlet explains that the seeming inconsistency of appearing under a new flag arose from the conviction that the conscientious man should recognise the will of God as expressed in the success with which the government had met. The publication was rewarded with a government pension, despite the dangerously cynical character of its thought[2];

[1] T. P. vol. 600.
[2] Cp. the excellent remarks of Gardiner, *Commonwealth and Protectorate*, I. 282–5.

and on the issue of the first number of the *Mercurius Politicus* a few weeks later, Needham takes his place as one of the author-ised exponents of the policy of the government. The sincerity of his republican professions was further vouched for by the fact that he became 'a great crony' of Milton[1].

The opening pages of *The Excellency of a Free State* present us with a view of Monarchy very similar to that which we found in the works of Cook. It is credited with no merits. When the people are entrusted with the government, on the other hand, they are so fully occupied in looking after the preservation of their own rights that they never think of usurping those of other men. That none but honest and public-spirited men will desire to occupy places of authority, the machinery of govern-ment should be so arranged that the public service becomes a burdensome occupation. A further precaution is taken by strictly limiting the duration of the tenure of power, since, in political as well as physical bodies, motion is the grand preventive of cor-ruption. By this means no time is afforded for self-seeking to ripen into faction, and legislators speedily experience the results of their own activity. A free state also brings with it many positive advantages. A popular *régime* secures that the door of honour stands open to all that ascend by the steps of merit and virtue. And yet, however much success or service entitles a man to the gratitude of the nation, it is a prime principle of State that he be hindered from being too powerful or popular.

Anarchy is as impossible in a free State as oppression; for when we talk of the people, we do not mean the confused and promiscuous mass of men, nor those who have forfeited their rights by delinquency, apostasy or even neutrality. The govern-ment is conducted by the worthy members of the community

[1] Wood's *Fasti*, Part II. 414.

and by no others[1]. Concerning this system, the most suitable to
nature and reason, certain misunderstandings are rife. The most
common, perhaps, is that which regards it as incompatible with
the existence of society. But, in fact, it is only in a popular
government that the preservation of property is guaranteed, since
in monarchy every man's right is placed under the will of another.
No precedent can be cited by the enemies of freedom against the
people's government, for it will always appear that the people
were not in fault but provoked by craft or injustice. A second
mistake is also widely prevalent. It is thought that successful
government demands judgment and experience, and that in
consequence the perpetual presence of inexperienced members
in positions of importance would involve a lack of steadiness and
decision. The inference is unwarranted. The chief duty of those
who hold the reins is to provide remedies for the ills of the
country, and, since matters of grievance are matters of common
sense, there is no need of any special skill or judgment in devising
laws for their remedy[2]. But though Needham is convinced that
a free State is not open to any damaging indictment, he feels
that certain principles of policy should be borne in mind. It is
most essential, for instance, that a community in a state of freedom should keep close to the rules of a free State, so that in any
alteration of government the seeds of Monarchy may not sprout
forth. It is important, too, that every child should be educated
in the principles of freedom, and at a suitable age should solemnly
abjure the principle of kingly government. Respect for the
authority of the votes of Parliament should also be inculcated at
an early age, and treason against its majesty should be made a
capital crime. All should be accountable, yet frivolous charges
against those in authority must be avoided. Above all, not

[1] 23–80, T. P. vol. 1676.   [2] 81–128.

'Reason of State, that strange pocus,' but honesty is to inspire the councils of the State. 'The Court Gospel taught in that unworthy book, *The Prince*, has gained thousands of proselytes; but in a free State nobody mistakes breaches of faith for policy.' Of more special directions Needham is sparing; but it is interesting to notice that a warning is registered against the union of legislative and executive power in the same hands[1].

The work contains some excellent principles of government, but it is disfigured by not a little sophistry[2]. The passage in which the author attempts to answer the contention that in a democracy divisions and tumults are rife is an example. The people, says Needham, almost in the words of Burke, are never in fault; they are merely provoked by injustice or craft. But this distinction really surrenders the whole case, for it admits that disturbances occur, and that injustice and craft are to be found in a democratic community. Another instance is met with in his discussion of the objection that government needs judgment and experience. In the first place, his contention that the devising of remedies for the ills of the nation is the only important task of government implies a very inadequate notion of the function of the State; and in the second, the assertion that matters of grievance require no great skill to be remedied points to a lack of observation that is almost childish. A further example of loose thinking appears in connection with his recommendation of the separation of powers. In no case are the legislative and executive to be in the same hands; yet he pleads for a single chamber. The first vote of his assembly divides it into two parties, and the majority becomes omnipotent in every department of State.

[1] 145–246.
[2] It was exhaustively and acutely criticised by John Adams, *Works*, VI. 1–223.

In addition to those who thus indirectly supported the Government by their advocacy of republicanism, champions of the actual *régime* were not wanting. Mrs Hutchinson, who speaks for her husband, declared that the Parliament had restored the Commonwealth to a 'happy, rich and plentiful condition[1]'; and an anonymous adherent was convinced that with a fair trial it would take its place with Venice and other long-lived republics[2]. To the ecstatic fancy of Ludlow, the nation seemed likely to attain in a short time such measure of happiness as human affairs could experience[3].

[1] *Memoirs*, 362. [2] *Persuasive to Compliance*, 5, T. P. vol. 565.
[3] *Memoirs*, I. 343.

CHAPTER VII

The Antagonists of the Oligarchy

THE events which culminated in the death of the king gave a new impetus to democratic ideas[1]. The resemblance, however, between the *régime* that followed and the ideals that had been formed extended no further than that the government of England was not monarchical. The rule of the Rump was as essentially the government of a minority as had been that of the king; and it rested on the sword. The country was ruled, not by laws of its own making, but by the arbitrary proclamations of a body of men which by successive mutilations had come to represent nobody.

In addition to the fact that the form of the government was not 'such as the people approved,' its spirit was such as to exaggerate the anomaly of its position. The State Papers of the time reveal to us a picture of what can only be described as tyranny. As was frankly replied to Sir Roger Twysden, when pleading against the confiscation of his estates, the House did not look at the nice observance of the law[2]. The principle which was consistently followed was to stifle every expression of opinion throughout the country. 'Keep a watchful eye on the confluence of the people on any pretence,' were the instructions of the

[1] It was typical that the abolition of the veto of the Court of Aldermen over the Common Council, though vainly attempted for years, was now accomplished without effort. Sharpe's *London*, II. 303.

[2] Bisset's *Commonwealth*, II. 426. It was in vain, for instance, that the seamen told the Government that they 'apprehended it inconsistent with the principles of freedom to force men to serve.' Single Sheets, B.M., 669, f. 19, No. 33.

Council of State to their representatives in the counties, 'especially in times like these. The most diligent care must be taken to prevent such meetings of the multitude that may make use of pretence to begin insurrection or carry on designs to the interruption of the public peace[1].' No entry is so common as the notice of a warrant against the circulation of books and newspapers[2], and Mabbott, the licenser, was dismissed for laxity[3]. Orders were issued to seize all the private presses in the counties and to arrest the hawkers of books[4]. How tyrannical was the effort to muzzle the press is shewn by the fact that, despite the utmost activity of the Government, its exertions were to a great extent fruitless[5]. The religious freedom of the people was as little respected. It was ordered that 'nothing by pretence of pulpit liberty should be suffered in prejudice of the peace and honour of the Government[6].' The Council of State did its best to suppress even the observance of Christmas[7]. It was only because the country was in large measure paralysed with the effort of the struggle, because the majority was split up into parties among whom combination, at least for the time, was impossible, and above all the fact that the minority possessed control of the army that the Government was able to maintain itself. The single merit of the Oligarchy was that its members were good administrators[8].

---

[1] C. S. P. 1651, 286.
[2] Cp. *ib.* 1650, 533 for a specimen page.
[3] *ib.* 1649, 50, 127.
[4] *ib.* 1650, 185.
[5] *ib.* 1651–2, 444.
[6] *ib.* 1651–2, 115.
[7] *ib.* 1650, 484.
[8] Cp. Coke's *Detection*, II. 30–1.

I

The most powerful opposition proceeded from the Levellers. After the reconciliation of soldiers and officers early in 1648, the current of recriminatory pamphlets had again begun to flow[1]; but the revival of the royal cause induced Lilburne to seek a reconciliation with the enemy. If Oliver would act honourably, he was willing to forget the harsh treatment he had received from him, and to aid him with the last drop of his blood[2]. The danger passed away sooner than had been anticipated; but Lilburne continued to desire a *rapprochement*. Why should not representatives of the minority in Parliament, of the army and of the Levellers meet and draw up a final Agreement? The suggestion was well received, and the Royalists heard in alarm that the Independents and Levellers were agreed in aiming to 'root out the king[3].' The *Agreement* that was drawn up by the majority of the Committee which proceeded to sit at Whitehall naturally bore marks of its joint authorship. Yet the Levellers could congratulate themselves on the document as a whole. The Council was to act according to the instructions and limitations imposed on it by the Parliament which elected it, and the Parliament in like manner was to be subordinate to the electors. All cases were to be settled by a jury, and no branch of government was to possess any judicial power. Imprisonment for debt was to be abolished. No one was to contribute to the maintenance of Ministers of whose teaching he did not approve. A new

[1] *People's Prerogative and Privileges*, T. P. vol. 427 ; *England's Weeping Spectacle of John Lilburne*, T. P. vol. 40 ; *Windsor Projects and Westminster Practices*, T. P. vol. 442. [This period is particularly well treated in Pease, *op. cit.* chs. VIII–XI. H. J. L.]

[2] *Legal Fundamental Liberties*, 32.   [3] Cal. Clar. S. P. I. 464.

Parliament was to be urged to rid the kingdom of lawyers and establish Courts in every hundred[1].

The Levellers, who, on the strength of Ireton's approval of their scheme when it was first mentioned to him, had understood that the decision of the majority of the Committee was to be final, now thought that 'all had been done, as to any more debate upon it, and that it should without any more ado be promoted for subscriptions[2].' Incredible as it appears that they could have entertained such a notion, on discovering that it was to be submitted to the Council of Officers for discussion they considered the army leaders false to their pledges. All but the Levellers themselves saw that they were engaged in a hopeless task. 'The Grandees and the Levellers,' declared a Royalist journal tersely, 'can as soon combine as fire and water; the one aim at a pure democracy, the others at an oligarchy[3].' And this the debates of the officers, to which representatives of the Levellers were admitted, once more made clear[4]. The disappointment found expression in the *Plea for Common Right and Freedom* which was presented to Fairfax. If he had been honest in his declarations he had now the opportunity to convince the world of it. The opposition that was emasculating the *Agreement* must be brought to an end[5]. The exhortation was echoed in a Representation from the garrisons in Northumberland[6]; but the appeals produced no effect, and the *Agreement* was tendered to

---

[1] *An Agreement of the People*, 7–15, T. P. vol. 476. These points were taken almost without change from a Petition of the inhabitants of London to Parliament on October 23. It was doubtless composed by Lilburne or one of his friends. T. P. vol. 468.

[2] *Legal Fundamental Liberties*, 37.

[3] *Mercurius Pragmaticus*, Dec. 19, T. P. vol. 477; cp. Carte's *Original Letters*, i. 103, 4.

[4] *Clarke Papers*, ii. 75–131.

[5] T. P. vol. 536, 6.   [6] T. P. vol. 475.

Parliament almost apologetically in the very month of the king's death. 'The officers,' ran the communication to the House, 'were far from desiring to impose their private apprehensions on the judgments of any man, much less on members of Parliament. If it were not accepted, it might at least remain as a testimony of their endeavours for a settlement[1].' A month later the right of petitioning and of meeting in the army was strictly limited, and on March 1 the proposal for a revival of the General Council was rejected.

These measures led to a final outbreak in the army itself. A letter was presented to Fairfax attacking the officers with great boldness. The writers were expelled from the army, and in a few days their revenge was ready. *The Hunting of the Foxes from Triploe Heath to Westminster by five small Beagles* is one of the most effective pamphlets of the time. It put the question which half England was asking itself. 'We were ruled before by King, Lords and Commons, now by a General, Court Martial and Commons; and we pray you what is the difference[2]?' The protest was followed by a mutiny in London. Despite its easy suppression, the execution of Lockyer revealed the serious nature of the opposition which the army's policy had aroused. The corpse was preceded by 'a thousand' and followed by 'thousands,' clothed in black and bearing the green ensign[3]. In his dying speech the victim declared that, as he was brought thither to suffer for the people, he knew that God would make his blood speak liberty to all England[4]. A few weeks later, undaunted by the decisive measures of the officers, Captain Thompson mutinied in Oxfordshire and was joined by considerable numbers. His

---

[1] Rushworth, VII, 1358–61.   [2] *Somers Tracts*, VI. 52.
[3] Whitelocke, March 30, III. 24.
[4] *The Army's Martyr*, 6–7, T. P. vol. 552.

manifesto declared that, since it was notorious that the faith of the army had not been observed, no other means under heaven were left but to betake themselves to the law of nature to preserve their native rights. They were resolved to redeem their native country and to redeem it according to the principles of the *Agreement* of John Lilburne, and would endeavour to liberate him and his colleagues and to avenge any hurt that they might suffer[1]. The revolt, however, was subdued, and the discontent in other regiments took no active form[2]. When next the Levellers began to rise in the South and West, the soldiers whom they expected to take their part were ready to resist them[3]. With this repulse the final opposition by the Levellers within the army comes to a close[4].

The struggle was meanwhile being carried on by the civilian Levellers. True, Parliament had declared the people to be the original of all just power; but its reforming zeal had been contented with declarations[5]. At the end of February it was invited to lay seriously to heart certain proposals which found no place in the *Agreement*. No interval should elapse between successive Parliaments, which should be annual instead of biennial. No special courts should be erected, no tithes demanded, no imprisonment for debt permitted. The laws were to be reformed and liberty of religion ensured. Work and a comfortable maintenance

[1] *English Soldiers' Standard to repair to*, 11, T. P. vol. 550; *England's Standard advanced*, 1–3, T. P. vol. 553.

[2] *Declaration of Scroope's and Ireton's regiments; The Soldiers' Demand*, T. P. vol. 555.

[3] Whitelocke, III. 31–8; Clarendon, XII. 151.

[4] It was at this time that Denne deserted their ranks and wrote a pamphlet of recantation, *The Levellers' Design discovered*, T. P. vol. 556.

[5] Cp. *Declaration of the Parliament and grounds of settling government in the way of a free state*, 20, 25–7. Printed by order of Parliament. T. P. vol. 548.

should be provided for the poor and impotent; for the people in general had suffered through decay of trade and dearness of food, and had nothing left them but hopes of better times[1]. No party had so evidently transgressed against the light as their old colleagues[2].

For the Second Part of *England's New Chains*, Lilburne, Walwyn, Overton and Price—the four names occur henceforth in invariable connection—were forthwith arrested[3]. Petitions for their release at once began to pour in[4]. The women declared they could not eat nor drink in peace nor sleep in quiet for fear for their husbands and sons[5]. When a member of the House bade them stay at home and wash their dishes, they replied that they had scarce any left to wash, and were not sure of keeping these. If the lives of the four men were taken, they continued, as Cromwell appeared outside the House, nothing would satisfy them but his life[6]. Being ordered back to the closest durance after examination by the Council of State, Lilburne found means to issue a graphic account of the incident[7]. Indeed, as Mr Firth has remarked, it seemed utterly impossible to deprive him of ink. He had told the members that the laws and liberties of England were his inheritance and his birthright. They were not a Court of Justice, for the law made no reference to them; they were not a Council of State, for they had no commission from the people. When they asked him whether he had written the book, he

[1] *England's New Chains*, 2–12, T. P. vol. 545.
[2] *Second Part of England's New Chains*, 17, T. P. vol. 548; Overton's *Petition to the Supreme Authority of England*, 3, 4, T. P. vol. 546.
[3] C. S. P. 1649–50, 55.
[4] Petition in the *Moderate*, April 2, T. P. vol. 549; *Commons' Journals*, VI. 189, 200, etc.
[5] *Petition of Women*, 4–7, T. P. vol. 551.
[6] *Mercurius Militaris*, Ap. 17, II. vol. 551.
[7] *Picture of the Council of State*, T. P. vol. 550.

replied that the Star Chamber had been abolished for precisely such questions. On his retirement from the Council Chamber he heard Cromwell declare his conviction that there was no other way of dealing with them but to break them to pieces[1]. The narrative of their sufferings was closely followed by a remarkable declaration of their principles. None were born for themselves alone, but all were obliged by the Law of Nature and by Christianity to endeavour the happiness of the community. For this each must be able to enjoy his own with security. But this is only possible where the depravity of man is counteracted by institutions so designed as to give it no play. That because they demanded a good government they were for no government at all was an inference warranted neither by their conduct nor their teaching[2].

The high tone that had been regained by the party since the final breach with the army is maintained in the ultimate shape which the *Agreement of the People* assumed. The authors describe the document as 'the end and full scope of all our desires and intentions in government, wherein we shall rest absolutely satisfied,' and add that they trust it will 'satisfy all ingenuous people that we are not such wild, irrational and dangerous creatures as we are aspersed.' Parliament is to consist of 400 members, chosen, according to natural right, by all of the age of 21 who are not servants nor in receipt of relief. No office-holder may be a member, and no member may sit in two successive Parliaments. During adjournment the Government is to be conducted not by a Council but by a Committee. The Representative has power to preserve order, to regulate commerce, to supervise the coinage. On the other hand, Parliament may not legislate in matters of religion,

[1] 1–25. The experiences of the others were very similar, 25–54.
[2] *Manifesto of those unjustly styled Levellers*, 3–7, T. P. vol. 550.

nor may it impress for service. It may not grant monopolies, nor impose taxes on food. Passing to the judicial part of the scheme, we meet the familiar requirements, equality before the law, definite penalties, abolition of imprisonment for debt. No one is compelled to witness against himself; prisoners are allowed counsel; all cases must be settled within six months. Capital punishment is reserved for murder, and for the attempt to destroy the *Agreement*. Tithes are to be abolished, and each parish is to make its own arrangements with Ministers as to terms and salary. All public officers are to be elected locally and to serve for a year only. No forces can be raised but by agreement of the Parliament and the people, the former electing the General and higher officers, the latter choosing the rest in proportion to the population. Finally, the *Agreement* is incapable of being altered by any Parliament[1].

During the summer of 1649 the leader of the party remained in prison, issuing pamphlets, as usual, at short intervals. *The Legal Fundamental Liberties* once more insisted that representatives from the army and each county should meet and draw up an *Agreement* which should be beyond repeal[2]. *The Impeachment of High Treason against Cromwell and Ireton*, surpassing in violence anything that had yet appeared from Lilburne's pen[3], determined the Government to silence its author[4]. The speech of the defendant at the trial which ensued, filled though it was with quibbles and technicalities, was followed by such 'an extraordinary great hum' that three more companies of foot were ordered to the Court. For the jury as for the onlookers, the question of treason resolved itself into the broader issue whether the country should be governed

---

[1] T. P. vol. 552.   [2] p. 30.   [3] 2–4, T. P. vol. 568.
[4] C. S. P. 1649, 50, 544. Lilburne professed to fear assassination. *Memorials of the Verney Family*, III. 142–5.

by the sword or according to its own will[1]; and the verdict of acquittal was greeted by a shout which lasted for half-an-hour, and was commemorated by the striking of a medal[2].

The significance of the movement in the history of political thought comes to an end at this point[3]. With more truth than any other body of men of the time, the Levellers could claim to be considered as the people's party. Their thought rested on the conviction that the ordering of the life of a nation should be in accordance with certain moral principles which every man finds implanted in him. Of these the most important was that liberty is a right demanded by the very nature of human beings: not merely a freedom from the restraint of others, but a conscious and deliberate share in such arrangements as the community finds it necessary to make. From this right of the individual springs the

[1] Report of the trial in T. P. vol. 584; cp. comments of Bisset, *Commonwealth*, I. ch. 4; and Gardiner, *Commonwealth and Protectorate*, I. ch. 7, especially 186–8.

[2] C. S. P. 1649, 50, 357–61. In December, the Government thought it necessary to issue orders to seize all narratives of Lilburne's trial. 558. A further proof of his popularity occurred soon after in his election as a Common Councilman. The election, however, was disallowed. *C. J.* VI. 337.

[3] What had failed in England it was hoped might succeed in France. A document, emanating from Bordeaux during the civil war of 1651, demanding the articles of the Leveller programme, would seem a forgery, had it not been found by Cousin among the papers both of Mazarin and Condé. Cousin's *Madame de Longueville*, II. 465–76. Though the movement had no issue, the negotiations were followed with interest. Prophecies of change of government in France were applied to Condé, *Old Prophecies*, T. P. vol. 55. Cp. the remarks of Firth, Introduction to *Hane's Journal*, 15–17, and Chéruel's *Mazarin*, I. 56–60. The state of democratic thought in Bordeaux preceding the arrival of the Leveller emissaries is described in D'Aumale's *Princes de Condé*, VI. 108–10. Republicanism in France was sporadic. *Bibl. des Mazarinades*, I. 419, 201, 202; C. S. P. 1648–9, 334, 5; *Corresp. de Mazarin*, III. 1090, IV. 221, etc. [For a discussion and comparison of the Civil War in England and the Fronde cp. Henri Sée, *Histoire des Idées Politiques en France au* XVII*me Siècle*, ch. IV. H. J. L.]

sovereignty of the people, a sovereignty bounded, however, by social duty and by justice. Of the fundamentals which are inseparable from their well-being the people may not deprive themselves[1]. The subsidiary principle on which the teaching proceeded was the confirmation which was afforded by history to the ideas inseparable from man's nature. Appeal was made, in the first place, to certain definite constitutional rights inherited from their ancestors, recorded in Magna Charta and the Statute Book; in the second, to a contract that had been entered into by their forefathers in pre-historic times.

In this argumentative structure two elements of weakness reveal themselves. The appeal to natural right, as Ireton pointed out, is in its essence anarchic, and a historical basis which is but half historical does not cure the defect. In the second place, the human unit is credited with possessing more wisdom than, it is to be feared, it can claim. The 'natural aristocracy,' which, as Harrington was shortly to maintain, is the life-blood of successful democratic government, finds no place in the system elaborated by Lilburne and his fellows. We are sometimes tempted to forget the solid worth of many of the ideas of the Levellers in the unworthiness of their representatives; yet it is impossible not to recognise that behind their opportunism and their self-seeking, behind their doctrinaire habits of thought, lies a treasure of political counsels unequalled in its variety and suggestiveness by any system of the age save in that of Harrington.

[1] 'All authorities acting against the well-being of the people are void by the laws of God and Nature.' The *Moderate*, Oct. 31, T. P. vol. 470. Cp. Cornewall Lewis, 'When the State of Nature is merely a picture into which the painter has collected all those particulars which he considers characteristic of political and social excellence, it is naturally held up to imitation.' *Observation and Reasoning in Politics*, II. 281.

II

Though it was unlikely that in an age where the soil was so deeply ploughed some forms of Communism should not appear, it is too little known that the English revolution presents some of the most remarkable communistic speculations in history[1]. In commenting in the House on the petitions for the disendowment of the Church, the poet Waller foretold that the people would not stop with a plea for equality in ecclesiastical matters. 'Our laws and the present government of the Church,' said he, 'are mixed like wine and water. I look on the episcopate as an outwork or barrier, and say to myself that if this is stormed by the people and the secret thereby discovered that we can deny them nothing which they demand, we shall have a task no less difficult to defend our property against them than we had lately to preserve it against the prerogative of the Crown. I therefore counsel the reform and not the abolition of the Church[2].'

The Church was destroyed, and, as Waller had foretold, an attack was made on property itself. The common cry that the slavery of the people dated from the Norman Conquest provided a convenient plea for a revision of the system of property which had been instituted by that event. With this position the name of John Hare is specially connected. In 1647 he published a pamphlet bearing the characteristic title of *St Edward's Ghost*, urging the people to revolt[3]. A few weeks later, *Plain English to our Wilful Bearers of Normanism* laments both in its title and preface that the previous pamphlet had ' obtained no regard.' The

---

[1] The honour of the discovery of Winstanley belongs to Bernstein, *Geschichte des Sozialismus in Einzeldarstellungen*, 1. 589 f., 1895.

[2] *Parl. Hist.* 11. 826–8. Cp. the conclusion of the *Short History of the Anabaptists*, 56, T. P. vol. 148.

[3] *Harl. Misc.* VIII. 103.

author therefore devotes himself to proving that, while the right of conquest is recognised, the privileges of the Law of Nature and the necessities of the Salus Populi are alike forgotten[1]. In the following year, Hare blew a third blast before the walls which obstinately refused to fall. On this occasion he indicated *England's proper and only way to an establishment in honour, power, peace and happiness*; and, in reply to the objection that the rooting out of the innovations would be a difficult and troublesome matter, retorts that the nation had taken more pains over things of less importance[2].

Hare, however, had rather vague notions of what he desired to substitute for the system of property that he attacked. The many-sided Hartlib, on the other hand, elaborated an Utopia of singular interest. In the famous kingdom of Macaria, the government is carried on by a Great Council, divided into five committees, dealing with Agriculture, Fishing, Trade by land, Trade by sea, and Plantations. In other words, the State is an economic institution and directs and supervises every branch of production. For this reason, the conduct of the individual is the concern of the State, and if anybody holds more land than he is able to improve to the uttermost, he is first to be admonished of the great hindrance to the Commonwealth which thereby ensues. If his husbandry does not amend in a year's time, he incurs a penalty which every year of contumacy doubles. If time shews him to be incorrigible, he is banished and his lands are forfeited to the community[3]. Further traces of the conviction that the time was

---

[1] *Harl. Misc.* IX. 90–5. [The fullest treatment of this subject is by L. H. Berens, *The Digger Government*, which, however, contains a good deal of irrelevant matter. See also N. Beer, *History of British Socialism*, vol. I. p. 58 f. H. J. L.]

[2] *Harl. Misc.* VI. 36–47.

[3] *ib.* I. 580–5. Hartlib's plan was not the trifling of an idle moment.

approaching for drastic changes in the economic system of the country are to be found. While Hare had attacked the prevalent constitution of society as a lawyer and Hartlib as a philanthropist, Chamberlen approaches the subject from the standpoint of a trained economist. The *Poor Man's Advocate* declares on its first page[1] that the most necessary work of man is to provide for the poor. For this the author proposes no mere alteration of the Poor Laws, but the nationalisation of all Crown and Church possessions and the rescue of all common lands that had been enclosed[2]. This mass of property is to form a National Stock and to be administered for the benefit of the poor[3]. In rejecting the assumption that laziness ensues when men are guaranteed immunity from starvation, Chamberlen takes care to point out that his proposal is for the genuine poor and not for beggars.

Some years later, a Dutchman, named Peter Cornelius, propounded a *Way to the Peace and Settlement of these Nations, to make the poor in these and other nations happy*[4]. He congratulated the country on the liberty it had possessed since the abolition of the hierarchy, but declared that tithe remained as the chief cause of persecution and discontent[5]. It was desirable therefore that this and the old system of society with which it was connected should come to an end, and that Christendom should become a world-state under the rule of a single magistracy. With this object

Nearly twenty years afterwards he told Boyle that its scope was to endeavour the reformation of the whole world, and wrote to Worthington that he was sanguine that Macaria would soon have a visible being. Worthington's *Diary*, I. 163, Chetham Society.

[1] T. P. vol. 552.
[2] The proposal reoccurs in an undated pamphlet by W. Goffe, 'How to advance the trade of the nation and employ the poor,' *Harl. Misc.* IV. 385–9.
[3] *Poor Man's Advocate*, 2–20.   [4] T. P. vols. 972 and 984.
[5] *Peace and Settlement*, 3–30.

individuals were to form joint-stock associations in which they lived together, but in which they might retain the control of their property. It was expected, however, that the members of each 'little Commonwealth' would form in every respect one household. They were to elect a governor from among themselves for a year, and might re-elect him if they chose. Only the 'honest and rational' people, and of these only those who were skilled in some trade or occupation, were to be admitted as members, and any who proved to be unsuitable were to be expelled. Those unfit for admission were to be employed by the household, and on reaching a certain standard of good conduct to be allowed to enter[1]. All vices arising from riches and poverty, inequality, exploitation and the like, would vanish[2]. Though these remarkable pamphlets emanated from a Dutchman, they were written in English and with a full knowledge of English affairs. And from the fact that such speculation was unknown in the Low Countries at this time[3], it is hardly fanciful to attribute them to English influence.

We have found that men representing various classes entertained views and elaborated proposals in some measure communistic, without actually being communists themselves. Is anything more systematic and far-reaching to be found among the Levellers? The organ of the party, *The Moderate*, certainly speaks for the largest section, and on the whole deserves the name it bears[4]. Lilburne himself was very far from being a Leveller,

[1] *Way to Make the Poor Happy*, 5–29.　　　　　　　　[2] 14.

[3] Except, of course, that of Labadie. Heppe's *Niederländischer Pietismus*, 240–374 ; Ritschl's *Pietismus*, 1. 194–268.

[4] For striking manifestoes of its moderate position, see Sep. 7, 1648, T. P. vol. 463; Oct. 10, T. P. vol. 468. It is difficult to know on what grounds Lord Leicester wrote in his Diary, 'The *Moderate* always tries to incite the people to overthrow all property.' Blencowe's *Sydney Papers*, 77–9.

and expressly disclaims any sympathy with the notions of the Diggers[1]. Walwyn, on the other hand, was more extreme in his notions, and many stories were abroad of his questioning spirit. Though he did not publish any heretical opinions, he seems to have been careless who was present when he was talking. At any rate he was pilloried in 1645 in the first volume of the *Gangraena* as a dangerous man[2]. Several years later we meet with accusations of a more explicit character. 'In order to work on the poorer sort,' we are told that he declared 'he could wish there was neither pale, hedge, nor ditch in the nation, for it was an unconscionable thing one should have £10,000, and another, more useful and deserving to the Commonwealth, not be worth twopence.' He had been overheard declaring in conversation that it would never be well till all things were common. 'But will that ever be?' 'We must endeavour it.' 'But that would destroy government.' 'There would be no need of government, for there would be no thieves or criminals[3].' Since the vindications of Walwyn confine themselves to the charges of heresy and evil character we may consider it probable that he, alone of the Levellers, was to a great extent a convinced communist[4].

[1] *Legal Fundamental Liberties*, 20. Edwards fails to notice the existence of the two wings; and mentions the heresy 'that the land should be equally shared' in connection with Lilburne and Overton. *Gangraena*, vol. 3, p. 52.

[2] He at once published an indignant reply, *Whisper in the Ear of Mr Edwards*, T. P. vol. 328. The description was repeated in the 2nd volume issued in the following year, with anecdotes of his disrespect to the Trinity and his contempt for monarchy, to prove that he was a 'desperate man, a Seeker and a Libertine,' 25–50. To these charges Walwyn replied with dignity, and predicted Edwards' recantation of his slanders and his conversion to some of the opinions he had reviled. *Antidote against Master Edwards, his old and new prison*; and *Prediction of Mr Edwards' Conversion and Recantation*. Both in T. P. vol. 1184.

[3] 16.

[4] *The Charity of Churchmen*, T. P. vol. 556; and *Fountain of Slander*

When the monarchy was gone, the time seemed to have come for the transition from theoretical to practical communism. Though the working-classes had stood aloof from the great struggle, they shared the general expectation that the establishment of the Republic would usher in the era of reform. The rise of prices consequent on the discovery of new supplies of the precious metals was followed but slowly by the increase of wages, and the hardship was heightened by the monopoly prices demanded for many of the necessities of life[1]. To these chronic evils was added, during the fifth decade of the century, that of a series of unusually bad harvests[2]. The war, too, had brought with it on the one hand a large increase of taxation, and, on the other, the intolerable vexation of free quarter. Though the miserable condition of the poor was constantly discussed and the proposals for amelioration were numerous[3], the pamphlets and newspapers of the time are full of lament that no improvement was being effected[4].

Discovered, T. P. vol. 557. That Henry Marten was a Communist rests on the evidence of Clement Walker alone. 'He now declares himself for a community of wealth,' wrote Walker in 1648, and 'protests against Parliament and all Magistrats, like a second Wat Tyler.' *Hist. of Independency*, Part I. 139. For corroboration of the statement he refers to a book recently published by Marten, *England's Troublers Troubled*. But no copy of the work has ever been found, and nothing that we know of Marten leads us to believe that he entertained such opinions. If he had done so, it would have been made use of in the innumerable attacks upon him.

[1] Usefully collected in Overall's *City Remembrancia*, 213–27. D'Ewes computed them at 700, *Autob.* I. 171.

[2] Rogers' *Agriculture and Prices*, V. 779–99.

[3] In addition to those already mentioned, cp. Cook's *Unum Necessarium, or the Poor Man's Cause*, T. P. vol. 425. The suggestions include the appointment of a Poor Man's Lawyer, Doctor, etc., and the State control of public-houses. Similarly thoughtful proposals were made by Herring, *Nickolls' Letters to Cromwell*, 99–102. Cp. Eden's *State of the Poor*, I. 148–73.

[4] *The Address of the Poor to the King* had hoped he would earn the name

Although it was not till 1649 that public attention was directed to the appearance of a new doctrine, the outlines of it are to be found in a pamphlet published in December, 1648. The *Light Shining in Buckinghamshire* announces in its sub-title a discussion of the main cause of the slavery of the world. By the grant of God all were free alike, and no individual was intended to exercise rule over his fellow-men. 'But man, following his sensuality, became an encloser, so that all the land was enclosed in a few mercenary hands and all the rest made their slaves.' Of these robbers the most desperate was made king in order to protect the rest in their misdoings. Each should have a just portion, so that none need to beg nor steal for want. The government should be carried on by elders chosen by the people, who would decide all questions in every town and hamlet without any further trouble. At the present time we were governed by nobles and priests. All our nobility and gentry were originally the servants of William the Conqueror; their rise was their country's ruin, and the putting them down would be the restoration of our rights. 'The base priests preach all our powers and constitutions to be Jure Divino. Shake off these locusts and be no more deluded by them; cast off these abominable deceivers[1].'

Four months later, the exhortation 'To your tents, O Israel,' with which the earlier pamphlet had closed, bore fruit. On April 16, the Council of State received the following intelligence. 'On Sunday sennight last, there was one Everard, once of the army but cashiered, who termeth himself a prophet, and four more came to St George's Hill in Surrey and began to dig, and

of 'The Poor Man's King,' T. P. vol. 205. Cp. *The Poor Man's Pension*, T. P. vol. 10, etc. Not until the ascendancy of Cromwell did the burden become lighter (Macpherson's *Annals*, III. 479–80), and then but for a while.

[1] T. P. vol. 475, 1–10.

sowed the ground with parsnips, carrots and beans. On Monday following they were there again, being increased in their number. On Friday they came again, twenty or thirty, and wrought all day at digging. They do threaten to pull down and level all park pales and lay open and intend to plant them. They give out that they will be four or five thousand within ten days, and threaten the neighbouring people they will make them all come up to the hills and work.' The letter was at once forwarded by Bradshaw to Fairfax, with a request that he should send some horse to disperse the disorderly and tumultuous people. A force was at once dispatched, and three days later Fairfax was informed that the affair was not worth notice. There had never been above twenty of the diggers. They had met Everard and Winstanley, their leaders, and they had promised to appear before Fairfax; but he would be glad to be rid of them again[1].

The following day the leaders appeared before the Council of State and explained their conduct[2]. All the liberties of the people, declared Everard, had been lost by the coming of the Conqueror. The time of deliverance was now at hand, and God would restore them their freedom to enjoy the fruits of the earth. A vision had appeared to him, and a voice had bidden him dig and plough the earth and receive the fruits thereof. Their intention was to distribute the benefits of the earth to the poor and needy, to feed the hungry and clothe the naked. They did not intend to meddle with property nor to break any enclosures, but only to take what was common and untilled and to make it fruitful. They were willing to live in tents as their forefathers, whose

---

[1] *Clarke Papers*, II. 209–12.
[2] *Declaration and Standard of the Levellers of England*, T. P. vol. 551. The speech appeared in print on April 23. The account in Whitelocke, III. 17–18, is transcribed almost verbatim from the pamphlet.

principles they took for a model, had lived. The speaker had kept his hat on in the presence of the General, remarking that he was their fellow-creature. No further steps were taken by the Government at the time. They felt, perhaps, that rumour had exaggerated the importance of the diggers, whom after Everard's speech they were inclined to regard as harmless fanatics. A week after the examination, however, appeared a manifesto revealing the fact that behind the artless confession to which they had listened lay a philosophy which threatened every existing institution.

The *True Leveller's Standard Advanced, or the State of Community opened and presented to the sons of men*, published on April 26, was a 'declaration to the powers of England and to the powers of the world why the common people had begun to dig on St George's Hill.' 'In the beginning,' runs the manifesto, striking a new note in the first sentence, 'the great creator Reason made the Earth a common treasury for beasts and man.' Not a word was said by which one man could claim rule over another. But man falling into blindness was brought into bondage, and became a greater slave to his own kind than the beasts of the field to him. Hereupon the earth, made for a common treasury or relief to all, was bought and sold, and was hedged in by the rulers and kept in the hands of a few. For a certain time the creator, the spirit Reason, thus suffered himself to be rejected; whence arose wars to uphold dominion and riches, the curse under which creation groans. But when the earth again becomes a common treasury, as it must, for Reason and all the prophecies of Scripture point to it, all enmity will cease; for none will desire a larger share than another[1]. Passing from an exposition of their philosophy to a vindication of their recent conduct, the authors declare that they

[1] T. P. vol. 552, 6–11.

have met with resistance because they maintain an universal liberty, which was not only their birthright, but which they had bought with their money and blood in the war. All landlords lived in breach of the commandment 'Thou shalt not steal.' They had induced the plain-hearted poor to work for them with small wages, and by their work had made great fortunes. By their very labour the poor raised up tyrants to rule over them. The authors then state that it had been revealed to them in dreams where they should begin to dig, and that though the earth might be barren they should receive a blessing from the spirit. 'You Pharaohs, you have rich clothing and full bellies, you have your honours and your ease; but know the day of judgment is begun and that it will reach you ere long. The poor people you oppress shall be the saviours of the land. If you will find mercy, let Israel go free; break to pieces the bands of property[1].'

The Diggers still remained quietly employed at St George's Hill. When Fairfax came from Guildford to London at the end of May, he visited the locality and found twelve of them hard at work. To a short admonition from the General, they replied that they were digging crown lands, and that, the king who possessed them by the Norman Conquest being dead, they returned to the common people[2]. The day after the visit of the General appeared another manifesto of the party, directed to the Lords of Manors[3].

[1] 11–22.

[2] *Speeches of Fairfax to the Diggers*, May 31, in T. P. vol. 531. A 'Declaration of the Well-Affected in Bucks,' contains the only positive approval that I can find that the colony met with. The locality suggests something more than a coincidence. *Messenger*, June 15, 58, 59. A fuller, though later, account appeared in the *Moderate*.

[3] The rapacity of landlords had been the theme of every economist for half a century. Rogers, vol. v. ch. 2. A remarkable document, denouncing the landlords and asking that 'our natural inheritance shall return to us again,' emanated from Hertfordshire in 1647. Urwick's *Nonconformity in Herts*. 832, 3.

It was prompted by the fact that they were in all directions cutting down and selling trees on common lands and thereby impoverishing them[1]. 'God has enlightened our hearts,' said the writers, 'to see that the earth was not made purposely for you to be the lords and we to be your slaves'; but they still declared that they had no intention of resorting to force. This appeal producing no effect, a letter was soon after dispatched to Fairfax. He had been mild and moderate to them in Court and when he had come to see them, and the author was thereby emboldened to plead with him for justice. The laws that had been made in the days of monarchy had given freedom to the gentry and clergy, but had done nothing for the people[2].

In July the persecution which they had so remarkably escaped fell upon them. Winstanley and two of his comrades were brought before the Court at Kingston for trespass, and the jury consisted of 'such as stood strongly for the Norman power.' They were forbidden to speak and were heavily fined. Thereupon they sent an account of their arrest and sentence to the House of Commons, once more explaining their position and defending their claims. They enclosed a list of some of the abominations which William the Conqueror introduced into England, among which were those of tithes and lawyers[3]. At the end of November a more serious attack was made upon the little community. A party of soldiers appeared, pulled down the two houses in which they were living and carried the wood away in a cart. A long and eloquent letter from Winstanley followed. The arguments are for the first time wholly devoid of the familiar Digger philosophy. There is

[1] *Declaration of the Poor Oppressed People to Lords of Manors*, 4, in T. P. vol. 557.
[2] *Letter to Fairfax and the Council of War*, T. P. vol. 560.
[3] *Appeal to the House of Commons*, 15–17, T. P. vol. 564; *Watchword to the City of London and to the Army*, T. P. vol. 573.

not a word about Natural Right. They claim nothing more than the fulfilment of a contract. Parliament had virtually said to them, Give us taxes, free quarter, excise, venture your lives with us to cast out the oppressor, and we will make you a free people. They had agreed, and the victory had been won. The spoil should be equally divided between those who went to war and those who stayed at home and paid them. They claimed freedom in the common land by virtue of their conquest over the king, for they had bought it by their blood and money. If the Government denied them their request, it would have to raise money for their support; whereas, if they were allowed to reclaim the waste land, England would be correspondingly enriched. Besides, it was a stain on a Christian nation that there should be so much waste land and that so many should starve for want[1].

The destruction of the houses seems to have put an end to the little settlement; at any rate we hear no more of it[2]. But the leader of the Diggers was far from losing heart or bating a jot of his principles. In *A New Year's Gift for the Parliament and Army*, Winstanley attempted to demonstrate that branches of kingly power still remained. Tithes had been promised to the clergy by the Conqueror on the condition they would 'preach him up.' Our old law-books were still in use and should be burnt in Cheapside. If the government was to be new, let the laws be new also. England was a prison; the subtleties of its laws the bolts and bars; the lawyers its jailors[3]. The second part of the pamphlet[4] contains

---

[1] *Clarke Papers*, ii. 217–21.

[2] Under April 4, 1650, iii. 170, Whitelocke writes that a letter was sent from the diggers and planters of commons with the usual requests. It must have emanated from one or two individuals, for it makes no reference to any colony. A petition of Cumberland tenants to Oliver in 1654 is full of digger phraseology; but it would be fanciful to suggest any direct connection. C. S. P. 1654, 294.

[3] *New Year's Gift*, Jan. 17, in T. P. vol. 587, 7–10.

[4] *The Curse and Blessing that is in Mankind.*

one of the most arresting passages Winstanley ever wrote, and prepares us for the work on which he was about to engage. 'At this very day poor people are forced to work for 4*d*. a day, and corn is dear. And the tithing-priest stops their mouth, and tells them that "inward satisfaction of mind" was meant by the declaration "The poor shall inherit the earth." I tell you, the scripture is to be really and materially fulfilled...You jeer at the name Leveller. I tell you Jesus Christ is the head Leveller[1].'

Winstanley had gradually won the position he now occupied as the acknowledged leader of the English Communists. His name had appeared at the head of the list of the fifteen who signed *The True Levellers' Standard Advanced*, and of the forty-five who subscribed to the declaration to the Lords of Manors. Since then, almost every work produced by the movement had appeared in his name alone. The snatches of rhyme that are scattered through his pamphlets render it probable that the Diggers' Song discovered among Clarke's papers is from his pen, while the similarity of position assumed in the *Light of Buckinghamshire* to that of the later pamphlets forbids us to believe that he was not author, or at least joint author, of the earliest manifesto of the movement. In striking contrast to his importance and ability is the impenetrable obscurity in which his early history is involved[2]. He prefaces his *Watchword to the City of London* with a few lines of autobiography. 'I was once a freeman of thine, but beaten out of estate and trade by thy cheating sons in the thieving art of buying and selling. I was therefore forced to live a country life, where likewise with taxes

[1] pp. 41-3.
[2] His early works, *The Mystery of God* and *The Breaking of the Day of God*, are purely theological disquisitions, remarkable for nothing but their attack on the Church. Their mysticism evoked charges of heresy, to which Winstanley replied in *Truth lifting its head above scandal*. They must have had but a small circulation, for they were all missed by Thomason. They may be found in B.M. 4377, A 1, 2, and 4372, AA 17.

and free quarter my weak back found the burden heavier than I could bear.' While his worldly prospects were at a low ebb he received consolation from an unexpected source. 'Not a year since[1], my heart was filled with sweet thoughts and many things were revealed to me I never read in books nor heard from the mouth of flesh; and when I began to speak of them, some people could not hear my words. Then I took my spade and began to dig on St George's Hill.' The experiment, as we have seen, had not been encouraging, but, undismayed by its failure, he now set himself to elaborate the constructive part of his system. In Feb. 1652 it was ready, and *The Law of Freedom* appeared, with a dedication to 'All the Nations of the Earth[2].'

The Dedicatory Epistle informs Cromwell that he and his officers had not conquered by their unaided efforts but by the help of the common people, whose right in consequence it was to share in the victory, and whom a change of names without a change of things would never satisfy. The clergy were opponents of liberty; yet tithes still swallowed up the savings of the poor. Even where the laws were good they were tampered with by magistrates. Worst of all, the landlords still ruled the country as tyrants. It might be asked how the clergy and the landowners were to exist if tithes and service were withdrawn. The answer leads us to the kernel of Winstanley's teaching. A different system must be introduced.

In the new society there must be no buying nor selling, for with bargaining came deception and from deceit sprang oppression. With the disappearance of buying and selling, there will be no more lawyers. But may not one be richer than another? For two reasons he may not. In the first place, riches give men power to

---

[1] He is writing in the autumn of 1649.   [2] T. P. vol. 655.

oppress their fellow-men and stir up wars. And, secondly, riches are impossible to obtain by honest means. A man can never become wealthy by his unaided efforts; and if he is assisted by others, a share in the result of their joint exertions belongs to them. In the first chapter Winstanley proceeds to declare that freedom is to be found only in the unimpeded enjoyment of the land. Property there must be, but all must possess it. A similar transformation must be effected in relation to magistracy. All bearers of office must be elected, and none may hold a post for more than one year[1]. Passing to the economic ordering of the new state, production is to be carried on both by individual and cooperative activity. Exchange, however, is purely communistic; each brings what he has produced into the common store and takes what he needs either for maintenance or for his work. A certain quantum is expected from each, and, if it is not forthcoming, the worker is placed under supervision and if necessary is punished. Should any abuse arise in drawing from the common stock, a similar course is followed. Education, which is universal, includes technical instruction. Work is expected from all under forty, and may be continued after that age at will[2]. Those who have reached the age of sixty superintend the well-being of the entire community. The town and county officials compose the county Parliament and Court. Members of the national Parliament must be over forty, unless specially distinguished, and are chosen by all over twenty. The chief duty of the clergy is to provide instruction, on the weekly day of rest, consisting of a relation of the chief events which have happened during the week, readings from the laws of the land, and lectures on subjects of general interest. The priest is to confine himself to what he has learned from study and observation. For to know the secrets of Nature is to know the

[1] pp. 39–67. [2] pp. 68–78.

works of God, and to know the works of God is to know God Himself. Marriage is a civil rite, and may be terminated for sufficient reasons by a declaration of the parties before an officer and witnesses. Buying and selling are punished with death, and to declare that the land is the property of any special individual subjects the speaker to branding[1].

Of Winstanley there is little more to relate[2]. Soon after completing the presentation of his thought, he seems to have joined the Quakers. His latest work, *The Saints' Paradise*, appearing in 1658[3], combines something of his old spaciousness of thought with a quietism that is largely new. We notice with interest the blending of Quakerism and the Digger philosophy. 'The heart that thinks it cannot live without money, lands, the help of man and creatures, is tempted of the devil; the pure spirit or holy law within tells the heart he must be stript of all these and trust to Providence for subsistence[4].'

It would be easy to exaggerate the importance of the little colony of Diggers on St George's Hill. The greater number of them, beyond all doubt, had no other views than were common to the Franconian and Thuringian peasants of 1525, or those who followed the standard of Ket in 1549. On the other hand, it would be difficult to overestimate the significance of their spokesman in the history of thought. Alone of his English contemporaries, he recognised the well-being of the proletariat as constituting the criterion not only of political but of social and economic conditions. Determining that their rights were not

[1] 76–89.
[2] The letter of Winstanley to Fairfax and the Council of War, dated Dec. 8, 1649, *Clarke Papers*, II. 217–21, is wrongly inserted in the Calendar of State Papers for 1652, 3; and this mistake has led Bernstein (*Geschichte*, I. 592–3) to record a final appearance of the diggers in 1653.
[3] T. P. vol. 2137.   [4] pp. 32, 3.

secured in the actual state of society, he proceeded to develop a complete scheme of socialism. That he looked in a different direction from the other thinkers of the age constitutes his unique interest. In the earnest spirit which breathes through his scheme, Winstanley is perhaps equalled by Vairasse and Meslier and Cabet; in his consideration for the poor, he may be matched by the author of the *Utopia*. But in the completeness with which he anticipates modern developments, he stands alone. By his very weaknesses, too, he is curiously modern. Human nature is capable of transformation if certain changes are effected. The knowledge of the scholar is despised, for culture breeds contempt. 'Practical instruction' is to be followed by the study of natural science, and 'fantastic speculations' are to be forbidden. Equally unsatisfactory is the reading of history. But when all reservations are made, he can claim to have seen that certain ideas nominally accepted by the conscience of mankind involved far-reaching social and economic transformations, and to have proclaimed that until society was organised on a moral basis no political changes could bear fruit.

CHAPTER VIII
Monarchy without Kingship
I

WHEN the end of the oligarchical government came in 1653, the country was ready for it. The statement of the Protector that not a dog barked[1] is confirmed by the State Papers, the Memoirs, and the Correspondence of the times. Indeed the event called forth not a little enthusiasm; and where there was no enthusiasm there was no regret[2].

In attempting to explain Cromwell's political theory, one of two mistakes has been almost universally made[3]. Either it is affirmed that the later part of his career merely carried out designs formed in the earlier; or it is contended that his philosophy was the child of opportunism, and that no mind was less governed by general ideas. The dominant note is struck in his earliest recorded speeches in the Council of Officers. 'I am very often judged for one that goes too fast[4],' said he, during the discussion whether the Army

---

[1] Speech I.

[2] Except, of course, among the commonwealthsmen. C. S. P. 1652, 3, 298, 304, 313; Bates' *Elenchus*, 159–71; Baxter's *Life*, 70; *Hatton Corresp.* I. 7, C. S.; Salvetti's *Corresp.* XIV. 53–7; Pauluzzi's 103rd letter, *Venetian Transcripts*, R. O. vol. 12, etc. It had been hoped for much earlier. 'This quarter,' wrote Farington in Sept. 1651, 'will tell you what great man we shall have either as King or Protector. We must have something; I do not see how it can be avoided. I wish it to-day rather than to-morrow.' *Farington Papers*, 167, 8, Chetham Society.

[3] [Lives of Cromwell with estimates of his views have been written by S. R. Gardiner and Sir Charles Firth. The Life by Lord Morley is also notable as the judgment of a distinguished man of letters who was also a practical politician. H. J. L.]

[4] The story recorded by Holles, *Memoirs*, 208, and Baillie, *Journals*, II. 245, that in the attack on Manchester he expressed himself opposed to all titles arose from a misunderstanding. See Preface to *Manchester's Quarrel with Cromwell*, C. S.

should march up to London and threaten the Parliament in the summer of 1647. 'Give me leave to say this to you. For my own part I have as few extravagant thoughts of obtaining great things from the Parliament as any man; but have what you will have, that you have by force I look upon it as nothing. I do not know that force is to be used except we cannot get what is for the good of the kingdom without force[1].' It was indeed commonly remarked that the Lieutenant-General rarely expressed decided opinions. 'He seemed to have great cunning,' said Waller, his old commander, long afterwards, speaking of his early days, 'and while cautious of his own words, not putting forth too many lest they betray his thoughts, he made others talk till he had, as it were, sifted them and known their designs[2].' But the seeming hypocrisy arose from the real difficulty that he felt in forming a judgment.

The cautious temper maintained in spite of the exasperating conduct of Parliament finds its counterpart in his attitude towards the proposals of the Levellers. When the *Agreement of the People* was handed in, he was almost staggered by the number and magnitude of the changes that it suggested. 'Truly this paper does contain in it very great alterations of the government of the kingdom, alterations from that government that it hath been under, I believe I may almost say since it was a nation. How do we know if, whilst we are disputing about these things, another company of men shall gather together and put out a paper as plausible as this? And not only another, but many of this kind? And if so, what do you think the consequence would be? Would it not be utter confusion[3]?' On being induced to discuss the document, the Lieutenant-General took exception to the proposal of universal suffrage. Unlike Ireton, he did not deny the contention

---

[1] *Clarke Papers*, I. 191, 2, 202; 368–70. [2] Waller's *Recollections*, 125–7. [3] *C. P.* I. 236–40, 247–50, 288–92.

of its adherents that it was a birthright of every man; his philosophy was not sufficiently definite to decide upon the point, and he employed the argument from probabilities. 'The consequences of this rule tend to anarchy, must end in anarchy. For where is there any bound or limit set if men that have but the interest of breathing shall have voices in elections[1]?'

The attitude towards Monarchy is equally moderate. After the capture of Oxford, for instance, it is recorded by James II that he alone of all the officers knelt to kiss the prince's hand[2]. But Cromwell was well aware that other forms of government were feasible. 'We all apprehend danger from the person of the king and from the Lords. I think that if it were free before us whether we should set up one or the other, there is not any intention to set up one or the other. So neither is it our intention to preserve them if they be a visible danger to the public interest[3].' But that they were such a danger he had not yet convinced himself. The course of the negotiations with the king we have already seen. When he had visited Charles, he told Berkeley he had seen the tenderest sight his eyes ever beheld, the interview of the king with his children; 'and he wept plentifully at the remembrance, saying: Never was man so abused as he in his sinister opinions of the king, who, he thought, was the uprightest and most conscientious man of his three kingdoms[4].' However coloured the story be by its narrator, at any rate Cromwell risked his popularity in his endeavour to arrive at a settlement, and earned the title of 'the King-ridden' from Henry Marten[5].

A year later, after the crisis of the second Civil War, he had received assistance from the logic of events. 'Authorities and

[1] *Clarke Papers*, I. 309, 328.
[2] *Life of James II*, I. 29.
[3] *C. P.* I. 378–83.
[4] Berkeley's *Memoirs*.
[5] Carey's *Memorials*, I. 355.

powers,' he writes to Hammond[1], 'are the ordinance of God. All agree there are cases in which it is lawful to resist. Not to multiply words, dear Robin, the query is whether ours be such a case. I desire thee to consider what thou findest in thy heart to two or three plain questions. First, whether Salus Populi be a sound position? Secondly, whether this Army be a lawful power, called by God to oppose and fight against the king? My dear friend, let us look into providences; surely they mean somewhat. They hang so together; they have been so constant, clear, unclouded. Malice, swollen malice against God's people now called Saints, to root out their name; and yet they, these poor Saints, getting arms, and therein blessed more and more!' Yet he still repeatedly expressed his desire to maintain the old framework of the constitution; and even when all thoughts of compromise had passed away, and though he was determined that the king should be brought to trial[2], he desired that his life might be spared[3]. But of the justice of the sentence he had no doubt. Burnet relates that when the Scotch Commissioners came to beg for the king's life, Oliver 'entered into a long discourse of the nature of the regal prerogative according to the principles of Mariana and Buchanan. He thought a breach of trust ought to be punished more than any other crime whatever[4].' The story that in after times he tried to excuse himself from a share in the incident by the plea that he had been compelled thereto by Ireton[5]

[1] Nov. 25, 1648, Carlyle, Letter 85.
[2] Letters in *Clarke Papers*, II. 140–4.
[3] We know that animated debates took place in the Council of Officers; and though we have not Clarke's reports, we learn from the newspapers that Cromwell contended 'there was no policy in taking away his life.' Gardiner, IV. 283.
[4] *Own Time*, I. 72.
[5] Cal. Clar. S. P. II. 212, June, 1653.

must be a fable, though there is no reason to doubt that he was deeply affected by the execution[1].

Eighteen months later he wrote to the Governor of Edinburgh Castle that they had 'turned out a tyrant, in a way which all tyrants in the world would look at with fear,' while many thousands of Saints in England rejoiced to think of it[2]. It is beyond doubt that from the time of the execution of the king, and still more after the Irish and Scotch victories, Cromwell was looked to by thousands to redress the evils under which the country was suffering[3]; and this must be continually borne in mind in studying his conduct during the following years. Until now there is no reason to suppose that the thought of becoming supreme had occurred to him[4]. After Worcester, however, he invited several members of Parliament to a meeting, and told them that, the king being dead and his son defeated, he held it necessary to reach some settlement of the nation. ' My meaning,' said he, ' is that we should consider whether a republic or a mixed monarchical government will be best; and if something monarchical, then in whom power shall be placed.' At the end of the discussion he remarked: ' It will be a business of more than ordinary difficulty. But really I think that a settlement of somewhat with monarchical power in it would be very effectual[5].' The dis-

[1] Peck's *Memoirs of Cromwell*, 53, 4; Spence's *Anecdotes*.

[2] Carlyle, III. 63, Sept. 12, 1650.

[3] Nickolls' *Letters addressed to Cromwell, passim*. Cp. Salvetti's *Corresp.* vol. 13, *passim*, especially 261 b, 268.

[4] The truth is that he came very slowly to the knowledge of his own abilities. ' He had then,'—Waller is speaking of the early years of the war,— ' no extraordinary parts, nor do I think he did believe he had them.' *Recollections*, 124. Mrs Hutchinson naïvely remarks that he acted ' by such degrees that it was unperceived by all that were not of very penetrating eyes.' *Memoirs*, 342. That designs had been attributed to him by his enemies from an early date does not prove that he had entertained them.

[5] Whitelocke, III. 372–4.

cussion proved that the soldiers were one and all republican, but that the lawyers preferred some form of monarchical government, the proposal of choosing one of the younger sons of the late king finding most favour.

For nearly a year Cromwell was silent; but in November, 1652, he reopened the question in a conversation with Whitelocke. 'There is very great cause for us,' he began, 'to improve the mercies and successes which God hath given us, and not to be fooled out of them and broken in pieces by our particular jarrings and animosities against each other.' The army, he continued, had conceived a strong dislike for the Parliament. 'And I wish there were not too much cause for it. For really their pride and ambition and self-seeking, their daily breaking forth into new factions, their delays of business and design to perpetuate themselves; these things, my lord, do give too much ground for people to open their mouths towards them. So that, unless there be some authority so full and so high as to restrain and keep things in better order, it will be impossible to prevent our ruin.' But they had been acknowledged as the supreme power, remarked Whitelocke; how then could they be restrained? To which Cromwell replied by another question, 'What if a man should take upon him to be king?' After Whitelocke's remonstrances, he continued, 'Surely the power of a king is so great and high and so universally understood and reverenced by the people of this nation that it would be of great advantage in such times as these[1].' Six months later the hostility of the army had become still more pronounced, and, urged on by Harrison, Cromwell by a sudden resolution brought the existing *régime* to an end and became Protector[2].

[1] Whitelocke, III. 468–74.
[2] Cromwell's own version of the story must be finally accepted since

There is no reason to doubt that his disapproval of a permanent Parliament was deep and genuine. His faith in the disinterested virtue of the Commonwealthsmen had been shattered on learning that they were forcing through a bill to perpetuate their own power. 'We could not believe such persons would be so unworthy,' he observed in his first speech; 'we remained till a second and third messenger came with tidings that the House was really upon that business and had brought it near to the issue. We should have had a Council of State and a Parliament executing arbitrary government without intermission.' Things had now been changed. 'They come and tell me they do not like my being Protector. What do you want me to do? "Pray turn these gentlemen of the Long Parliament all in again. We fear you will exercise arbitrary government." They fear, these objectors, arbitrary government by me; but if arbitrary government were restored by reinstatement of the Long Parliament, then they are not afraid of it. Such hypocrisies, should they enter into the heart of any man that hath truth or honesty in him[1]?'

What, then, were the proper duties of a Parliament? Certain points were altogether beyond its province. 'In every government there must be somewhat fundamental, somewhat like a Magna Charta, which should be unalterable. That Parliaments should not make themselves perpetual is a fundamental. Liberty of Conscience is a fundamental. That the command of the Militia should be placed so equally that no one party in Parliament or out of Parliament have a power of ordering it is a fundamental.'

Mr Firth's publication of extracts from the Clarke MSS. in *Eng. Hist. Rev.* July, 1893. It is impossible, for instance, to believe that Blake was sent to Scotland to be out of the way, and that the famous 'Declaration of the Generals at sea' was concocted by Oliver and entrusted to Deane a week or two before the event. Deane's *Life of Deane*, 617–19.

[1] Carlyle, III. 215, 16.

But he cannot trust the Parliament to preserve the fundamentals. 'Of what assurance is a law to prevent an evil if it be in the same way legal to unlaw it again? Are such laws like to be lasting[1]?' In a word, a Single Person must be constantly at hand in times of crisis to protect the people against itself. As he himself remarked, his duty was to act as police constable to the warring factions of the country; and in this aspect he was very commonly regarded[2]. Yet he is aware that this might seem dangerous, and will minimise the risk by excluding the hereditary principle. 'If you had offered me this one thing, that the Government should have been placed in my family, hereditarily, I would have rejected it; and this hath been my constant judgment, well known to many who hear me speak[3].'

Cromwell had been but little concerned with administration, and he entered on his duties with a comparatively light heart. It was regarded as significant of his conviction that he was able to bear the burden alone that he left the post of Lieutenant-General vacant[4]. But the creation of his brain to some extent broke down in its practical application, and this led to a slight modification of theory. His numerous protestations of inability to remain 'Sole Director of England,' as he was addressed by the Czar[5], may be taken to express his new-born conviction that the destinies of a great nation were beyond the strength of a single ruler to control. Read in this light the decided expression of his preference for a free Parliament in his Second Speech loses its seeming insincerity[6]. Yet the Parliament is to represent the

---

[1] Third Speech, September 12, 1654.
[2] Cp. Waller's *Panegyric to my Lord Protector*, Lines 169–73, etc.
[3] Fourth Speech, IV. 9.   [4] *Relazioni Veneti, Inghilterra*, 389.
[5] Thurloe, *State Papers*, III. 257.
[6] September 4, 1654. What may be called the constitutional side of Oliver's mind was a profound mystery to Carlyle.

worthy alone, and, among the worthy, only those who have a stake in the country. Nobody who had opposed the Parliament since the commencement of the Civil War, ran Oliver's Reform Bill, could elect or be elected; none but persons of known integrity and good conversation were eligible; none with property amounting to less than £200 were to possess the franchise[1]. Oliver's ideal, in a word, was that a Parliament, elected by the worthy members of the nation, assisted by an executive, should in ordinary circumstances carry on the government, and that a Single Person should be invested with a dictatorship if any difficulties were to arise, resigning his power after the circumstances which made it necessary had passed away. 'I called not myself to this place,' he declared after eighteen months of rule. 'A chief end of calling this Parliament was to lay down the power which was in my hands[2].'

The new Parliament did not inspire him with confidence, and the burden became at times intolerable. He caught at every opportunity to beg advice from his opponents. On one occasion Hertford had lost several of his children, and Oliver followed up his letter of sympathy with an invitation to dinner. 'I am not able to bear the weight of business that is on me,' said he; 'I am weary of it. Pray advise me what I shall do[3].' On another occasion the Protector asked Roger Boyle the news of the City. '’Tis said you are going to marry your daughter to the king.' 'What think they of it?' asked Oliver. 'The wisest thing you can do.' 'Then Cromwell made a stand and looking steadfastly in my face, said, "And do you believe so too?" "Yes," I replied; "you cannot trust your party; you must secure yourself."' The Protector, however, ended the conversation with the repeated

[1] *Inst. of Government*, §§ 14, 17, 18.   [2] IV. 45-51.
[3] Lady Lewis' *Friends of Clarendon*, II. 121.

assertion that the king could not forgive his father's death[1]. Physical signs, too, that the strain was proving too much for him were not wanting[2].

Two objects took almost complete possession of the Protector's thought,—to satisfy the godly and to settle the government on a legal basis. 'I know it is a trouble to my Lord,' wrote Thurloe to Monk, 'to have any one who is a saint in truth to be grieved or unsatisfied with him[3]'; and confirmations of these remarkable words are numerous. It was this feeling which prompted him to implore Harrison to desist from the plots in which he was losing himself[4], to urge Colonel Hutchinson to return to public life[5], to seek the friendship of Sir Richard Fanshawe[6], to augment the stipend of his outspoken critic, John Shaw[7]. While the greater number of the protests that crowded in[8] left him unmoved, the remonstrance from three of his old comrades, written more in sorrow than in anger, must have filled him with grief[9].

That the settlement of his government on a more legal basis was equally desired the proofs are manifold. When a pamphleteer maintained that possession was the only right to power, Cromwell expressed the utmost abhorrence for the doctrine and ordered the book to be burned[10]. The proposal to assume the

---

[1] Boyle's *State Letters*, 21, 2.
[2] Sagredo wrote that he had seen 'che mentre stava scoperto gli tremavo la mano con la quale stringeva il cappello.' Berchet's *Cromwell e Venezia*, doc. XXIII.
[3] *Clarke Papers*, II. 246. Gardiner (*Commonwealth and Protectorate*, II. 479) declares that after the attack on the West Indies Cromwell 'gave the first place to mundane endeavour'; but this judgment need not be taken to conflict with the statement in the text.
[4] Thurloe, II. 606.   [5] Mrs Hutchinson's *Memoirs*, 375.
[6] Lady Fanshawe's *Memoirs*, 117.   [7] Shaw's *Diary*, 149, Surtees Society.
[8] A collection in Single Sheets, B.M. 669, f. 19.
[9] Okey, Alured and Saunders to Oliver, Rymer's *Foedera*, XX. 736–8.
[10] White's *Ground of Obedience*, T. P. vol. 171. The Major-Generals,

title of king, almost universally regarded at the time as one
more sign of his contempt for legality, arose from his very
respect for it. He told Parliament that he would 'rather have
any name from it than any name without it[1].' It was this desire
too that led to the *Petition and Advice*, the object of which,
though granting the power to the Protector of appointing his
successor, was to increase the power of the Commons and, by
instituting a Second Chamber, to revive at least the outward
form of the historic constitution[2].

The same resolution to change as little as possible, even at
the cost of alienating old supporters, appears in Cromwell's
relations to the Church. The complaint of Evelyn[3] is not borne
out by the evidence, and in the pages of Walker's *Sufferings of
the Clergy* his name has but small place. The expulsion of in-
cumbents he found for the most part already consummated, but
such as had escaped he allowed to remain. The Anglican service
was used publicly, and the sermons of Gunning, Fuller and
others in the metropolis were thronged[4]. Ussher had his library
restored to him, and he was told that all restraints should be
removed from the Episcopalians if they would leave politics

instead of being the instruments of lawless oppression, were primarily
administrators of the Protector's numerous schemes for the well-being of
the people. See Rannie's valuable article, ' Oliver's Major-Generals,' *E. H. R.*
April, 1895. An interesting summary of this too-little known department
of Oliver's work is in Inderwick's *Interregnum*, 1–116. The taxes, though
very heavy, were more justly assessed and better collected. Dowell's *Taxation*,
II. ch. I.

[1] Speech on the Title, April 13, 1657.

[2] As Bordeaux wrote to his master, ' Il fait toujours profession de ne vouloir
rien changer.' Guizot's *Histoire de la République d'Angleterre*, II. 273. Nothing
more admirable has ever been written on Cromwell's instinct for legality
than Godwin's pages, *History of the Commonwealth*, IV. ch. 34, especially
606–8, old as they are. Cp. Hoenig, *Oliver Cromwell*, I. 14, III. 379, etc.

[3] *Diary*, Aug. 3, 1656.

[4] Fuller's *Life of Fuller*; Pepys, etc.

alone[1]. In Howe royalists and episcopalians found a sort of consul ever ready vigorously to plead their cause[2]. It was pointed out that the country possessed religious freedom; that that alone had been worth fighting for; and that those who were meddled with were punished merely for the sake of civil peace[3]. His breadth of vision is further illustrated by his interference to protect individuals and sects in danger of persecution[4], and by his welcome of the Jews, in opposition to the prejudices of his contemporaries[5].

A final point must be mentioned in connection with the Protector's political ideals. The three kingdoms were to be drawn closely together, above all through representation in a single assembly. The most friendly relations with New England were maintained, and Cromwell was, perhaps, the first English states-man with a true sense of the importance of the colonies to the mother country[6]. With the Dutch Republic, reports of the fabulous prosperity of which were still taken home by travellers[7], the Protector desired to enter into the closest union. The diplo-matic efforts of the Oligarchy had met with scanty success, and the Navigation Act had not induced a more friendly attitude. This feeling of hostility it was Oliver's special wish to eradicate. Accosting the Dutch ambassador soon after the expulsion of the Rump, he remarked, 'If we two could understand each

---

[1] Elrington's *Ussher*, 271.   [2] Calamy's *Howe*, 16, 17.
[3] Richardson's *Apology for the present Government*, 1654, T. P. vol. 812. Cp. Döllinger's remarkable judgment, *Vorträge*, III. 55, 6.
[4] Burton's *Diary*, I. etc.
[5] Kayserling's *Manasseh Ben Israel*.
[6] Cp. the Letters from the Colonies in Hutchinson's *Massachusetts*, Appendix.
[7] Huet's *Commerce des Hollandois*, 25, etc. ed. 1717, etc. The Dutch Diurnal was at this time instituted exclusively for news of the Low Countries, T. P. vol. 726, etc.

other, we would dictate to Europe[1].' A scheme was accordingly
drawn up by the Council, 'not necessitating the alteration of
the municipal laws of either, but setting the whole under one
superior power, to consist of persons of both nations, and all the
subjects of each country having the privileges of the other without any difference in distinction.' When the plan found no
response with the Dutch, who were at this time hopelessly
divided in their political preferences[2], he brought forward a
scheme in which there should be a joint army and navy and
free-trade between the two countries. This, in turn, met with
such determined opposition that no further attempt at union
was made[3].

II

Despite his efforts, Cromwell's government failed to give
entire satisfaction even to those whose affection and admiration
for him were unbounded. Since Milton had expressed himself im-
perfectly satisfied with the rule of the Oligarchy[4], it might have
been supposed that he would approve of the form of government
which followed it; and this expectation is at first sight fulfilled.
The *Defensio Secunda* published in 1654 contains a full-length
portrait of the Protector. 'He has either extinguished or learned
to subdue the whole host of vain hopes, fears and passions which

[1] He was unconsciously labouring to fulfil the desire of Bacon. *Occasional
Works*, IV. 27.

[2] Many were satisfied with things as they were, Aitzema's *Netherlands in*
1651, 2, ed. 1653, 166, 7; some contended for a monarchy, 688; De Witt
wished to introduce more of the aristocratic element of Venice, 255.

[3] Geddes' *De Witt*, I. 333–456. Vreede's *Nederland en Cromwell* is of small
value.

[4] 'Our form of Government is such as our present distractions admit of,
not such as could be wished.' *Defensio Prima*, Preface.

infest the soul.' Addressing Oliver directly, he proceeds, 'While you are left among us, that man has no proper trust in God who fears for the security of England. We all willingly yield the palm of sovereignty to your incomparable ability and virtue, except those few who, ambitious of honours they have not the capacity to sustain, envy those conferred on one more worthy than themselves, or who do not know that nothing in the world is more pleasing to God or agreeable to reason than that the supreme power should be vested in the best and wisest.' Milton is still an ardent Oliverian. No such belief in the wisdom of Parliaments existed in his mind as rendered the very conception of a Protectorate inconsistent with true republicanism.

Yet reading between the lines we discover that his satisfaction was not unqualified. If the eulogy on Fairfax, buried in his country-seat, signifies little, the praise of Bradshaw and Sydney, the representatives of Parliamentary republicanism, and of Overton, at the very moment suspected of countenancing plots against the Protector, was different. Milton preferred the political system of Cromwell to that of Bradshaw or Overton, but he desired the incorporation of their persons and certain of their principles in the machine of government. The eulogies mean that Milton was growing conscious that the rule of the Protector was becoming insufficiently national. His two fundamental political principles were that the government of a community should be carried on by all its worthiest members, and that a rational liberty should be secured for the individual. He had already convinced himself that the first was in jeopardy; and he was now unable to repress the suspicion that the second might also become endangered. Wittingly and purposely Oliver would not interfere with the liberties over which he had control; but it was in his power, if his conscience suggested or his policy dictated that he should do so. If liberty be withheld from conscientious motives, it is none the less withheld. This vein of uneasiness runs through and mingles with the panegyric itself. 'Reflect often what a dear pledge your land has entrusted to your care; that liberty she once expected only from the chosen flower of her talents and virtues she now expects from you only and through you alone hopes to obtain. If you, hitherto the tutelary genius of liberty, should hereafter invade it, the general interests of piety and virtue will be affected. In no other way can you perform them so readily, in no other way render our liberty at once so ample and secure, as by associating in your councils the companions of your dangers and toils.' The author, not content with suggesting a reconstitution of the Council, proceeds to further recommendations. Not only had Milton pleaded for the entire dissociation of the government from all religious connections in a series of tracts, but had inserted the demand for disestablishment in the forefront of the Sonnet to Cromwell. While religion was connected with civil magistracy, the temple of liberty lacked its roof. As the years passed away without the accomplishment of his wishes, he became more and more convinced that the power to grant or withhold the rights of the people should not lie in the hands of a single man, however disinterested and conscientious[1].

His anxiety was further increased by the fact that he hoped nothing from the action of Parliament. Nowhere in his former treatises do we find such outspoken condemnation of the shibboleths of current democracy. The voice of the people was as far from sounding to Milton like the voice of God as to Metternich. Every individual has his birthright to freedom, but for the claim to a share in shaping the destinies of the nation Milton

[1] Cp. the luminous remarks of Masson, *Life of Milton*, iv. 606–16.

has as much contempt as Ireton[1]. 'Who would vindicate your right of unrestrained suffrage or of choosing your representatives,' he asks in a strain of almost cynical disbelief in human nature, 'merely that you might elect the creatures of your own faction whoever they might be, or him, however small might be his worth, who would give you the most lavish feasts and enable you to drink to the greatest excess? Ought the guidance of the republic to be entrusted to persons to whom nobody would entrust the management of his private concerns, or the treasury left to the care of those who had lavished their own fortunes in infamous prodigality? Who would suppose he would ever be made a jot more free by such a crew of functionaries[2]?' The *Defensio Secunda* reveals a state of mind that must have been common at this time. Despite his admiration for the Protector, Milton is dissatisfied with the rule of a single person; despite his belief in the sovereignty of the people, he has no faith in representative government.

Of those to whom Cromwell had for long been an object of suspicion some were won to his side by closer acquaintance. Whitelocke, who lacked the fierce passions and the deep emotions of his age, found himself invited to undertake an important embassy to the Swedish Court. Regarding the proposal as part of a policy of removing obstacles from the ruler's way, he was unwilling to accept it. 'If you stay,' said his old servant, 'I doubt there may be much danger for you.' 'Why, what can he do to me?' replied Whitelocke. 'What can he do? What can he not

---

[1] Of the lies in Dr Johnson's *Life of Milton*, none is so barefaced as the accusation of 'telling every man he was equal to his king.'

[2] Many years later his opinion was unchanged. See the lines beginning
    'And what the People but a herd confused,
      A miscellaneous rabble?'
in *Paradise Regained*.

do[1]?' Following as usual the path of least danger, he set forth
on his journey to Sweden. Oxenstierna and the Queen received
him kindly[2] and pelted him with searching questions. 'I desire
to know what stability there is in your government,' said the
Chancellor. 'We hold the government to be the same now,
concerning fundamentals, as when we had a king.' 'But do you
hold a kingly government unlawful, that you have abolished it?'
'Every government,' returned Whitelocke astutely, 'which the
people chooseth is certainly lawful, kingly or other; and that is
best which they make choice of as best.' How could Whitelocke,
asked Christina, take service with a man, who had expelled the
Parliament from which he had received his commission? 'With
that I had nothing to do. If his power be unlawful, all the more
should I serve my country.' Such was Whitelocke's attitude to
the Protectorate in its earlier years. The mission was successful,
and he returned home in safety to receive the thanks of the Protector. From this time he again became less hostile to Cromwell,
and the old friendly relations were gradually resumed. 'Whitelocke,' says Ranke severely but not unjustly, 'had an irresistible
tendency to attach himself to the ruling powers, and to accept
personal promotion from them, provided they allowed the system
of English Law to remain as a whole such as it was[3].' His sense
of his own importance was flattered. He sat in the first two
Parliaments, was one of Oliver's Lords, and finally became a
member of his Council. 'The Protector,' he writes, 'often advised
with me and a few others about his great businesses, and would
be shut up three or four hours together in private discourse.
Sometimes he would be very cheerful and laying aside his greatness he would be exceeding familiar with us; and then he would

---

[1] *Embassy to Sweden*, ed. 1855, I. 28.   [2] I. 200–322.
[3] *Eng. Hist.* III. 9; cp. Clarendon, VIII. 248.

fall again to his serious and great business. And this he did often, and our counsel was followed by him in most of his greatest affairs[1].'

On the other hand the Protectorate had in the Commonwealthsmen and the Levellers two implacable enemies. Ludlow's dislike of Cromwell gradually passed into fanatical hatred. He had at first, he informs us, received no clear account of the events of April 20, and had known that certain of those who had shared in them were men of principle. He had also considerable hopes of reform in the Church and the Law from the Little Parliament, and had therefore felt himself at liberty to retain his post[2]. But with the promulgation of the Instrument of Government, and the dissolution of the Parliament, the full scope of the revolution was revealed. In his wrath he obstructed the proclamation of the new Government as long as he could, and refused to continue to serve as one of the Commissioners for the government of Ireland. To the suggestion that he should wait and see how the usurper would use his power, he replied that nothing could be reasonably expected of him[3]. He turned conspirator and dispersed incendiary pamphlets against the government[4]. After repeated interviews with Henry Cromwell and Fleetwood[5], and repeated refusals to surrender his commission, he was allowed an interview with the Protector. The unflinching republican reiterated the opinions which he was well known to entertain. He could not sign an agreement that he would not

---

[1] *Memorials*, IV. 237–91.   [2] *Memoirs*, I. 356, 7.

[3] I. 374–8. In the excess of his rage against the Protector, Bradshaw at this time 'spoke so respectfully of the royal authority within due bounds as if he had a mind to return into favour with kings.' Barwick's *Life of Barwick*, 159, 60.

[4] I. 406, cp. Cromwell's *Speech*, Sep. 17; Carlyle, IV. 194, 5; and Clarendon, XIII. 184.

[5] Thurloe, II. 150.

G

act when he met with any power, superior to the existent, from which he could expect the good of mankind. 'But who shall be judge of that?' asked Lambert; 'we ourselves think we use the best of our endeavours to that end.' Ludlow replied that everybody must govern himself by the light of his own reason[1]. At the second interview, a few weeks later, the same *impasse* was quickly reached. 'What can you desire more than you have?' asked the Protector. 'That which we fought for,' said Ludlow,— 'that the nation might be governed by its own consent.' 'I am as much for a government by consent as any man,' returned Oliver; 'but where shall we find that consent?' Ludlow, no doubt sincerely believing that he was indicating a practicable policy, replied, 'Among those who have acted with fidelity and affection to the public[2].' The greater number of the party soon after attempted to take their places in Oliver's second Parliament, but were excluded. 'Has such a blow,' asked an indignant pamphlet after furnishing the particulars, 'ever been given to the freedom of the nation since the Norman Conquest[3]?' When the period of obscuration came to an end, its concluding scene was worthy of its entire duration. The hypocrite 'manifested so little remorse of conscience for his betrayal of the public cause and sacrificing it to the idol of his ambition that some of his last words were rather becoming a mediator than a sinner, recommending to God the condition of the nation that he had so infamously cheated and expressing a great care of the people whom he had so manifestly despised[4].'

It is a fact of special interest and importance that Vane began his public career in New England. Crossing the Atlantic when

[1] *Memoirs*, I. 432–7.
[2] II. 10, 11; cp. the interview of Hutchinson, Mrs Hutchinson's *Memoirs*, 374–8.
[3] *Harl. Misc.* IV. 451.
[4] *Memoirs*, II. 44, 5.

scarcely more than a boy, though setting forth with well-defined intentions[1], he was without delay appointed Governor of Massachusetts. At his return, hopes were expressed that he had left his 'former misguided opinions behind him[2]'; and indeed there is no evidence that he brought back more than a vague mysticism from his three years' sojourn[3]. But events moved fast, and in the summer of 1644 he was chosen to undertake the secret mission to the Generals to urge the actual or virtual deposition of the king. Vane was a revolutionary; but he abhorred revolutionary violences, and protested against the execution of Charles. 'For six weeks,' said he later, 'I was absent from my seat here, out of tenderness of blood[4].' He was none the less the most influential civilian member of the government which followed the death of the king. It was only when he was excluded from public life that he seems to have commenced systematic thinking.

The Retired Man's Meditations were the earliest fruit of the two years of enforced leisure spent at Raby and Belleau. The single chapter dedicated to politics is of singular interest[5]. Magistracy 'hath its place and bears its part in the reign of Christ over men[6],' before the Fall as after. 'For it is not only useful to restrain from unrighteousness and disorder occasioned by sin, but also to conserve men in the good order and right disposition of things wherein by their creation they were placed[7].' It must however be according to its primitive constitution and right exercise. 'When the Scriptures say the rule of magistrates is over men, we are to understand the proper bounds and limits of

---

[1] C. S. P. America, I. 211.   [2] Strafford, *Letters*, II. 114.
[3] Baxter singles him out as the only sectary in the House in 1640, but does not say what opinions he was supposed to hold. *Life*, 25, 47.
[4] Burton's *Diary*, III. 173, 4.
[5] T. P. vol. 485, ch. 24, deals with Magistracy.
[6] 286.   [7] 391.

the office, which is, not to intrude themselves into the office and proper concerns of Christ's inward government and rule in the conscience, but to content itself with the outward man. It ought not therefore to be condemned or disobeyed by any as accounting it a part of the Fourth Monarchy[1].' Passing from the general to the particular, Vane expresses a cheerful confidence that the difficulties through which the nation has passed are designed for some commensurate purpose. 'He hath not emptied us from vessel to vessel without some teaching thereby what was bad and may be left behind, nor without some dawnings and intimations of what is good and is yet before us, to be prosecuted and followed after. God cannot leave us when the work has come, as it were, to the birth, and is upon the very anvil to be formed into what may answer the common good of men[2].'

In the following year the Protector invited suggestions for the improvement of the machinery of government, and Vane composed and published his *Healing Question*[3]. Cromwell had contemplated proposals of a strictly limited scope, and was altogether unprepared for a fully developed rival system. What possibility remained, asked Vane, of reconciling and uniting the judgments of honest men within the three kingdoms who still pretended to agree in the spirit, justice and reason of the same good Cause as of old? Neither blood nor treasure should be thought too dear to keep it from sinking. What was the Cause? 'The whole body of honest men are to enjoy the freedom to set up meet persons in the place of supreme authority, whereby they may have the benefit of the choicest light and wisdom of the nation for the government under which they will live.' The government being composed of the right men, it must act in the right way. In a good government, naturally, the good alone may share. Privileges

[1] 388, 9.   [2] 394.   [3] *Somers Tracts*, VI. 304, 13.

are therefore to be confined to those who have on all occasions shewed themselves lovers of freedom in civil and spiritual things. Once elected they were to be supreme. 'None are judges of the power of Parliaments,' said Vane at his trial, 'but themselves. Admit their judgment may be called in question by private persons, the fundamentals of government are plucked up by the roots[1].' According to their will the supreme power may, of course, be placed in one or a few. The new *régime* is to be founded by 'a great Convention, wherein fundamental constitutions shall be agreed upon and subscribed.'

This uncompromising work, for such it was, though its author may have been a 'quiet, harmless, dove-like person[2],' met with a response in the country only comparable to that of *Killing no Murder*. On September 4, Vane was summoned before the Council on the charge of writing 'a seditious book tending to the disturbance of the government[3].' He owned the writing, Thurloe told Montague, 'but in very dark and mysterious terms, as his manner was. His arrest was a necessity, not only for peace but to let the nation see that those who govern are in good earnest[4].' Vane found himself unable to give security not to act against the government[5], and the refusal was followed by a few months' imprisonment. From this time forward, he was an uncompromising antagonist of the Protectorate. Henry Cromwell told Thurloe that he expected he would ally with the Quakers against the Government[6]. That he engaged in Royalist plots is improbable. A few weeks after his departure from Carisbrook, it was suggested to Hyde by one of his agents that the king should

---

[1] *State Trials*, VI. 157.   [2] Sikes' *Life of Vane*, 105, 6, ed. 1662.
[3] C. S. P. 1656, 7, 98.
[4] Carte, *Original Letters*, II. 111, 112. Cp. Thurloe, V. 349.
[5] *State Trials*, V. 791–802.   [6] Thurloe, IV. 508.

write letters of grace to him[1]. If this was done, Vane seems to have taken no notice of it.

Far more dangerous was the opposition of the Levellers, who had recently broken up into two parties. Immediately after his trial, it had been reported that Lilburne had a hand in the negotiations which sprang up with royalist agents[2], and on his banishment in 1652 the rumours again began to circulate[3]. Authentic accounts, however, of what he said or promised are lacking. Here is a specimen of the rumours, introduced by the confession that the story was at second hand. 'I am told,' wrote Secretary Nicholas[4], 'that Lilburne said that if the king will promise if he be restored he will put all his castles, ships and militia into the hands of the people and be governed by Parliament in all affairs, he will undertake to make him king, having, as he saith, 40,000 men that will rise on these conditions.' While he may have mixed in royalist circles, there is no real evidence that he ever plotted to restore the king[5]. On the expulsion of the Rump, Lilburne, considering his sentence to be terminated, returned to England, only, however, to find himself immediately arrested. The general impression was that he had at last 'brought his neck into a noose' and would be hanged[6]; but his hold on the people was found to be as great as ever.

The trial provoked extraordinary excitement. Twenty citizens offered bail of £2000 each[7]. To a judge's remark that he would be

---

[1] Cal. C. S. P. III. 245.
[2] Hist. MSS. Comm. 13*th Report*, Portland MSS. I. 591, 2.
[3] Cal. Clarendon S. P. II. 141, 146, 213.
[4] 1652, *Nicholas Papers*, I. 291, C. S.
[5] His letters at this time are filled with quotations from the lives of Plutarch's republicans. *Lilburne Revived*, Pt. I. 5, 6, Pt. II. 10–23, T. P. vol. 689.
[6] C. S. P. 1652, 3; Thurloe, I. 320.
[7] Cal. C. S. P. II. 221.

executed it was rejoined that it would be the bloodiest day England had ever seen[1]. During the trial, three regiments stood under arms and six or seven thousand citizens were estimated to be present, many of them armed[2]. The crucial nature of the struggle was obvious even to foreigners[3]. The incidents of the trial were very much like those of the former; but on the present occasion, Lilburne succeeded in procuring a copy of the indictment, which he proceeded to lay before Counsel,—a feat, as Sir James Stephen reminds us, achieved by nobody else before the Bill of Rights[4]. The conduct of the judges, as before, gave him opportunities of which he was not slow to avail himself. In the narrative which he published shortly after, he related, for instance, that one of them asked him what they had to do with the Law of God[5]. That his acquittal was followed by renewed banishment, though 'for the peace of the nation[6],' raised public indignation to the highest pitch. It was not to be imagined how much esteem he had got for vindicating the ancient laws and liberties[7]. The Protector, comments Clarendon justly, looked on it as a greater defeat than the loss of a battle[8].

Lilburne was sent over to Jersey and so strictly guarded that no more was heard of him than if he had been dead[9]. His memory,

---

[1] *ib.* 224. Lilburne's popularity with the women is remarkable throughout his entire career.

[2] Thurloe, I. 366, 7, 442.

[3] Cp. Letter of the Dutch Ambassador to De Witt, Rymer, XX. 684.

[4] *Hist. Criminal Law*, I. 364–7.

[5] *Afflicted Man's Outcry*, 1, 2, and *John Lilburne's Trial*. Both in T. P. vol. 711.

[6] C. S. P. 1653, 4, 101.

[7] Intercepted letter in Thurloe, I. 367, 8. It added fuel to the furnace of Ludlow's hatred. *Memoirs*, I. 417, 18.

[8] *Hist.* XIV. 52. Five years later, *Lilburne's Trial* still appeared in the booksellers' catalogues of 'the most vendible books.' T. P. vol. 955.

[9] Baillie to Spang, Dec. 1655, III. 290.

however, remained, and the Government organ chronicles illustrations of 'the Lilburnian spirit[1].' At intervals a pamphlet from his busy pen would appear in London, repeating that all commonwealths were weak where injuries were daily offered to the people[2], or defending himself from charges of turbulency of spirit[3]. At times, too, a petition for his release would be presented[4]. Whatever the Government had contemplated in the agitation inspired by the trial, the prisoner remained unmolested[5]. In 1657 he received permission to return to England and died, a member of the Quaker body[6], in the summer of 1658, a few days before his great enemy[7].

Far less respectable was the conduct of the main body of the party. Fulfilling certain prognostications, its members became royalist intriguers in indignation at the establishment of the Council of State[8]. In September, 1649, Hyde forwarded to Nicholas a paper which he had drawn up to serve in any negotiations with the Levellers that might ensue. There were several reasons why application should be made to this party in preference to any other. Their propositions were extravagant and impracticable, and would for the most part fall of themselves. Since they were great enemies to arbitrary government, they would gradually be reduced to a reverence for the laws. Above all, they had power and interest in the Army and Navy and

---

[1] *Faithful Scout*, Feb. 9, 1654, T. P. vol. 479.

[2] *Declaration to the freeborn people*, May, 1654, 6, T. P. vol. 735.

[3] T. P. vol. 711.   [4] C. S. P. 1635, 203, 4.

[5] A Committee had been appointed to 'suggest what to do...with speed.' *Commons Journals*, VII. 306–9.

[6] Neal, *Puritans*, IV. 18.   [7] C. S. P. 1657, 8, 148.

[8] In a remarkable conversation with Overton, Lady Halkett had remarked, after listening to his story, 'And you will find reason to change every government till you come to beg the king to come home and govern you again.' Lady Halkett's *Autobiography*, 69–71, C. S.

many towns and garrisons[1]. Negotiations were soon on foot, for in the same month the Council of State warned the governors of garrisons that royalist designs were being carried on in all parts of the country by joint endeavours with the Levellers[2]. The negotiations thus begun in 1649 grew to importance in 1655, when they became focussed around the personality of Sexby, whom Thurloe recognised as a great foe of the government and whose papers he begged his agents to strain every nerve to secure[3]. Declaring that he would be contented to see the king reinvested with all his legal rights, so that the people were assured of their liberties[4], Sexby was naturally welcomed with open arms[5]. The royalists were penniless and the Spaniards were called in to finance the scheme. It was known that 'Spaniards, Cavaliers, Papists and Levellers' had entered into a confederacy, and that Sexby had undertaken the assassination of the Protector[6], and the surrender of a port and garrison[7].

Turning to the actual history of the intrigues revealed in the Clarendon papers, we derive the impression that the danger from this quarter was rather less than it appeared to those who knew little about it[8]. The negotiations were complicated by difficulties of principle and method. The Levellers insisted that the king

[1] *Nicholas Papers*, I. 138–47. Cp. Whitelocke, Sep. 8, III. 101.
[2] C. S. P. 1649, 50, 303.
[3] Cal. C. S. P. III. 70. Wildman had been secured in the previous year. A full account in *Every Day's Intelligencer*, Feb. 9, 1654, T. P. vol. 479.
[4] *Nicholas Papers*, II. 341.
[5] Not a few of the royalists, however, regarded him with suspicion from the first. *Nicholas Papers*, III. 39, 145, etc.
[6] Thurloe, V. 45 and 694.
[7] *ib.* 319 and 349; cp. Cromwell's speech, Sep. 17, 1655; Carlyle, IV. 194, 5.
[8] The only definite attempt at a rising was Overton's effort to seize Monk and secure the army in Scotland; but it was suppressed without any difficulty. Thurloe to Pell, Pell's *Correspondence*, I. 118–21.

should abolish tithes and episcopacy and surrender his veto[1]. The royalists no less decisively refused to promise to alter the fundamental government of the kingdom, to the support of which nine-tenths of the people were really disposed[2]. The other difficulty was equally unsurmountable. Spain refused to supply any considerable sum till the Levellers began operations, while the Levellers professed themselves unable to effect anything without money. The original plan had included an invasion combined with the murder of Cromwell; but as time slipped by, the programme was lightened by throwing over everything but the latter design[3]. Several of the royalists pretended to believe that this was on the point of execution[4], but the confident assertions of Sexby lost impressiveness by repetition[5]. He had founded his hopes on the acceptance of the kingship by the Protector, and after his refusal he grew morose and altered[6]. In the summer of the same year, the 'grand traitor' was captured as he was crossing over to Holland[7]. 'The loss of his person,'

[1] E.g. Sexby's paper to the king, Dec. 1656, Clarendon S. P. III. 315; and Clarendon, *Hist.* XV. 119, address signed by Wildman and others.

[2] Hyde's reply, Clar. S. P. 315–17; and *Hist.* XVI. 133. The proposals usually included the abolition of episcopacy and tithes, amnesty for all but the adherents of the Protector, etc., e.g. Cal. C. S. P. III. 145.

[3] The authorship of *Killing no Murder*, Harl. Misc. IV. 289–305, which, in Heath's words, 'frightened Oliver exceedingly,' *Chronicle*, 295, remains a mystery. It is often attributed to Sexby and is almost certainly the work of the Levellers. One of them was taken with two bundles of copies. Thurloe to Henry Cromwell, VI. 311. [*Killing no Murder* was reprinted by Henry Morley in his volume *Famous Pamphlets*. A copy in the possession of Mr H. J. Laski has a note in the handwriting of Sir Dudley North attributing it to Sexby. H. J. L.]

[4] Cal. C. S. P. III. 41, 220, as indeed it was; Burton's *Diary*, I. 332–4; II. 486–8, etc.

[5] Cal. C. S. P. III. 160. There seems no need to suppose with Brosch that Sexby had never had any genuine political plans and was merely playing for money. *Die Puritanische Revolution*, 472–3.

[6] Cal. C. S. P. III. 294.   [7] C. S. P. 1657, 8, 48.

wrote Talbot to Hyde, 'is very great; but the business is not lost[1].'

With the arrest of Sexby, the story not only of the Levellers' intrigues with the royalists but of the Levellers themselves comes to an end. Those who remained alive took no part in the resistance to the Restoration or threw in their lot with the Common-wealthsmen[2], and the one manifesto put forth by professing Levellers in the year of anarchy bears a closer relationship to Harrington than to Lilburne[3].

[1] Clar. S. P. III. 357.
[2] Ludlow, II. 246, 7. There was a rumour that the army had chosen new agitators, Hartlib to Boyle, Boyle's *Works*, V. 287; but the report is not corroborated by other evidence.
[3] *Harl. Misc.* IV. 543–50.

CHAPTER IX

The New Religious Bodies

IN addition to the discontented republicans the Protectorate had
foes of a widely different character to face. At the end of the
first decade of the great struggle the Independents had been the
dominant sect; at the beginning of the second, they were so no
longer[1]. For many Independency served merely as a halting-place
on their passage from the Church to other religious bodies, of
which the Millenarians, the Baptists and the Quakers were the
most prominent[2].

I

The very name of Millenarians or Fifth Monarchy Men
suggests the outlines of a political philosophy. The fourth monarchy was drawing to its close, and was to be followed by the
reign of the saints. In view of this great certainty all political
arrangements now in being become of necessity transitory. So
far all were agreed. But the Millenarians of the English revolution,
like the Millenarians of the German Reformation, split into two
sections on a further question. What was to be their attitude
towards the existing order of things? Should they quietly await

---

[1] They had not so great congregations of the common people, says
Clarendon of them at this time, 'but were followed by the most substantial
citizens,' *Hist.* x. 175; cp. Hoornbeeck's *Summa Controversiarum*, 662, ed.
1653.
[2] [See L. F. Brown, *Baptists and Fifth Monarchy Men*; and H. A. Glass,
The Barbone Parliament. There is interesting material on this as on the
other religious aspects of the period in W. A. Shaw, *The English Church during
the Civil Wars and the Commonwealth.* H. J. L.]

the arrival of the inevitable? Or should they endeavour to hasten its advent by combating the powers which occupied the place it was destined to fill?

"'Tis certain,' wrote Thurloe to Henry Cromwell in 1655, 'that the Fifth Monarchy Men, some of them I mean, have designs of putting us into blood[1].' Of the two wings thus indicated the more moderate may be traced in the camp after Naseby. The new opinion, if not welcomed by Cromwell for selfish purposes as his enemies said, was not opposed by him and soon spread widely through the army. Harrison, Overton and other leaders became its adherents, and Fleetwood was suspected of something more than sympathy. About the time of the king's death a revolutionary wing began to emerge. One of its members declared that the form and not the power of monarchy had disappeared, and that Parliament was no less absolute and tyrannical[2]. Another proclaimed that nobles and mighty men were about to become subject to the saints, that it was lawful to combat Christ's enemies with the material sword, and that the saints should then possess riches and reign with Him on earth[3].

The penman of the party, John Rogers, had been ejected as an Anglican, had turned Presbyterian, and on the growth of Millenarianism had become a convert[4]. *Sagrir or Domesday drawing nigh* professed to expose the ungodly laws of the fourth monarchy and the approach of the fifth. The origin of all good laws was in the people, but successive conquests had robbed them of their rights[5]. The two plagues of the nation were the priest and the lawyer, who would need to be removed before the Church of

[1] Thurloe, IV. 191.

[2] Salmon, *A Rout, A Rout*, 3, T. P. vol. 542.

[3] Cary's *The Little Horn's Doom and Downfall*, T. P. vol. 1274, April, 1651, 133, 212–327.

[4] Rogers' *Life of Rogers*.   [5] 45–109, T. P. vol. 716.

Christ could be reformed. The fourth monarchy was breaking up apace and would suddenly 'tumble and kick its heels in the air.' By 1666 the fifth would be visible throughout the world, and in about 40 years it would have prevailed. Men therefore should buy no more lands nor estates, seeing it would 'make such mad work in the world[1].' In a treatise which immediately followed, the duties of the saints in preparation for the event are described. It was most important that they should belong to no religious organisation[2]. No compulsion was to be exercised either over action or thought, for the worst heretic might live to reform. Magistrates, indeed, were superfluous[3].

Harrison's share in the expulsion of the Rump, together with Rogers' hopeful appeal to the Protector and the extreme gentleness of Cromwell's references to the sect[4], prove that the party, if not an active supporter of the new *régime*, at least did not oppose it[5]. When there seemed no chance of the erection of a Council of Seventy, in imitation of the Sanhedrim, in accordance with the wishes of Harrison[6], the Millenarians fixed their hopes on the Barebones Parliament, which consisted to a large extent of their own adherents[7]. Nor did the assembly disappoint their expectations[8]. It attacked the clergy; it demanded the abolition of Chancery; it declared nobility contrary to the Law of Nature. In a word 'their prate was to make way for Christ's Monarchy on earth[9].' On the dissolution of the Parliament the left wing of the

---

[1] 124–54.

[2] *Chanuccah, or A Tabernacle for the Sun*, 69–127, T. P. vol. 716.

[3] 162–79.　　　　　　[4] Speech 11. Carlyle, IV. 27, 8.

[5] Baxter's *Life*, 58; Clarendon, XI. 221; Ludlow, II. 6–8; Clarke MSS. in *Eng. Hist. Rev.* July, 1893, etc.

[6] Ludlow, I. 358.　　　　　　　[7] *Sagrir*, ch. 4.

[8] Feake's *Beam of Light*, 50–2, T. P. vol. 980.

[9] Coke's *Detection*, II. 38–44, ed. 1719; Baillie's *Journals*, III. 289; cp. *Scheme of Law Reform, Somers Tracts*, VI. 177–240.

party entered upon a career of the utmost violence. Harrison began to plot and was arrested. Rogers denounced Cromwell as Anti-Christ, the Man of Sin, the Great Dragon[1]. The party increased rapidly, and drew to itself many of the most violent and desperate spirits[2]. 'Men impoverished by long troubles,' wrote Pell at this time, 'must needs have great propensions to hearken to those that proclaim a golden age at hand, under the name of Christ and the saints, especially as so many prophecies are applied to these times. The end of Paganism was in 395, to which they add 1260. Others pitch on 1656, because the lives of the patriarchs in Genesis make this number. Therefore Christ will come this year or next[3].' The party first rushed into the arms of the Levellers, and meetings were held to discuss common principles of action with a view to taking arms[4]; but the negotiations were interrupted by a series of arrests[5]. Nor did the relations with the more turbulent members of the Baptist party about the same time have any practical issue[6].

The Millenarians were strong enough to stand alone. As early as the autumn of 1653, an anonymous correspondent had warned the Protector against danger from a secret assembly at Blackfriars[7]. The agent whom Thurloe dispatched heard Feake and Powell explain the position of the party. 'Lord,' prayed Feake, 'Thou hast suffered us to cut off the head which reigned over us, and Thou hast suffered the tail to set itself up and rule over us in the

[1] *Morning Beams*, in Rogers' *Life of Rogers*, 169–71. Cp. Thurloe to Monk, *Clarke Papers*, II. 242–6.
[2] Cp. *Life and Death of Mr Blood*, *Somers Tracts*, VIII. 438–47.
[3] Pell's *Correspondence*, I. 155, 6.
[4] Carte, *Original Letters*, Thurloe to Montague, II. 111.
[5] Pell's *Correspondence*, I. 144, 5.
[6] Thurloe, IV. 629.
[7] Rymer, XX. 719. It was, however, largely attended. Cowley satirised it in *The Cutter of Coleman Street*, *Works*, ed. 1707, 844.

head's place[1].' The preachers were arrested[2], but when Needham again visited the meeting he found things little changed. 'The place was crowded, the humours boiling, and as much scum came off as ever.' Though it was but a 'confluence of silly wretches,' he recommended the total suppression of the meeting[3].

Feake's temporary detention did not moderate the violence of his utterances and, on being once more arrested, he declared at his trial that God would destroy not only unlawful but lawful Government, not only the abuse but the use of it[4]. A diminution in their popularity, however, seems to have followed the outburst of violence, and, in the summer of 1656, Thurloe wrote that their credit and numbers were declining[5]. Their fanaticism, however, remained the same. In the same year a report of a meeting reached Thurloe in which it was debated when was the time for destroying Babylon and its adherents, who should do it, and how it should be done. They had concluded that the saints must do it, 'the time to be now and the means the sword[6].' The resolution was soon put into practice, for in April, 1657, occurred their first insurrection. 'The number and quality of the persons engaged,' runs Thurloe's report to the Council, 'were truly very inconsiderable and indeed despicable. Though they speak great words of the reign of the saints, and seem to invite none but the holy seed, yet the baits they lay to catch men are the taking away customs, excise, taxes, tithes[7].' The enactment of the Petition and Advice inflamed them to still greater heights of daring. Rumours that Harrison, Okey, Rogers and Canne had proclaimed

---

[1] C. S. P. 304–8; cp. Thurloe, I. 21, and Cal. C. S. P. II. 398.
[2] C. S. P. 1635, 308, 9.　　　　　　　　　　[3] C. S. P. 393.
[4] Brooks' *Lives of the Puritans*, Feake, III. 308–11.
[5] Thurloe, IV. 698; and Carte's *Original Letters*, II. 102–6; cp. Thurloe, V. 220.
[6] Thurloe, V. 197.　　　　　　　　　[7] *ib.* VI. 184–6.

their resolutions to destroy all who should oppose them were frequent[1]. 'These incendiaries,' wrote Henry Cromwell, 'are very dangerous and of an inveterate temper[2].' Baillie feared that if the party increased there would be wholesale slaughters[3]. A Book of Characters was discovered and, when deciphered, proved to contain the names of individuals marked for destruction[4]. Pagitt found it necessary to alter the account he had given of the opinions of Millenaries in earlier editions of his *Heresiography*. They now taught that all the ungodly must be killed, and that the wicked had no property in their estate[5].

In this turbid torrent one pamphlet alone had pretensions to sanity[6]. The writer, returning to the idea of Harrison, desires a Sanhedrim or Supreme Council, 'men of choicest light and spirit.' Borrowing a principle to which the Levellers had given currency, he withheld the power of altering the foundations of common right and freedom, religious liberty chief among them. Popular control was to be further guaranteed by the rotation of

---

[1] Thurloe, VI. 291, 349, etc.   [2] *ib.* 790.   [3] *Journals*, III. 323.
[4] Burton's *Diary*, Feb. 26, 1659, III. 494, 5.
[5] 157, 8, 6th edition, 1661. A remarkable example of the more mystical Millenarian spirit is found in the case of Pordage, who was credited with having said that he cared no more for the higher powers than for the dust under his feet. Ere long there would be no Parliament, nor magistrate nor government in England, and the saints would take the estates of the wicked for themselves and the wicked should be their slaves. Fowler's *Daemonium Meridianum*, 172–7, T. P. vol. 840. The charges were repeated in a second part, T. P. vol. 868. He would admit nothing, however, but that he preferred mystical theories and ascetic practice. *Innocency Appearing*, 57–9, T. P. vol. 1068. Despite this attack, Pordage attracted a number of kindred spirits and instituted the 'Philadelphian Society.' The best descriptions are in Horst's *Zauberbibliothek*, I. 314–27, III. 349–51, and Corodi's *Gesch. des Chiliasmus*, III. 330–74, 403–21. The story presents the closest resemblance to that of Labadie, though the movement was less considerable and Pordage a man of far less ability.
[6] *Principles and Declarations of the Remnant*, T. P. vol. 910. *The Diapoliteia*, T. P. vol. 1995, cannot be called an exception.

the councillors and the absence of an executive. With this exception, the party never paused to consider the trivialities of constitution-making.

Closely allied to the Millenarians at this time, in popular belief, were the 'Anabaptists.' The *coup d'état* of 1653 was welcomed by a large proportion of the sect. Whether the Bedfordshire Baptists who wrote to the Protector that they had 'groaned' under the recent government were telling the truth or were merely attempting to curry favour[1], many of the party were at this time closely connected with Harrison, who was the chief author of the revolution[2]. The majority remained quiet if not contented. In a representation sent to the Protector on the rumour getting abroad that he intended to purge the army, the authors challenged him to declare when their church had been unfaithful to him[3].

So far as there was a revolutionary wing to the party during the Protectorate, it was to be found in the army that was stationed in Ireland[4], though here, as everywhere, the mistake of confusing the general with the particular is possible[5]. At the end of 1653 it was considered that in the plot to set up an Anabaptist general the greater part of the soldiers was engaged[6]. Their conduct made people declare that their pride and uncharitableness would ere long bring them low[7]. Henry Cromwell, whose conciliatory

---

[1] *Confessions of Faith*, 320, 1.

[2] Report of the Dutch Ambassadors, Thurloe, I. 395, 6; Neal, III. 137.

[3] Thurloe, II. 150, 1.

[4] The Scotch Baptists were never charged with extremism, though their numbers were considerable. Nicoll's *Diary*, 105, 6.

[5] An intercepted letter of Dec. 1653, attributes the famous Monday evening lecture at Blackfriars of Feake and Powell and Rogers and Simpson to 'the Anabaptists.' Thurloe, I. 621, 500, 1.

[6] Hist. MSS. Comm. 13*th Report*, Portland MSS. I. 672.

[7] Thurloe, IV. 314.

policy was praised by his opponents[1], complained that they openly denied the position of his father and reviled those who recognised him[2]. The connection with the Fifth Monarchy Men was still very close, many conversions from one party to the other being recorded[3]. Towards the end of the Protectorate, however, the violence, activity and importance of the radical party seems to have diminished[4]. Multitudes of those who had been classed as Baptists became Quakers, and a final blow was given to the left wing when Monk purged his army[5].

Except in the case of Canne, who was more a Millenarian than a Baptist, every authoritative declaration of principle leads us to regard the English Baptists as an orderly and relatively conservative society[6]. Baxter, no friend of the party, confessed that 'most of them were persons of zest in religion and godly, sober people, and differed from others but in the point of infant baptism[7].' Though Jeremy Taylor selects them as an example of an exception that might have to be made in the 'Liberty of Prophesying,' it is because they held that it was unlawful to take up defensive arms, to kill malefactors, to take oaths, and other tenets soon to become characteristic of the most peaceable of

[1] Baxter's *Life*, 74.
[2] Thurloe, IV. 348. The address, however, of William Howard to the king in 1656, Clarendon, XV. 121–30, was the work of an individual, not of a party. And the king took no notice of it, though it raised hopes in certain quarters. *Nicholas Papers*, III. 282, C. S.
[3] Thurloe, I. 621; V. 187; IV. 629, etc.
[4] Thurloe, VI. 708, 9; cp. VII. 403 and 527. 'The Anabaptists seem, in deep silence, to take no notice of the weal or woe of the present times.'
[5] Clarendon S. P. III. 664.
[6] All evidence of antinomianism in their teaching comes to us at second hand. Lamb, for instance, the pastor of the largest Baptist Church in London, was 'charged with antinomianism.' Brooks' *Lives of the Puritans*, III. 461–6. This has been forgotten by Neal, *Puritans*, III. 137, etc.
[7] *Life*, Part II. 140, 1. Cp. Evelyn's *Diary*, Dec. 3, 1649.

men[1]. The typical Baptist is to be found, not among those who haunted the meetings of the Millenarians, but in such men as Tombes, the friend of Clarendon and Sanderson, in the learned Jessey, and in the saintly Hanserd Knollys.

II

The most important incident in the religious history of the second decade of the revolution was the rise of the Quakers[2]. The commonest theories of their origin were that they sprang from the Anabaptists or the Ranters. That they did not respect the laws of the land was the ground of their supposed relationship with the former[3]; that they set the dictation of an inward monitor above the established conventionalities of thought and phrase seemed to point to a connection with the latter[4]. Though Baxter, after giving an account of the Ranters, naïvely adds that they were so few that he had never seen one, he declares that the Quakers were but the same party with another name[5]. On the other hand, Roger Williams made the sect the mother, not the daughter, of 'Rantism[6].' Pagitt gave up the attempt to determine

[1] *Liberty of Prophesying*, § 19, *Works*, VIII. 212–31.

[2] [On the political philosophy of the Quakers see a forthcoming work with that title by P. S. Belasco. On the Quaker movement generally, W. C. Braithwaite, *The Beginnings of Quakerism*, and *The Second Period of Quakerism* are of primary importance. The text should have laid emphasis on the Quaker denial that human nature is inherently evil, and the inferences drawn therefrom; cp. especially Howgill, *The Inheritance of Jacob* (1656) and *Truth Lifting up its Head* (no date). H. J. L.]

[3] Pell to Morland, Pell's *Corresp.* II. 309, 10; Kennett's *Register*, 396; Baxter's *Quaker's Catechism*, and *Answer to the Quaker's Queries*, T. P. vol. 842, *passim*; Underhill's *Hell Broke Loose*, 1–12, T. P. vol. 770; Joanne's *Becoldus Redivivus, or the English Quakers and German Enthusiasts revived*, T. P. vol. 2137.

[4] Leslie's *Answer to the Switch*, § 22, *Works*, ed. 1832, VI. 297–315, etc.

[5] *Life*, 76, 7.   [6] *George Fox digged out*, *Works*, V. 43.

their relationship, and contented himself with declaring that the Ranters and Quakers were 'unclean beasts, much of the same puddle[1].'

To calmer observers it is obvious that the new movement most nearly resembled the Mennonist Church whence the Baptists had sprung[2]. So close is the connection indeed between these sister bodies that it is sometimes said that Fox was rather the organiser than the founder of the new society. The General Baptists went over almost in a body to the Friends, taking many of their own ideas and practices with them[3]. The relationship is further illustrated by the fact that, in the rare instances where Quakers deserted their communion, they rejoined the Baptists[4]. Yet, though the framework was to some extent borrowed and adapted, the spirit which animated the leaders distinguished it from every other contemporary organisation. A time arrives in the history of every church when the feeling that the spiritual life of the individual is being lost behind the machinery of its organisation leads to a protest, which in certain cases produces a permanent separation from the main body. From this point of view Quakerism was as inevitable in England as Pietism in Germany. It was pledged to no definite opinions, observances or organisation. The way-faring man, as described by Fox, had visited in turn the Papists, the Common-prayer men, the Presbyterians, the Independents, the Baptists, but by none had he been told that the only religion was that of spirit and of truth[5]. So great was the revolution involved in these words that even a man of moderate principles

[1] *Heresiography*, 259, 6th ed. 1661.
[2] Barclay, *Inner Life*, 221–48.
[3] The parallels are usefully collected in Tallack's *Fox, the Friends and the Early Baptists*, 68–88, 160, 1.
[4] *Broadmead Records*, 53, etc. Hanserd Knollys Society.
[5] Fox's *Letters*, No. 260, ed. 1698.

like Thorndike declared that the Quakers were not to be reckoned as Christians at all[1]. The dream of Luther was first realised in England in all its fulness and clearness in the Quaker movement. 'What!' asks Fox in a letter, realising that the words may seem strange to his readers, 'are all Christians priests? Yes; all Christians[2].' From this principle the rest follows as a matter of course. In the first place, the movement appealed to the poorer classes as no other had done. Against no other sect does Pagitt bring the accusation that it was 'made up of the dregs of the common people[3].' As one of its more friendly critics pointed out, it did the magistrates yeoman service in reclaiming 'such as neither Magistrate nor Minister ever speak to[4].' Distinctions of sex no less than position were obliterated by this all-embracing equalitarianism[5]. In the same letter as that in which he stated that all Christians were priests, Fox asks, 'Are women priests?' and answers, 'Yes; women are priests[6].' A further distinction was equally inadmissible. Clarkson used to say that Fox was the first Englishman publicly to declare against slavery, and more than one slave-owner received a letter severely declaring that God was no respecter of persons[7].

[1] *Forbearance or Penalties, Works,* v. 487.
[2] Letter 249.   [3] *Heresiography,* ed. 1661, 244.
[4] *Light shining out of Darkness,* 88, T. P. vol. 770. The author is perhaps Stubbe.
[5] So prominent was the position occupied by women that it was at first rumoured that the sect was confined to the female sex. Clar. S. P. ii. 323. From the very beginning of the struggle of king and Parliament, indeed, women had begun to occupy a new position. *Discovery of six women preachers,* 1641, is the first evidence of the kind, T. P. vol. 166; but their claims had found as much ridicule as acceptance. *A Parliament of Ladies,* 1647, was a clever skit, T. P. vol. 384.
[6] L. 249. It followed as a matter of course that women might preach. Turner's *Quakers,* 71, 91–4. The fullest exposition of Fox's views concerning women occurs in L. 320.
[7] *ib.* 153, 354, etc.

Combining these principles of the priesthood of the believer with that of the supremacy of the Inner Light[1], which, though held by the majority of the sects of the time, meant far more to the Quakers, the movement would have been democratic at whatever time it had taken its rise. But there were several reasons in the moment of its appearance why its implicit radicalism should become explicit. The general dislocation of the established order prepared the country for further innovations; and the drive of the movement was increased by the fact that there was not an universally recognised abuse to be attacked, but an order of things which considered itself and was thought by many to be the remedy of that abuse.

On the other hand the character of the founder of the society went far to influence its nature in a contrary direction. In his positive teaching, Fox was steadily opposed to every form of antinomianism. 'Any such as cry, away with your laws, we will have none of your laws, are sons of Belial[2].' At Exeter he refuted the charge of political disaffection with the greatest warmth. 'You speak of the Quakers spreading seditious books and papers,' said he. 'I answer, we have no seditious books or papers. Our books are against sedition and seditious men and seditious books and seditious teachers and seditious ways[3].' The party was implicated in no attack on the Protectorate, in no intrigue for the recall of the exiled family[4]. As presented by the founder and his immediate followers, there was nothing in Quakerism to interfere with the performance of the ordinary duties of citizenship. On one occasion alone did Fox meddle with politics. When the report spread abroad that Oliver would become king, 'I warned him

[1] Cp. Lechler's *Englischer Deismus*, 62–6; Möhler's *Symbolik*, 492–505, etc.
[2] *Letters*, 251. [3] *Journal*, I. 342.
[4] Clarendon's statement that they shared in the address taken by Howard to Charles in 1656, XV. 103, is not confirmed by other evidence.

against the issue of divers dangers,' wrote George in his Journal, 'which, if he did not avoid, would bring shame and misery on himself and his posterity. He seemed to take it well and thanked me[1].' For the Protector had learned the real character of his outspoken critic[2]. It is difficult none the less to understand why Fox should have opposed the change of title. He was no such friend to the exiled family that he thought it sacrilege for anyone else to occupy the throne, and he could not but realise that the Protector was already king in everything but name. The explanation is rather to be looked for in a conviction that the step would prove disastrous for Cromwell himself, by turning his thoughts to considerations of personal glory[3].

Called by the same name and sharing many of the same principles, their very existence resolutely denied by the apologists of the party at large, it is with the violent spirits of the party that the age connected the Quaker movement. In the teaching and conduct of the founder himself there was a vein of fanaticism. Fox commenced his apostolate by interrupting a service[4], and Lichfield was denounced as 'a bloody city' because martyrdoms had taken place in the town under Diocletian[5]. Such extravagances were soon outgrown; but as he became more moderate, radical tendencies grew into temporary prominence. This was accomplished the more easily owing to the atomistic nature of the early Quaker community[6]. In the four or five years after the institution

---

[1] *Journal*, I. 432. The Letter in Sewel, I. 303.　　[2] *Journal*, I. 240-2.

[3] Cotton Mather declares that Fox used to say that he read not there were kings but among the apostate Christians and in the false Church. *Magnalia*, II. 536. Leslie collects a number of eulogies of the king's execution from various schools of Quaker opinion. *Snake in the Grass*, § 18, *Works*, IV. 204-42. Perhaps the best explanation of Fox's political opinions is that he had none of a very definite character.

[4] *Journal*, I. 105.　　　　　　　　　　[5] *ib.* I. 137.

[6] Barclay, *Inner Life*, 414-24.

of the society, a series of events took place directly calculated to foster such a transformation. With the Baptists who entered the ranks of the new body arrived a number of the more antinomian spirits of the same party[1]. Not a few of the Fifth Monarchy Men also joined the movement, and with them came the disposition to look upon the dissolution of Oliver's First Parliament as the signal for the revolt of the Saints[2]. While bearing in mind that the moderate wing led by Fox continued active and influential, it is impossible to deny that with 1653 begins a second period in the history of Quakerism, and that by the alliance of the new party with the extremest tendencies of Church and State the movement itself is for some years compromised. Communistic tendencies never appeared in official Quakerism; yet there is some reason to believe that private property was one of the institutions against which many a Quaker meeting may have inveighed. We have no direct evidence of such teaching in England, but the apostles who went to Holland caused the greatest excitement by preaching that all goods should be common[3].

Early in the summer of 1654 news reached the government of 'various tumultuous meetings by persons under the name of Quakers' in the Midlands[4]. Missionaries who began to wander up and down the country were charged with scattering seditious books and papers, to the disturbance of the peace of the Commonwealth[5]. In their madness they made no discrimination between

[1] Cp. Oliver Heywood's *Autob. and Diary*, IV. 7.
[2] Hubberthorn's *Horn of the Goat Broken*, T. P. vol. 883, is a remarkable proof of the way in which the movement was impregnated with Millenarian ideas. Its extent was much under-estimated by Corodi, *Geschichte des Chiliasmus*, III. 252–80.
[3] *Gesch. des Sozialismus*, I. 671. In the settlement in Amsterdam all things were in common. Wagenaar's *Beschryving van Amsterdam*, II. 206, 7.
[4] C. S. P. 1654, 210, 11. [5] Hamilton's *Quarter Sessions*, 164, 5.

the worthy and the worthless. Bursting into Bull's parish church while he was preaching, they shouted, 'George, thou art a hireling and a false prophet. Come down[1].' It was learned that, though they were never seen with a weapon in their hands, several had been found carrying pistols under their cloaks[2]. A Quaker took up his position at the doors of Parliament and drew his sword on a group of members. When questioned, he replied that he was inspired by the Holy Spirit to kill every man that sat in the House[3].

Quakers found their way in considerable numbers to Ireland, and in the beginning of 1655 Henry Cromwell was convinced that he had to deal with a serious problem. 'Our most considerable enemies,' he wrote to Thurloe, 'are the Quakers. Some of our soldiers have been perverted by them, and I think their principles and practices not very consistent with civil government, much less with the discipline of an army. Some think them to have no design, but I am not of that opinion. Their counterfeited simplicity renders them the more dangerous[4].' Large numbers, too, crossed the border, and secured a large following at the expense of much disorder[5]. Baillie considered that they must be possessed with a devil; 'they furiously cry down magistracy and ministry, and their irrational passions and bodily convulsions are very great[6].' It was considered by many ministers that they would 'soon be ripe to cut throats'; and it was thought that, if they dared to do so, their principles would not prevent them[7]. The

[1] Nelson's *Bull*, 27, 8.
[2] Thurloe, III. 116; Salvetti, *Corresp.* XV. 194, b. 627 b.
[3] Whitelocke, IV. 163.   [4] Thurloe, IV. 508 and 530.
[5] Nicoll's *Diary*, Bannatyne Club, 147–78.
[6] *Journals*, III. 323. The charges may be substantiated by a collection of anecdotes published in 1655, T. P. vol. 844, and by Ives' *Quakers' Quaking*, 1656, T. P. vol. 883.
[7] Thurloe, V. 187.

people were called to arms on the score that 'the Quakers were up[1].' A childish panic sometimes prevailed. 'When a great storm arose,' relates Wood, 'some thought the Anabaptists and Quakers were coming to cut their throats[2].' A constant fire of warning and denunciatory letters was directed against the government, and redoubled when the report spread abroad[3] that Oliver would take the title of king. Of the new spirit Edward Burroughs was the chief literary spokesman. In an almost endless series of pamphlets he declared war against every section of political and religious feeling. The Protector read that he had 'fallen low[4]'; citizens of London had to listen to a scathing denunciation of their commercial and personal character[5]; the leaders of the different religious bodies were attacked one after the other[6]. In discussing obedience to the laws, Burroughs only allows himself a haughty *petitio principii*. 'We do not wilfully disobey the laws of men but for conscience sake; and herein we are justified by the law of God[7].'

In addition to plots against the government, the more violent party came into collision with their fellow-citizens in relation to certain points of personal conduct. Of these the peculiarity which provoked the greatest disapproval was the rumoured practice of appearing in public without clothes[8]. The greater number, when replying to the charge, declared that they had never seen any

---

[1] Newcome's *Autob.* Chetham Soc. I. 109.
[2] Wood's *Life*, I. 280.
[3] Sewel's *Quakers*, I. 92–4, 136–40, 275–80, 313–16.
[4] Burroughs' *Works*, folio, 1672, *Trumpet of the Lord*, 96.
[5] *Testimony concerning London*, 214–22.
[6] *Gospel of Peace against Bunyan*, 144–52; *Answer to Baxter*, 310–24, etc.
[7] *Case of the Quakers once more stated*, 893.
[8] C. S. P. 1661, 472; Williams' *Fox digged out*, 13, 59, 242; Fuller, IV. 126–30, in the dedication to Book 8; Leslie's *Defence of the Snake, Works*, V. 40–6.

such thing themselves and would condemn it if they did[1]. Others contended that it had the sanction of the prophet Isaiah, and asked why Quakers should not be prophets too[2]. But this formed a small part of the indictment that was brought against them on all sides. The new settlements in America present a more perfect mirror of what may be called their political antinomianism. It was in Massachusetts that the battle chiefly raged, and we may take Cotton Mather's account as typical. 'When they came over in 1657, they induced many to oppose good order, sacred and civil. They manifested an intolerable contempt of authority. It was very enraging to hear these wretches saying among the people, "We deny thy God, thy Christ; thy Bible is the word of the devil." There was the frenzy of the old Circumcellions in these Quakers. I appeal to all the reasonable part of mankind whether the infant colonies had not cause to guard themselves against these dangerous villains[3].' In the replies that greeted the appearance of the *Magnalia* it was contended that they were punished 'for neither broaching opinion nor principle nor doing any other thing, but barely for being such as were called Quakers[4].' To Mather's contention that their conduct was incompatible with the existence of society, it was retorted that they could not own a government to be of God unless the light of Christ in the conscience witnessed to it[5]. The great martyrology of Besse quietly omits all compromising matter[6]. Soon after, however, the gentler form of Quakerism began to appear in America and was

---

[1] Answer of Stubbe, Burnyeat and Edmundson to Roger Williams, *Fox digged out*, 14, etc.

[2] Ellwood's *Life*, 4, 6.   [3] *Magnalia*, II. 522–8.

[4] Bishop's *New England Judged*, ed. 1703, 315–34. Cp. Sewel, I. 566–80.

[5] Whiting's *Truth and Innocency defended against C. Mather's Calumnies*, 93, ed. 1702.

[6] *Sufferings*, II. 177–278.

recognised by Mather himself[1]. To Roger Williams' antiquated taunts his opponents could truthfully reply that they were for righteous government and righteous laws, and for none to rule by force[2]. Williams was himself obliged, as we have already seen, to confess to the Commissioners that they lived peaceably among the settlers. But this mistake on the part of the founder of the most liberal settlement in the New World is a condemnation of the earlier phase of the movement. It was, in fact, no more like the generation which succeeded it than is the mountain torrent swollen with melting snows and turbid with débris like the stream which lazily trickles over the pebbles in summer.

Of the various forms which were taken by the extreme wing of the Quakers, none created such a sensation as that with which the name of James Naylor is connected. Without accepting the view which regards the episode as of far-reaching political importance[3], it remains an interesting and unique illustration of certain principles implicit in the movement. Naylor had fought in the Parliamentary army, and in 1652, on hearing Fox, had felt a 'call[4].' He had thereupon become an itinerant preacher and met with success scarcely less than that of his master. He expressly denied as a lying slander[5] Baxter's charge that their members affirmed self-perfection. While residing for a while, however, near Bristol, an hallucination seized certain women of his following. Naylor was hailed as the Messiah, the King of Israel, and accepted the title. The Quaker movement was charged with responsibility

---

[1] *Magnalia*, II. 522–8; cp. the report from Barbadoes, C. S. P. America, I. 483.

[2] *George Fox digged out*, 311, 312.

[3] Weingarten's *Die Revolutionskirchen Englands*, 268.

[4] 'I converted James Naylor near Wakefield,' *Journal*, I. 138.

[5] Answer to Baxter's *Quakers' Catechism*, 11, T. P. vol. 351. And Answer to the *Perfect Pharisee under Monkish holiness*, 1–20, T. P. vol. 735. But the *Power and Glory of the Lord* is ominously self-righteous, T. P. vol. 711.

for the occurrence[1]. The vague and incoherent recantation that Naylor put forth did not serve to win the suffrages of his judges[2]; and even the interposition of the Protector did not avail to save him from the execution of a cruel sentence and an imprisonment of three years[3]. The tragi-comedy at Bristol gave a sensible check to the revolutionary current of Quakerism[4]. The Kingdom of the Saints on Earth from this time gradually vanishes from their vision, and even zealous opponents of the Protectorate recognise that the time had come for a more purely spiritual activity[5].

[1] Thurloe, v. 694, 708, 9; Burton's *Diary*, I. 10–167.
[2] *Somers Tracts*, VI. 22–5.   [3] Burton, II. 246–58, 265, 6.
[4] Naylor himself fully recanted; see his recantations in Sewel, I. 244–51.
[5] Sewel, I. 447–55, 404, 5. Stubbe's able tract of 1659 defends the Quakers as 'an innocent sort of men.' *Light shining out of Darkness*, 81–8, T. P. vol. 770.

CHAPTER X

The Years of Anarchy

THOUGH the intrigues of the Levellers came to an end, though the Commonwealthsmen were disarmed, though the violence of the sects had diminished, and though there was no royalist outbreak after 1655, Cromwell's position was as far as ever from being assured. The closing months of the Protectorate were, indeed, its most tranquil period; but there can be little doubt that had his life been prolonged he would have witnessed not the consolidation[1] but the dissolution of his power[2]. For some weeks Oliver ruled England from his urn. It soon became evident, however, that the tenure of his successor was in the highest degree uncertain, and when the new Parliament met in January, 1659, the republicans who now re-entered public life began a systematic crusade against the Protectorate.

The first important speech of Vane, their leader, was prompted by the discussion on the Bill which Thurloe introduced to recognise the title of Richard Cromwell. 'Consider what it is that we are upon,' said Vane, 'a Protector in the office of Chief Magistrate. But the office is of right in yourselves. I advise you give not by wholesale so as to beg again by retail. Instead of the son of a conqueror by nature, make him a son by adoption[3].' The plea was in vain. Richard succeeded to his father's position, and Vane could now only seek to limit his authority as much

1 See Goldwin Smith's Lecture in *Three English Statesmen,* and Seeley's remarks, *History of British Policy,* II. 99.

2 This is forcibly put by Gardiner, *Cromwell's Place in History,* Lecture v. Burton's *Diary,* III. 171–80.

as he could. A week after the former speech, he pleaded that the veto should be withheld. 'The denying of the negative voice to the chief magistrate is fit and requisite. They that wish him safety and honour will agree that he shall have power to do everything that is good and nothing that is hurtful[1].' On March 1, the question arose by what right the Upper House continued to sit, and Vane once more attacked the Constitution. 'We have as much power as those that made the Petition and Advice. Cannot we dispatch the business of the Parliament alone? Besides, the power to nominate another House was given singly to the late Protector[2].' The effect of the speech was so great that the Upper House was only saved by the votes of the Government's nominees. Against these, a week later, Vane directed the whole force of his indignant eloquence. 'A greater imposition never was by a single person put upon a Parliament, to put 60 votes upon you. By this means, it shall be brought insensibly upon you for Scotch and Irish members to enforce all your votes hereafter[3].' To the disapproval of the office which Richard held was added contempt for his person. 'The people of England are renowned all over the world for their great virtue; yet they suffer an idiot without courage, without sense, to have dominion in a country of liberty. One could bear a little with Oliver Cromwell, though he usurped the government, his merit was so extraordinary. But as for Richard, his son, who is he? Is he fit to get obedience from a mighty nation? For my part it shall never be said I made such a man my master[4].' With such opposition, the Protectorate could not last very long. When the Parliament treated the army with equally little consideration, the officers compelled Richard to dissolve it. Lenthal was thereupon

---

[1] Burton, III. 318–20.   [2] *ib*. III. 565, 6.
[3] *ib*. IV. 104, 5.   [4] Hosmer's *Vane*, 466, 7.

invited to summon the members excluded six years before by Cromwell. On the reassembling of the Rump, the Protectorate came quietly to an end.

I

The number of parties and opinions in 1659 was almost infinite[1]. 'The great officers,' runs the classical passage in Ludlow, 'were for a select standing senate to be joined to the representative of the people; others laboured to have the supreme authority to consist of an assembly chosen by the Parliament, and a Council of State chosen by that assembly to be vested with the executive power. Some were desirous to have a representative constantly sitting but changed by a perpetual rotation; others proposed there might be joined to the popular assembly a select number of men in the nature of the Lacedaemonian Ephors, who should have a negative in things wherein the essentials of government should be concerned. Some were of opinion that two Councils should be chosen by the people, the one to consist of about 300, and to have the power only of debating and proposing laws; the other to be in number about 1000, and to have the power finally to resolve and determine; every year a third part of each to go out and others to be chosen in their places[2].'

Of the rival schemes thus outlined by Ludlow incomparably the most important and influential was that of Harrington[3]. The author of *Oceana* had gone with the Parliamentary Commissioners to Newcastle, but entered the king's service as Gentleman of the Bedchamber. 'Finding him to be an ingenious man,' said

[1] Cp. *Hudibras*, Part III. Canto II.   [2] Ludlow, II. 98, 9.
[3] [The standard treatise on Harrington is by H. F. Russell Smith, *Harrington and his Oceana.* An excellent edition of the *Oceana* has been published in Lund with valuable notes by G. B. Liljegren. H. J. L.]

Wood, 'his Majesty loved his company and did choose rather to discourse with him than with the others of his chamber. They had often discussions concerning government; but when they happened to talk of a Commonwealth, the king seemed not to endure it[1].' The man who talked of Commonwealths with the king in the dreary days of his captivity, yet won his love and gave his own in return, is a figure of peculiar interest and fascination. The very fervency of interest in the mighty problems at issue which drove others into active life saved Harrington from its allurements[2]. When Lauderdale roughly asked him why he, 'a private man,' had speculated on government, he replied that nobody engaged in public affairs had ever written sensibly on the subject[3].

The period of foreign travel occupies a place in the career of Harrington of unique importance. He used to say in later life that before he left England, he knew of monarchy, aristocracy, democracy, oligarchy, only as hard words to be looked for in a dictionary. After visits to Denmark and France, he passed into Italy, where the true political schooling of his life was to begin, taking up his station for the greater part of the time at Venice[4]. Thirty years before Harrington arrived, the attention of Englishmen had been directed in a special degree towards the Italian republic[5]. While England was still hot with indignation at Gunpowder Plot, Venice had quarrelled with the Pope over the claims of the clergy and the Jesuits to independence of her laws[6].

---

[1] *Athenae*, III. 1115–22.
[2] He fruitlessly contested a seat in 1642, but did not again attempt to enter Parliament. Wood.
[3] Toland's *Life of Harrington*, 30.
[4] Toland, 11–13.   [5] Welwood's *Memoirs*, 30–2.
[6] Friedberg's *Grenzen zwischen Staat u. Kirche*, 688–704; Döllinger's *Bellarmine*, etc.

When Paul V had excommunicated the state and the Jesuits had been expelled, the Protestant world believed that Venice was about to follow the example of the northern nations. Sarpi himself was regarded as already more than half a Protestant. The stir had been felt nowhere more than in England. James had sent his *Apology for the Oath of Allegiance* by special messenger to the Grand Council[1]. Sir Henry Wotton had become a channel of communication between the two states[2]. Bedell, the chaplain of the English Embassy, had been closeted with Father Paul himself[3].

When the eyes of England had once been turned in close scrutiny on the ecclesiastical constitution of the republic, it was impossible but that its political arrangements should also engage attention[4]. By the opening of the seventeenth century the Venetian government had become extremely despotic[5]. Its nature was clearly recognised in England, and Twysden contrasted it with the democratic republicanism of the United Provinces[6]. To many thinkers in England this characteristic deprived it of all claim to admiration. 'In Venice,' wrote Needham, 'the people are excluded from all share in government, from making laws and from bearing offices. 'Tis rather a Junta than a Commonwealth[7].' Except, indeed, in writers who were more or less

[1] Sarpi's *Lettere*, I. 287–92.   [2] Walton's *Life of Wotton*.
[3] Bedell's *Life*, C. S. Cp. *Reliquiae Wottonianae*, 229, 30.
[4] Robespierre was later to order a description of the Government of Venice. Daru's *Histoire de Venise*, VI. 173.
[5] Ranke, *Zur Venetianischen Geschichte*, Aufsatz I.
[6] *The Government of England*, 6, C. S. Cp. Filmer's *Observations on Aristotle's Politics*, ed. 1679, 49–52; and Osborne's *Essays and Paradoxes*, 254, T. P. vol. 1900.
[7] *Excellency of a Free State*, T. P. vol. 1676, 62. In the great struggle, Venice was on the side of the king as long as she dared. See the remarkable story of her offer of aid in Ellis' *Original Letters*, 2nd Series, III. 318–22. Cp. *Letters of Henrietta Maria*, 354.

directly influenced by Harrington, little trace of any enthusiasm for its institutions is to be found in the works of English political writers of the popular party[1]. The only direct debt, in fact, which the English republic owed to the Italian seems to have been in the appropriation of certain details of the etiquette observed in public ceremonies[2]. What gives such peculiar importance, therefore, to Harrington's study of the Venetian system is not only that he was its first genuine student[3], but that he alone of the distinguished thinkers of the time derived many of his proposals from it.

Harrington returned to England with opinions which prevented him from throwing in his lot unreservedly with any party. Yet no treachery to his principles can be discovered in his close connection with the king, a connection, it is needless to say, that was purely personal. For he, finding the king 'quite another person than he had been represented to him, became passionately affected with him and took all occasion to vindicate him in what company soever he might be[4].' The story of their political discussions went abroad, and dutiful royalists declared that the king had worsted Sir James in an argument[5]. Possessing the confidence of both sides, Harrington naturally used his influence to procure a compromise; but his friendly interventions on the king's behalf

---

[1] Under the name of Adriana, Howell praises the Constitution; *Dodona's Grove*, 59–63, T. P. vol. 19; cp. Howell's *Letters*, 68–70. A glowing eulogy also occurs in a pamphlet called *A Plea for the present Government compared with Monarchy*, T. P. vol. 655, 5, 35, etc.

[2] See the report of Sir Oliver Fleming, Master of the Ceremonies, in C. S. P. 1649, 50, 117.

[3] The political instincts of travellers were usually very weak. Fynes Moryson, for instance, noticed little more than the buildings, *Itinerary*, 75–90. Philip Sidney, *Corresp. with Languet*, 9, ed. 1845; and Raleigh, *Works*, VIII. 296, etc. were the chief students.

[4] Wood.

[5] Cal. Clar. S. P. 1. 368.

were misunderstood, and he was removed from his post and imprisoned[1]. The friends never met again, and Aubrey often heard Harrington say that 'nothing ever went more near to him than the death of the king[2].'

When the monarchy was gone, Harrington set to work, in the maturity of his powers, to shew what form of government, since men were now free to choose, seemed best. We do not need the charming story of Lady Claypole's interposition with her father for the 'stolen child[3],' to make us believe that the *Oceana* was the pride of its author's heart. He had been preparing for it for 20 years, and spent six years on its actual composition. It is, indeed, the complete exposition of the completed system. The numerous works which followed were merely abridgements, or replies to criticisms, of his great work.

Harrington begins[4] by pointing out that the true principle by which governments should be estimated is that of the balance of power, a discovery made by the founders of the Venetian Commonwealth. The perfection of the government is to be found where the sovereignty is not limited but 'librated.' At first sight, it might seem that this brings us to the familiar expedient of mixed government, but the resemblance is merely in the bare fact of the division of power. All power in a state is of two sorts, external and internal, deriving from wealth on the one hand and from intellectual distinction on the other. It is the function of the material power to guarantee equality in the foundation, of the intellectual to secure freshness in the superstructure.

But how are these results to be achieved? The answers constitute the essence of the system. The equality of material well-being on which the State rests is produced by an Agrarian

---

[1] Herbert, *Memoirs*, 128–30. [2] Aubrey's *Lives*, II. 370, 371.
[3] Toland, 16, 17. [4] *Works*, ed. Toland, 1771, 35–72.

law; the freshness of life by which the State makes progress is effected by rotation[1]. The Agrarian law, we are informed, is of such virtue that no state where it has obtained has met destruction, and no government which has neglected it has long survived. Since the accession of Henry VII land had been passing from the nobility to the people, and power must follow it. The tendency to the break-up of great estates was to be accelerated by limiting the quantity of land held by an individual to the value of £2000 a year, and also by the division of property among all the children. Harrington's capital contribution to political thinking was to shew that the distribution of power must in the long run correspond to the distribution of property.

Rotation ensures that, as the blood of the body circulates and is prevented from becoming stagnant by being pumped through the heart, the individual members of the community take their share in the government of the commonwealth. Since the full advantages of rotation are only to be enjoyed where the suffrages of the people really express their will, it is necessary that this freedom of pronouncement be secured by the ballot. Bearing these principles in mind, the construction of the machine of government becomes easy. A Commonwealth is merely a society of men. Take any twenty and a difference will at once reveal itself. Six will at any rate be less foolish than the rest, and these will lead. In other words, a 'natural aristocracy' is diffused throughout the whole body of mankind, and it is as natural for the one to guide as for the other to follow. The duty of its members is to be counsellors of the people; their task to debate and afterwards to give advice in what they have debated. If they

---

[1] A very elaborate scheme of rotation had been put forth by Wither, in *The Perpetual Parliament*, 51, 2, *Works*, III. ed. Spenser Society. It appeared in 1652, but is not noticed by Harrington.

could do more, the government would not be equal; consequently there must be another council to decide. As the senate would represent the wisdom of the community, which lies in the aristocracy[1], the assembly should represent its interest, which lies in the whole body of the people. The duty of the assembly is to accept or reject the proposals of the senate. The government, completed by the election of the magistracy, may be summed up as 'the senate proposing, the people resolving, the magistracy executing.' There is no other Commonwealth, adds Harrington, in art or nature.

Before passing to a detailed exposition of the desired form of government, the author glances at the reasons why the recent constitution of the country broke down[2]. Alone of his contemporaries, Harrington understood that the causes of the great upheaval which had been witnessed needed to be sought in underlying social and economic transformations. A rapid review of the history of Oceana brings us to the period when power was still divided between the king and the nobility. King Panurgus, however, reflecting on the power and the inconstancy of those who had raised him to the throne, 'to establish his own safety began to mix water with their wine, and thus to open those sluices that have since overwhelmed not the king only but the throne.' The wise king of Bacon's imagination becomes the most short-sighted. 'For whereas a nobility strikes not at the throne but at some king they do not like, popular power strikes through the king at the throne, as that which is incompatible with it.' The work was continued by his son and successor, who by his dissolution of the abbeys turned the balance still more to the side of the people. There

---

[1] Cp. *A discourse shewing that Parliaments with a council sitting during the intervals are not to be trusted for a settlement*, 575–8.

[2] Second Part of the Preliminaries, 57–72.

was nothing further wanting to the destruction of the throne but that the people, not naturally apt to see their strength, should be allowed to feel it.

Since the author feels that there is no reason why a Commonwealth should not be as immortal as the stars in heaven, no efforts are to be spared that the methods by which this is to be attained may be put in force. True government resting on persuasion, weekly classes for the explanation of the constitution are to be held, and a thousand officials are to traverse the country to give the people their first lessons in the mysteries of the ballot— a familiarity more essential to be acquired since all elections, local as well as general, are conducted on this principle. The discussion of the Agrarian law is noticeable for its thoroughness[1]. The thirteenth article of the constitution of Oceana enacts that no individual shall own land in value above £2000 a year. Since this law strikes at the root of primogeniture, the heir-apparent of a noble house rose at the council-table and attacked the proposition. It was destructive to families, reducing all their members to poverty. Such assaults on men's estates would cripple industry by discouraging the accumulation of capital. The Lord Archon immediately rose to defend the measure. Even if such a measure were to destroy the families which it affected, who would dare to balance the interests of a few hundred with that of the nation? But it would not destroy them. The essence of a Commonwealth was equality. How could it be better described than as the destruction of a family, when we used our children like puppies, taking one and feeding it with choice morsels and drowning five? The nobility and gentry would no longer achieve their position in the state by riches, but by their education and their capacity for the public service.

[1] 94–103.

When their intrinsic merit, weighed by the judgment of the people, was the only path to honour and preferment, the amassing of possessions would become an ambition of rarer occurrence.

The religious life of the nation and the maintenance of religious liberty are under the control of a national council of religion. On the vacancy of an ordinary parochial benefice, two representatives of the parish are to repair to one of the Universities—which should be prudently reformed—and petition the Vice-Chancellor and Convocation for a probationer[1]. The candidate selected by the University returns to the parish and, after one year, the suffrages of the parishioners are taken by ballot. If two-thirds of the voters indicate their approval, the probationer enters on his duties as the fully recognised minister. That suitable candidates may be induced to enter the Ministry, every benefice in the nation shall be augmented to at least the value of £100 a year[2]. That liberty of conscience may be guaranteed, no coercive power may be exercised by any man or body of men. 'Where civil liberty is entire it includes liberty of conscience; where liberty of conscience is entire, it includes civil liberty[3].' Religious liberty consists not simply in toleration, but in a total absence of religious disqualifications[4]. Disputed questions are to be settled by the divines of the two Universities, debating and deciding independently of each other. That the clergy may have no cause to neglect their duties, they are ineligible for any other employment. In this way the freedom of the people and the supervision of the most learned members of the state are

---

[1] *The Rota*, 595.   [2] 81–3.   [3] *Political Aphorisms*, 484.

[4] Lecky's statement, 'He alone anticipated the doctrines of the nineteenth century,' is exaggerated. *Rationalism*, II. 76. Nevertheless, a markedly secular spirit may be noticed throughout his works, without having recourse to the supposition of Burnet that he was a Deist. *Own Time*, I. 114, 115.

conciliated[1]. No political writer, indeed, has discerned with greater clearness than Harrington the importance of education in the life and well-being of a state. A better system of instruction had been one of the petitions of Milton to the Protector in the *Defensio Secunda*, and a scheme had been outlined in the *Letter to Hartlib*; but Harrington came forward with practical proposals, anticipating in a very striking way the modern system of universal and compulsory education under the control of the state[2].

Though the author of *Oceana* had loved Charles I, he was no lover of monarchy, still less of the monarchy that the approaching Restoration bade fair to introduce. Yet, republican as he was, he echoed the cry for a free parliament and a government in accordance with the popular wish. 'If it be according to the wisdom and interest of the nation upon mature debate that there may be a king, let there be a king[3].' But this faith in his system led him to believe that in a very few years empire would once again follow property and that a republic would again be erected[4]. Instead of the deposition of the king came the arrest of Harrington, his trial, his imprisonment and its pathetic consequences[5].

Harrington's reputation as a political thinker has not been what it deserves. His worth has been in part discerned by isolated writers, as by Hume, when he declared *Oceana* to be the only valuable model of a Commonwealth[6], and by John Adams, when he wrote that the honour of the noble discovery of the relation of empire to property belonged as exclusively to Harrington as the discovery of the circulation of blood to Harvey[7]. But the

---

[1] Cp. *System of Politics*, ch. 6.   [2] 171–7.
[3] *Ways and Means*, 507.   [4] Aubrey.
[5] C. S. P. 1660, 1, 413; Toland, 31–4.
[6] *Essay* 38, *Idea of a Perfect Commonwealth*.
[7] *Works*, IV. 428. Cp. the Eulogies in Coleridge's *Statesman's Manual*, Mackintosh's *Miscellaneous Works*, 609, Cartwright's *Works, passim*.

ordinary historians of political and social speculation have almost
without exception missed his significance, and the judgment of
Montesquieu[1] has perverted his successors[2]. It is only in the last
few decades that a truer appreciation of perhaps the most remarkable political thinker of an age pregnant with original ideas has
begun to appear[3].

The first aspect in which Harrington's importance is obvious
is that of method. To those who see in a fanciful presentation
the disproof of serious thinking this contention may seem para-
doxical. But it is necessary to remember that his selection of an
imaginative setting for his ideas was no proof of Utopian leanings,
but was dictated by the rigorous censorship of the Protectorate;
and that his political works were no mere speculative pastimes
but an earnest and practical exhortation to the Parliament and
its governors. A glance at the *Civitas Solis* of Campanella or at
almost any of the Utopias of the seventeenth and eighteenth
centuries convinces one of the fundamentally different character
of the *Oceana*. The form proves nothing as to the character of the
work, which is in reality one of the earliest examples in political
thinking of the historical method[4]. The *Oceana* ranks, in this

[1] *Esprit des Lois*, IX. 6.

[2] Mohl's judgment may stand for all. 'Harrington jener geistlosen Gattung
von Staatsweisen angehört welche in der Auffindung verwickelter Formen
Schutz, in der Beschränkung der nöthigen Amtsgewalt Freiheit, in der
genauen Bestimmung von Kleinigkeiten Dauer, in einer mechanischen
Zerschneidung und Zusammensetzung Ordnung suchen.' *Geschichte der
Staatswissenschaften*, I. 191. Cp. Hallam, *Lit. Eur.* ch. 30.

[3] Janet is an exception. His notice of Harrington is amazingly superficial.
Hist. de la Science Politique, II. 191–3. The most serious discussion of his
system is that by Franck, *Publicistes*, II. 202–52. Meritorious articles have
appeared by Dow, *Eng. Hist. Review*, April, 1891; Dwight, *Political Science
Quarterly*, March, 1887.

[4] This is strangely missed by most commentators. Roscher is an exception,
Englische Volkswirthschaftlehre, 53–7. The teaching of history in colleges
was one of the demands of the *Modest Plea for an equal Commonwealth*, 59–72.

respect, with the *Discorsi* of Machiavelli and the *République* of Bodin in the period preceding the appearance of Vico and Montesquieu. 'No man,' taught Harrington, 'can be a politician except he be first a historian and a traveller. For if he has no knowledge in history, he cannot tell what has been; and if he is not a traveller, he cannot tell what is. But he that neither knows what has been nor what is can never tell what must be or what may be. Harrington himself, as his fellow-attendant on the king records, was the 'best read man in history of all sorts' he had ever known[1]. When the Council of Legislators began to sit, 'the Lord Archons made it appear how unsafe a thing it was to follow fancy in the fabric of a Commonwealth, and how necessary that the archives of ancient prudence should be ransacked before any counsellor should presume to offer anything to the work in hand[2].' Even in the crisis of 1659, Harrington takes care to preface his *Model of a Commonwealth fitted to the present state of this nation* by a sketch of seven of the principal republican constitutions of history[3]. Though he stands fast by the notion of a right reason or natural law, every article of the constitution of Oceana must be judged at the bar of history before its admission. A further illustration of the historic spirit is to be found in his attempt to exhibit the intimate connection of the political and economic factors of the English revolution[4].

Despite his method, however, it would be idle to deny that there is something of the doctrinaire in Harrington. The generalisation that a political theory will be at any rate unconsciously moulded by the view of human nature that its author happens to hold is continually illustrated in the thought of the seventeenth century. While the extreme of absolutism is held by those who,

[1] Herbert's *Memoirs*, 65.   [2] *Works*, 73.   [3] 491–505.
[4] Cp. Bonar's *Philosophy and Political Economy*, 86–90.

like Hobbes, regard mankind as essentially evil, democracy is combated or qualified by Baxter and Ireton and Milton primarily on the ground of man's imperfection. Democratic ideas were accepted in reliance on human worth. 'Our fierce champions of a free state,' said L'Estrange with considerable truth, 'presuppose great unity, great probity, great purity[1].' Harrington champions the principle of rotation because he believes that there is an inexhaustible supply of worthy and capable men ready to play their part in the drama of government. He upholds the universality of the elective principle because, in the words of one of his critics[2], he is convinced that men are wise enough to choose the wise and good enough to choose the good. He believes that the different organs of government will be satisfied with the functions allotted to them in the Constitution. 'In this Constitution,' he announces confidently, 'the councils must of necessity contain the wisdom and the interest of the nation[3].' But in his enthusiasm for certain of the results secured by the constitutions of Sparta and Venice he forgets that liberty was almost lost in their intricacies. As Hume was to point out, no sufficient security for freedom or for the redress of grievances was to be found in a scheme where the senate was the sole legislature, and could negative a proposal before it ever reached the votes of the people[4]. It never occurs to him that the well-being of a community may slip on the polished surface of a theoretically faultless scheme.

His economics, again, are notably unsatisfactory. He is bound by the old prejudice in favour of agriculture, and has failed to learn one of the chief lessons which Venice herself taught. Industry

---

[1] *Harl. Misc.* I. 14. [2] Baxter's *Holy Commonwealth*, 230.
[3] *Ways and Means*, 507.
[4] Hume to his nephew, Burton's *Hume*, II. 481, 2.

involved accumulation, and accumulation was incompatible with equality[1]. The extension of his principle to property in general, however, was too obvious to escape the notice of his critics. But he refused to accept it, on the ground that, though all riches had wings, those in land were 'hooded and tied to the perch[2].' He is still enmeshed in the toils of Mercantilism at a time when some of the clearest heads were beginning to see through its fallacies. He proposed to introduce premiums on large families and to impose double taxes on the unmarried and childless[3]. Even when he hit upon the right track, as in his defence of usury, he involves himself in great obscurity and almost absurdity in discussing it[4].

In the works of Harrington there is nevertheless a solid fund of valuable thought. He is more than the Sièyes of the English Revolution[5]. He possessed a breadth of conception as remarkable as Milton's in combination with a genius for details that was his own. More clearly than any of his contemporaries, he saw that a good government was an organism, and that it must grow naturally out of the conditions of society. His critical and constructive power entitles him to rank among the foremost of those thinkers who have endeavoured to combine democratic principles with the interests of order.

It is not difficult to accept the testimony of Anthony Wood that the *Oceana* was greedily bought up. Such interest did it arouse in the minds of several men of distinction and ability, Nevile, Petty, Cyriac Skinner and others, that the Rota Club was formed for the discussion of its proposals. We are fortunate in possessing a spirited account of the proceedings of the famous

---

[1] *System of Politics*, 466.
[2] *Prerogative of Popular Government*, 243–5.   [3] 97.
[4] *Prerogative of Popular Government*, 229–32.   [5] Cornewall Lewis.

debating society, since Aubrey was one of its members. The doctrine, he informs us, was the more taking that there was, to human foresight, no possibility of the king's return. And the discourses themselves were the most smart and ingenious he had ever heard or expected to hear; the debates in Parliament were but flat beside them. The room was every evening as full as it could be crammed[1]. Wood adds, perhaps on the authority of Petty, that a special attraction was found in the use of the balloting box, which was brought into requisition at the close of each debate[2]. Pepys turned his steps thither more than once and found a 'great confluence of gentlemen' and 'admirable discourse[3].' Next to Harrington himself, the chief figure at the Rota Club was Nevile, a man to whom sufficient attention has hardly been paid. Hobbes used frequently to say, in referring to *Oceana*, that Nevile had a finger in the pie, and Aubrey, who knew both master and disciple, thought it not improbable[4]. In his criticism of the book, moreover, Stubbe invariably refers to its 'authors[5].' Nevile was at any rate the life-long friend of Harrington. It was he who introduced the principles of the Rota Club to the House of Commons, and secured eight or ten adherents; it was he who 'never forsook him to his dying day, and, during the year that his memory and discourse were taken by disease, paid his visits as duly as when his friend was in the prime of his understanding.'

Numerous tracts and broadsides, published in the interval between the deposition of Richard Cromwell and the Declaration of Breda, bear additional witness to the impression that

---

[1] *Lives*, II. 371.   [2] III. 1120.
[3] Jan. 10, Jan. 17, Feb. 20, 1660.   [4] II. 371.
[5] *Commonwealth of Oceana*, T. P. vol. 1956, *passim*; cp. especially, Preface, p. 2.

Harrington's principal proposals had made on the public mind[1]. They even effected an entrance among the ranks of other republican parties, and the system was adopted almost in its entirety by the few Levellers who survived[2]. In the autumn of 1659, Dr Barwick wrote to Charles that many of the Fifth Monarchy Men were 'taken with Harrington's new model[3].' A few weeks later, another correspondent informed his master that Haslerig was being supported by Nevile and Harrington's cabal and accepted their programme[4]. The greatest triumph was secured when a petition, suggesting the formation of a government on Harringtonian principles, was presented to Parliament, and the petitioners received the thanks of the House with the assurance that it was considered to be 'without any private end and only for the public interest[5].' Milton's *Ready Way*, published only a few weeks before the Restoration, bears witness that it was this scheme that secured the most general support.

It was impossible, however, that such a scheme should escape the jests that are reserved for novelties. It was queried whether it would not be expedient to ship all the gangrened members of the body politic to Oceana, piloted thither by Mr Harrington, 'our famous modern Columbus, discoverer of that floating terra incognita[6].' But more competent critics presented themselves. Of these, Baxter, the most distinguished, set himself to compose the outlines of a *Holy Commonwealth*. The first principles of the two men being so different, Baxter naturally disputes nearly all

---

[1] Above all, see the *Modest Plea for an equal Commonwealth*, T. P. vol. 1802. Wood assigns it to Sprigge, a Fellow of Lincoln. *Life*, I. 295.

[2] 59–72. *The Leveller; principles of Government and Religion asserted by those commonly called Levellers. Harl. Misc.* IV. 543–50.

[3] Carte, *Original Letters*, II. 202–4.   [4] *ib.* II. 223.

[5] *Petition of July 6*, 508–13.

[6] *Somers Tracts*, VI. 193. Cp. V. 425, and *Harl. Misc.* IV. 188–95.

Harrington's assumptions and disapproves nearly all his proposals;
yet he felt himself constrained to acknowledge that there was
much good interwoven in the mad scheme, of which use might
be made by righteous governors[1]. Of a widely different character
was the work of Matthew Wren. The author had published *Short
Considerations on Oceana*, and, in reply to Harrington's witty
retort[2], issued a formidable volume of polemic under the title of
Monarchy Asserted[3]. The Preface attacks Harrington in his
tenderest part, twitting him with his ignorance of affairs. 'Men
will suspect Harrington's ability in modelling a Commonwealth
till he has spent some years in the Government.' More sympathetic
was the attitude of Henry Stubbe, the gifted scholar and staunch
Republican[4] who, though dissatisfied with some of Harrington's
historical illustrations[5], warmly admits his obligations to his
works[6].

II

The executive appointed by the restored Rump consisted of
the army leaders and the Commonwealthsmen. A petition from
the former shews that such differences as their connection with
Oliver had involved between the two parties had come to an
end[7]. The prospect of unity, however, was overclouded by the
fact that Lambert was dissatisfied with his position, and that,
after quelling the royalist rising of Booth, he felt emboldened to
press his claims. But the House was blind to the danger, rejected
the demand that he should become Major-General of the army,

[1] 237, T. P. vol. 1729.   [2] *Politicaster*, 546–62.
[3] T. P. vol. 1853, 2, 3, 158.   [4] Wood's *Athenae*, III. 1067–83.
[5] *Oceana put in the balance and found too light*, T. P. vol. 1956.
[6] *Defence of the Good old Cause*, T. P. vol. 1956, Preface; cp. *Malice
Rebuked*, 42, T. P. vol. 1841.
[7] C. S. P. 1658, 9, 345.

and was forcibly dissolved by his soldiers. The Council of Officers thereupon appointed a Committee of Safety, in which the civilian and military elements were once more mixed. Lambert received the post he coveted, but at the expense of alienating Monk, who could not forgive the appointment of a superior officer in Scotland. So successfully, however, did he hide his resentment that he was invited to join his forces to those stationed in England.

While Monk was slowly marching south, the old antagonisms broke out once more in the Committee of Safety. A final effort was made by Ludlow to reconcile the conflicting parties. All differences were to be determined without appeal by 21 persons of known integrity, to be called Conservators of Liberty. The essentials of the cause should be clearly stated and be declared inviolable. The government was not to be altered from a Commonwealth by setting up a king, single person, or House of Peers. The legislative and executive powers were to be in different hands. Liberty of conscience should not be violated[1]. The essentially doctrinaire character of Ludlow's mind is nowhere more apparent than in his sole effort at constructive politics. 'The essentials of the cause' were to be declared 'inviolable by any authority whatsoever.' The Conservators were to be men of impartiality, whose ruling was to be final. No wonder that a constitution which would have been impracticable in a time of profound peace broke down at the very meeting that was called for its adoption. 'Whereupon,' relates the author of the scheme, 'my patience began to leave me, and I resolved to have no more to do with them[2].'

After other proposals, among them that of recalling Charles, the Rump was once more assembled, and proceeded to strike at the two leaders of the Republican party, Ludlow and Vane.

[1] *Memoirs*, II. 172, 3.   [2] II. 174.

Through good and evil fortune Ludlow had remained faithful to republican ideals as he understood them. This must be borne in mind if we are to restrain our irritation at the narrowness of his mind and the insufficiency of these ideals[1]. His life was passed in astonishment; and each fresh discovery of the perversity of human nature, instead of leading him to revise or suspect his own position, merely served to increase the tenacity with which he held it. On entering the service of Parliament at the beginning of the Civil War, it had seemed to him that the justice of the cause in which he had engaged was so evident that he could not imagine it would be attended with difficulty. For though doubtless the clergy and some of the courtiers and those who depended on the king for their subsistence would adhere to him, he could not believe that the people would strengthen the hands of the enemy against those who had the laws of God, nature, reason as well as the laws of the land on their side[2]. His attitude towards the Restoration is identical to that of Clarendon towards the Revolution. In both cases a national movement is represented as an act of apostasy from reason, a causeless flight from an Earthly Paradise. While Harry Marten recognised the king on the ground that, as he had been called in by the representative body of England, he had the best title under heaven, Ludlow continued to flaunt his banner of popular approval when it had become a thing of shreds and patches. The self-constituted champion of the people is found on this, as on almost every other occasion, in opposition to the popular will. 'The despotism of the Long Parliament,' in Guizot's words, 'first over the king, next over the nation when the nation desired

---

[1] This is what is not done in the exceedingly able though one-sided *Modest Vindication of Oliver Cromwell from Ludlow* which greeted the appearance of the *Memoirs* in 1696, *Somers Tracts*, VI. 416–42. No more merciless exposure of his weakness has been written.

[2] I. 38.

peace with the king; the despotism of the Rump and the Army over the people when, after the death of Cromwell, all England called for a free parliament; all these contradictory violences seemed just to Ludlow because they promised the destruction of the king or the success of the republican government. Before this name he immolated successively the laws, the liberties, the happiness of his contemporaries, and remained profoundly convinced that nothing but the treason first of the king, next of the parliament, then of Cromwell, finally of Monk, had caused the failure of himself and his friends in their patriotic designs[1].'

The Commonwealthsmen in truth stand alone among the parties of the time in transforming republicanism into a religion. By the side of its triumph, the loss of its democratic character was a trifle. And yet, at least in those who proved the sincerity of their faith by death or exile, an unmistakeable nobility shines through the fanaticism. While Colonel Hutchinson pleaded after the Restoration that he had been seduced, and Ingoldsby that Cromwell had guided his hand at the signature of the death-warrant, Scot was to beg that it might be recorded on his grave that he had condemned a king to die. To Cook and Hewson and Peters, to Scot and Harrison, though their testimony was given in the full dawn of the Restoration, it remained 'a cause which gave life in death to all the owners of it and sufferers for it,' 'a cause not to be repented of.'

It is impossible to number Vane with the Commonwealthsmen; for their thought was purely secular, their conduct governed by purely political considerations, whereas his inspiration was derived from and his ambitions dictated by his theology. He was described by James Naylor as 'drunk with imagination[2].' A report spread

---

[1] *Portraits Politiques*, 96–100.
[2] James Naylor to Margaret Fell, Mrs Webb's *Swarthmoor Hall*, 121.

abroad that a man had visited him and told him that he was sent by God to consecrate him king, and that Vane thereupon submitted to the imposition of his hands[1]. The impression made by his personality was unique. The learned Stubbe confessed that he fell into transports whenever his name was mentioned, and declared that not to honour it was to be an enemy of all that was good and virtuous[2]. Clarendon adds that he had 'an unnatural aspect which made men think there was something in him of extraordinary; and his whole life made good that imagination[3].' The 'slyness' of which Sir Philip Warwick accuses him[4] was nothing but an impression produced by his remarkable subtlety of thought. His practical ability and his intellectual aberrations were both sufficient to arrest attention; but their combination produced a phenomenon at which his age never ceased to marvel. 'Such vast parts and such strong delusions,' wrote Kennett in a sentence on which we cannot improve, 'so much good sense and so much madness, could hardly be believed to meet in any one man[5].' In the history of political thought, Vane is of importance as representing a peculiar phase of republicanism. In his appeal to abstract right, in his desire to limit Parliament by a fundamental Constitution, he was at one with most of the radical parties of the day. He realised, however, that government was a difficult matter; and his friend and biographer Sikes properly remarks that no man was more dissuaded from popular tumults[6]. But where

[1] Bordeaux to Mazarin, Dec. 18, 1659, Guizot, *Richard Cromwell*, ii. 304, 5.
[2] *Malice Rebuked*, Preface, and 7, T. P. vol. 1841.
[3] *Hist.* iii. 34.   [4] *Memoirs*, 246.
[5] *Register*, 711. There is no adequate life of Vane. The remarks of T. H. Green in his 'Lectures on the Commonwealth,' *Works*, iii. 277–364, display greater insight than the elaborate biographies of Forster, Upham and Hosmer.
[6] *Life*, 112.

he most widely differed from his fellow-republicans was in his attitude towards republicanism itself. To him it was nothing but a provisional expedient, better indeed than monarchy, but destined to give way to the rule of the saints.

On his march southward, Monk secretly visited Fairfax in his Yorkshire home[1], and from this time the Restoration became a certainty. On reaching London, the General was as lavish in his protestations of loyalty to republican ideals as any Commonwealthsman could desire; but the farce was soon played out. The House contrived to quarrel with the City, ordered Monk to dismantle the walls, and, on his demurring, sharply censured him. With this check to the authority of the Rump, the cry for a free Parliament became irrepressible, and the members who had been excluded in the forties were recalled. The appointment of a Presbyterian executive and the establishment of Presbyterianism quickly followed.

Since the death of the king little had been heard of the Presbyterians, though the quiet undercurrent of opposition continued to flow[2]. But with the downfall of the Protectorate, they had once more emerged from obscurity, and Presbyterian ministers encouraged the rising of Booth[3]. It was at this time, too, that their most venerated member gave to the world his mature political philosophy. Throughout his career Baxter held himself aloof from active participation in political life. His chief intellectual characteristic, the dislike of extremes, involved a middle position in political philosophy[4]. He declared that God

[1] See Brian Fairfax's 'Iter Boreale' in *Fairfax Corresp.* IV. 151–73.

[2] Rous alone accepted the rule of the oligarchy, contending in the *Bounds and Bonds of Public Obedience*, T. P. vol. 571, that the lawful commands of unlawful rulers should be obeyed.

[3] Whitelocke, Aug. 5, 1659.

[4] The inconsistencies are trenchantly exposed in Coleridge's *English Divines*, vol. 2.

and not the people was the foundation of power, though he admitted that the king's oath made him a mayor or bailiff[1]. But on entering the army he seems to have caught something of the spirit which animated it. The passages of exaltation in the *Saints' Rest* cannot but include a political reference. 'What rare and mighty works have we seen in England in four or five years! What a destruction of the enemy! What miracles have taken place and in what an unhoped-for way!' The later incidents of the struggle, however, were profoundly distasteful to him, and, though he did not resist the oligarchy, he sympathised with those who did[2]. In like manner, when he met the Protector after the only sermon which he preached before him, he told him that he took their ancient monarchy to be a blessing to the land, and asked how England had forfeited it[3]. On the other hand, he was convinced that it was Cromwell's design to do good in the main. Moreover, though it was unlawful to take any oath of allegiance to any governor save the king, it was not unlawful to submit.

Our knowledge of Baxter's political theory is completed by the work which was prompted by the success of the *Oceana*. The frank declaration of the preface, 'I like not the democratic forms,' may be taken as the epitome of the *Holy Commonwealth*. The people are not the original of power, for three reasons. They may choose the person, but they cannot give the power. If they are the original, they must not elect others. Thirdly, if the power is in the people, it must be in all or part. If in all, none can be subjects and therefore there can be no sovereign; if in part, then the people are not sovereign at all[4]. Relying on these arguments, the author proceeds to declare that the people's consent is not always necessary to the constitution of the government. The sovereign, too, is above all the positive laws of the Commonwealth; for he that is highest hath no higher to obey, and laws are merely significations of the lawgiver's will. Democratic government is the worst of all forms. The governors must be good as well as wise; but as the earth contains but few men that are wise and good, if they may rule but a little time, the bad must succeed them[1]. The unfitness of the people for employment in the public service is proved by a glance round a court of justice. 'I have thought of the excellency of democracy when I have sat and heard a learned judge opening a hard case to the jury, and they have stood by all the while as if he had been talking Greek or Hebrew, and gone their way and brought in their verdict as it first came to their tongue-ends, before they understood the case any more than the man in the moon, unless there were a crafty fellow among them, and then he rules the rest[2].' Is the government, then, to be absolute? The chief check is to be found in the influence of the moral law. St Paul only meant that the magistrate should be obeyed in the ordinary routine of life. Any other obedience would be treating him as an idol[3]. But the duty must be clear, and Baxter appropriately concludes with the warning reflection that it is dangerous for uncalled men to dream that every opportunity is a call[4].

Of less speculative interest but of greater practical influence were the writings of Prynne, whose pen, needless to say, had never been idle. Since the defeat of the Presbyterian cause, his implicit conservatism had become more and more explicit. Instead of saying directly that the people were wronged by the oligarchical government, he preferred to say that 'the whole

[1] *Holy Commonwealth*, 205.   [2] 230.   [3] 356–470.
[4] 509. Cp. *Christian Politics, Practical Works*, VI., especially ch. 3.

body of the laws were violently assaulted[1].' The law provided, in like manner, that the franchise should be confined to free-holders; and after twenty years of confusion Prynne has nothing to suggest but that the freeholders should elect a new representative[2]. Certain points of ceremonial had been observed in Parliament in the fourteenth century and should be revived[3]. The House of Lords was passionately defended, not on the ground of its utility, but because it would be 'the extremity of injustice to deny them their ancient hereditary right[4].' The attitude is always the same; the law of England is the measure of all things. Charles was the legal heir, and Prynne's philosophy did not allow him to ask himself if his return would be conducive to the well-being of the nation. 'He asserts the king's right so boldly,' wrote a royalist agent to Ormond when the Restoration became certain, 'that he may be called the Cato of his age[5].' The disposition on the part of the Presbyterians to obtain securities for the fulfilment of their desires had been general, and some had gone so far as to suggest that, if such were not forth-coming, Monk should be invited to become Protector or Stadt-holder[6]. But this mood was not widely shared and did not last long.

At the very moment when the establishment of Presbyterianism was taking place, Milton uttered a last despairing cry. The appearance in February, 1660, of the *Ready and Easy Way to establish a Free Commonwealth*, expanding the scheme lately

[1] *Seasonable, Legal and Historical Vindication of the Laws,* 5, T. P. vol. 488. Cp. *Brief Memento to the Parliamentary Junta,* T. P. vol. 537.
[2] *Short, legal, medicinal, safe, easy prescription,* etc. *Somers Tracts,* VI. 533, 4.
[3] Preface to the *Records in the Tower.*
[4] *Levellers Levelled,* 28, T. P. vol. 428.
[5] Carte's *Original Letters,* II. 312.
[6] Bordeaux to Mazarin, Guizot's *Monk,* 284.

presented in a letter to Monk[1], introduces us to his constructive
political opinions. The pamphlet itself is by far the boldest and
most passionate that he ever wrote. The worst apprehensions
that he had communicated to his friends[2] in the last days of
1659 had been realised. Where the old opinions are repeated, it
is without any qualifications. Kingship is now unnecessary,
burdensome and dangerous; the government of a single person
in any form is scouted. 'That people must needs be mad or
strangely infatuated that build the chief hope of their common
happiness and safety on a single person who, if he happens to be
good, can do more than another man, and if bad, hath in his
hands to do more evil without check.' A sovereign has little
else to do but to 'set a pompous lace upon the superficial
actings of state, to pageant himself up and down in progress
among the perpetual bowings and cringings of an abject people.'
Passing from the general to the particular, Milton cries out in
poignant anguish: 'That a nation should be so valorous and
courageous to win their liberty in the field, and when they have
won it should not know how to use it or value it, but basely and
besottedly to run their necks again into the yoke which they
have broken and prostrate all the fruits of their victory at the
feet of the vanquished, will be such an example as kings and
tyrants never yet had the like to boast of.' Equally decided and
uncompromising is his reference to the law of nature. 'We are
not bound,' he cries, 'by any statute of preceding Parliament but
by the law of nature only, which is the only law of laws truly
and properly to all mankind fundamental; to which no people
that will thoroughly reform but may and must have recourse.'

[1] *Present means and brief delineation of a Commonwealth, Prose Works*
II. 106–8.

[2] *Letter to Oldenburg, Prose Works,* III. 520; and *Letter to a Friend concerning the Ruptures of the Commonwealth,* II. 102–6.

With all his old confidence and certitude Milton remarks that he does not doubt 'all ingenuous and knowing men' agree with him that a free Commonwealth without Single Person or House of Lords is by far the best government. True, we have never reached it; but the opportunity has now arrived when we may establish it for ever in the land without difficulty or delay. If the people, laying aside their prejudices and considering their own good, elect their knights and burgesses, men not addicted to a Single Person or a House of Lords, the work is done. To the mind of the *doctrinaire* these impossible conditions are fulfilled as soon as conceived, and the 'Grand Council,' 'well-chosen,' already seems to exist. In this body the sovereignty, though only as a trust, is to reside. And now Milton produces his talisman. The Grand Council is to be perpetual[1]. The ship of the Commonwealth is always under sail; if those that sit at the stern steer well, what need to change them? The proposal is driven home by an onslaught on the alternative form of government, more fierce and bitter than that of the *Defensio Secunda*. 'How can we be advantaged by successive and transitory Parliaments? If they find no work to do, they will make it, by altering or repealing former acts or making and multiplying new, that they may seem to see what their predecessors saw not and not to have assembled for nothing, till all law be lost in the multitude of clashing debates[2].'

Resuming the championship of his scheme, Milton finds himself compelled by the imperfections of human nature to hold a compromise in reserve and selects the proposal of Harrington as

---

[1] A somewhat similar scheme had been advocated in Mayerne's *Monarchie Aristodémocratique*. Milton, however, does not appear to have been acquainted with the work.

[2] Milton had urged the Protector to content himself with little legislation, at the end of the *Defensio Secunda*.

the most popular. 'If the ambition of such as think themselves injured that they do not partake of the government cannot brook the perpetuity of others chosen before them, or if it be feared that long continuance of power may corrupt the sincerest men, there is the expedient lately propounded, that annually the third part of the senators may go out according to the precedence of their election.' But the qualification is allowed with a very bad grace. The author feels that this wheel is too much like the wheel of fortune. Rotation involves the putting in of many that are raw and inexperienced, and should therefore, if possible, be avoided. It is idle to expect anything from a floating foundation, and therefore the safest course is that none of the Council be removed but by death or on conviction of crime. Any possible ill-effects of this centralisation are to be counteracted by the institution of assemblies in the chief towns. With such a constitution, declares Milton, the people will have none to blame but themselves if the Commonwealth does not rival the United Provinces and all other states[1].

Absolutist critics were never weary of accusing their opponents of inconsistency, and against none was the charge better founded than against Milton[2]. It is impossible not to regret that the noblest champion of liberty to which the age gave birth should in the maturity of his powers and experience have pleaded for a slavery greater than that against which he had fought so zealously. We are tempted to quote Milton against himself. 'To sequester our-

[1] A final presentation of Miltonian philosophy appeared a few weeks later, *Brief Notes on Dr Griffiths' Sermon*. But it contained nothing of novelty or importance.

[2] Cp. above all, Filmer's *Reflections on the Original of Government*, 17–32, ed. 1679, a criticism of unusual power. The best recent discussions of his shortcomings are in Seeley's *Lectures and Essays*, and Stern's *Milton u. seine Zeit*, III. 74–7. Geffroy's *Étude sur les doctrines politiques de Milton* is worthless.

selves out of the world into Utopian politics which cannot be drawn into use will never mend our condition[1].' 'Can one read it,' asked John Adams[2], 'without shuddering? A single assembly to govern England? An assembly of Senators for life? If no better system of government was proposed, no wonder the people recalled the Royal Family.'

The paradox is not to be defended; but it may be in some measure explained. Milton held that liberty had 'a sharp and double edge, fit only to be handled by just and virtuous men[3].' Secondly, alone of his contemporaries, he saw the full scope of the Revolution that was in progress. Before his mind arose the vision of a new era. In the early days of the struggle he had fancied he saw a mighty and puissant nation awaking as a man out of sleep. When the strife was over, the triumph of freedom in England had become an event of universal significance. 'I behold all the nations of the earth recovering that liberty they so long had lost; I behold them spreading the blessings of freedom and civilisation among the kingdoms of the world[4].' The struggle was not merely against an evil king, but for 'the blessings of freedom and civilisation.' Liberty of thought, liberty of expression, liberty of action were the rights of mankind. It is the contrast of the unique opportunity that has arrived for the whole human race to take a step forward towards a higher civilisation with the unripeness of the great mass of his fellow-men for such

[1] *Areopagitica.*

[2] *Works,* IV. 465. Cp. Mirabeau, 'Je ne connaîtrais rien de plus terrible que l'aristocratie souveraine de six cents personnes qui demain pourraient se rendre inamovibles, après-demain héréditaires, et finiraient, comme toutes les aristocraties du monde, par tout envahir.' Speech on the Veto.

[3] Reflections on the War, from the third book of his *History of England.* Published in Maseres, *Tracts,* 813.

[4] *Defensio Secunda.*

a transition that accounts for Milton's apparently illiberal teaching. The contempt of the mountain eagle for the animals that crawl upon the earth is reflected in his imperial soul.

A fortnight after the appearance of Milton's pamphlet, Monk was made Commander-in-chief and joint Commander of the Fleet with Montagu. A few days later the House dissolved itself, and writs were issued for the summons of a new Parliament. On May 7, the king was recalled by the weary nation without terms; and Ludlow might well feel that the end had come when, on May 29, he witnessed 'the inconstant multitude burning the badges of their freedom, the arms of the Commonwealth.'

CHAPTER XI

Democratic Ideas in the Latter Part of the Seventeenth Century

I

'SUCH a restoration,' wrote Evelyn, on the day of the king's entry into London, 'has never been seen since the return of the Jews[1].' Sir Philip Warwick spoke of it as a regeneration[2]. A resident wrote to his friend in Paris, 'Were you here, you would say, Good God, do the same people inhabit England that were in it ten or twenty years ago? Believe me, I know not whether I am in England or no, or whether I dream[3].'

The change was reflected in the field of political theory[4]. 'We submit and oblige ourselves and our posterities to your Majesty,' said the Commons, 'for ever[5].' Such an utterance as the following is typical of the times. 'That Monarchy is the best of governments is a matter so preeminently above all question that one penfull of ink spent on that subject cannot but be esteemed waste[6].' Harrington, talking of models of government, was 'reputed no better than whimsical and crack-brained[7].' The works of Milton and Goodwin were banished from the Bodleian[8], and the book-

---

[1] *Diary*, May 29, 1660.   [2] *Memoirs*, 437.
[3] C. S. P. 1659–60, 428. It is interesting to compare the account of a similar transformation in France, in Gourville's *Mémoires*: 'Les jeunes gens qui n'ont eu connaissance que du temps où le roi établit son autorité prendraient ce temps de jadis pour un rêve.'
[4] [See C. B. Roylance Kent, *The Early History of the Tories*. H. J. L.]
[5] *C. J.* VIII. 16.
[6] *Appeal*, etc. T. P. vol. 1956.   [7] Kennett's *Register*, 567.
[8] Wood's *Life*, I. 319.

sellers lamented the disgrace their profession had incurred by printing so many works 'of Milton's strain[1].' In Scotland 'seditious books' were called in, and the works of Rutherford were burnt[2]. The writings of the past generation found few students and fewer converts[3].

The accomplished fact was recognised by the vast majority of the Nonconformists. Though the Presbyterians gained nothing by the event to which they had so largely contributed, no new outbreak of literary or political activity takes place. That their name was often connected with real or imaginary plots proves no more than the currency of the word Anabaptist in the preceding generation[4]. From the ranks of the Independents, after the removal of Peters, the voice of revolt is heard no more[5], and the Baptists

[1] *Stationers' Register*, III. xxvii.

[2] Nicoll's *Diary*, 301–4.

[3] 'I spent most of my time,' records Potenger, who went to Oxford at this time, 'reading books which were not very common, as John Milton's works; but they had not the power to subvert the principles I had received.' Fowler's *Hist. of Corpus*, 235. Cp. Evelyn's description of Edward Phillips, Milton's nephew, who became tutor to his son, Oct. 24, 1663.

[4] The Exclusion agitation was 'a Presbyterian plot.' Grey's *Debates*, VII. 354. Cp. I. 113. The Rye House incident was called 'a new Presbyterian plot.' *Hatton Corresp.* II. 22, C. S. Rosewell was tried for High Treason in connection with it, but satisfactorily vindicated himself. *State Trials*, X. 147–307; Burnet, II. 441–3.

[5] When Barwick went to counsel recantation on the day before the execution, he found Peters surly and impenitent. Barwick's *Life of Barwick*, 295. Burnet's ridiculous story, I. 115–16, that Goodwin was concerned in Venner's rising arose from the fact that the insurrection was concocted in the street where he lived. There is no more evidence for his statement that at the Revolution of 1688 the Independents were for a Commonwealth. III. 297. It is interesting, however, to notice that the gloom of Shaftesbury's exile in Amsterdam was lightened by the Brownists. Christie's *Shaftesbury*, II. 456. The famous preacher Bradbury received the sobriquet of Hugh Peters Junior; but there is nothing in his works more alarming than his statement that God approves revolutions which establish the rights of human nature. *Divine Right of the Revolution*, ed. 1709, 39–42.

generally accepted the Restoration[1]. The Quakers, though some of their members had manifested the most decided opposition to the recall of the king, petitioning Parliament not to neglect the Good Old Cause[2], and many even selling their land to raise money for its defence[3], now became the peaceable members of society that they have since remained. Though occasionally accused and suspected of unlawful designs[4], history has nothing worse to chronicle than a few eccentricities of conduct[5]. When their creed took definite shape with the publication of Barclay's *Apology* in 1676, the tenet of political submissiveness took the place from which it has never been removed[6].

The Fifth Monarchy Men alone were differently affected by the Restoration. Harrison died with the conviction that he would shortly return at the right hand of Christ to judge his judges[7]. Their courage rose with the obstacles that confronted them, and they may well have entertained the belief attributed to them that each should subdue a thousand[8]. In this spirit, some nine months after the return of the king, a small body of them broke into St Paul's, asking the first person they met for whom he was. For King Charles, was the reply; whereupon he was shot by

[1] *Tracts on Liberty of Conscience*, 299–308; *Confessions of Faith*, 343–52.
[2] Whitelocke, IV. 342.
[3] Clar. S. P. III. 730.
[4] When they settled in Scotland, Lauderdale expected they might prove 'more dangerous than men are aware of.' *Lauderdale Papers*, II. 181, C. S.; cp. Grey's *Debates*, V. 290.
[5] In the crisis of the Dutch war, a Quaker walked about Westminster Hall, with a chafing-dish of fire and brimstone on his head, crying, 'Repent, Repent.' Pepys, July 29, 1667.
[6] 474, ed. 1849. Even their old enemies admitted that the sect had been reformed. Baxter, *Life*, 77; Henry More's *Discourse of Enthusiasm*, ed. 1712, 18–19. Cp. *Hudibras*, Part II. Canto II.
[7] C. S. P. 1660–1, 569; and Pepys, Oct. 13, 1660.
[8] Phillips' *Contin. of Baker's Chronicle*, 735.

the rebels, shouting the while, 'We are for King Jesus[1].' But the second revolt of Venner was suppressed as quickly as the first[2], and the Millenarianism of action disappears from English history[3].

The reign of unquestioning loyalty and satisfaction did not last long, and the cruel punishments of the regicides produced a revulsion of feeling. By the death of Vane it was considered that the king had 'lost more than he would get again a good while[4].' The words of the dying Peters were received with 'the same veneration as if they had been oracles[5].' Cromwell's memory was still 'idolised' by his old adherents[6]. The publication of 'seditious books' recommenced[7]. The Cavaliers themselves grew disenchanted[8], and Pepys spent whole afternoons discussing 'the unhappy posture of things[9].' The sale of Dunkirk added strength to the growing indignation. 'If the Dutch war be unsuccessful,' wrote the French ambassador in 1664, 'the memory of the victories which they won during the interregnum will be revived, and the difference will be assigned to the nature of the government. They may, indeed, very well care to try a republic again[10].'

[1] C. S. P. 1660–1, 470–1; *State Trials*, VI. 67–119.

[2] Pepys, Jan. 19, 1661, etc.

[3] Shaftesbury, however, recommended the king to except the Fifth Monarchy Men from toleration. Christie's *Shaftesbury*, II. App. 1. The Revolution of 1688 was taken by many to herald the approach of the Fifth Monarchy; but no outbreak took place. Evelyn, April 24, 1689.

[4] Pepys, June 14, 18, 22, 1662.

[5] Barwick's *Life of Barwick*, 296–9.

[6] Bethel's *World's Mistake in Oliver Cromwell, Tracts of C. II*, 366–74. Some old republicans who lived in Yorkshire revolted in 1663. Hunter's *Heywood*, 154–6; cp. Hist. MSS. Comm. *3rd Report*, 92.

[7] *State Trials*, V. 514–66.

[8] Cp. a remarkable song, 'The Cavalier's Complaint,' of 1661, *Political Ballads of the Commonwealth*, 257–65, Percy Society.

[9] May 5, 1663, etc.; cp. Clarendon's *Life*, I. 358.

[10] Cominges to Louis, May 5: 'Ils pourraient bien vouloir goûter une

The comparison with the days of the Protectorate was drawn even in the House of Lords[1], and the restoration of Richard Cromwell was mooted[2].

The discontent was so widespread that the exiles felt that the time for action had arrived[3]. The support of France and Holland was first to be obtained, and Sydney entered into negotiations with Louis. Though the French king had spoken with horror in 1662 of the mere supposition that his kingdom might be harbouring any of the regicides[4], he now entered warmly into the scheme. The Dutch fleet was to be invited to join the French in a descent on the English coast in order to encourage the malcontents to open revolt[5]. Charles was sufficiently alarmed to induce him to dispatch a band of assassins to seek for Sydney[6], and to send Mrs Aphra Behn, of unenviable notoriety, to Antwerp to learn their secrets[7]. The *Gazette* attributed the Fire to the republicans, regarding it as a signal for the outbreak of the Great Plot[8]. De Witt, however, refused to entertain the proposal of joining in the scheme, and with the conclusion of the peace of Breda the negotiations came to an end[9]. Both abroad and at home, however, the air continued to be thick with plots

---

deuxième fois de la république.' Jusserand's *Cominges*, 226. The opinion was shared by Sorbière, who visited England at this time. *Voyage en Angleterre*, 58, 130, ed. 1664. Cp. Bennet's Report, Lister's *Life of Clarendon*, III. 198.

[1] Buckingham's *Works*, I. 387–93, ed. 1715.

[2] C. S. P. 1665–6, 281, 340.

[3] The *State Papers* reveal the anxiety with which the Government had watched their movements from the very beginning of the reign.

[4] *Ambassades d'Estrades*, 1637–62, 242, ed. 1718.

[5] *Lettres d'Estrades*, 1663–8, II. 479–80, ed. 1709; cp. *Œuvres de Louis XIV*, II. 203.

[6] Ludlow, II. 382; cp. *Apology of A. Sydney*, 3.

[7] C. S. P. 1666–7, 44, 82, 145.   [8] Echard, 831–2.

[9] Some of the republicans had fought on the Dutch side. Arlington's *Letters*, I. 373.

and the rumours of plots. It was believed that orders had been sent by one of Cromwell's Justices of the Peace to the 'retired brethren' to hold themselves in readiness for a revolt[1]. The smallest disturbances were connected with far-reaching schemes of violence. When the apprentices rioted in the City, it was believed by many that they were the advanced guard of an army of Oliver's old officers and soldiers[2].

While in England discontent merely smouldered, in Scotland the exasperation produced by the atrocious cruelty of the administration was leading to an explosion. That obedience to the government was conditional on the performance of its duties had long been an axiom to the Scotch nation[3], and the cry was now raised that the rulers had failed to carry out their part of the contract. The most outspoken of the protests came from James Guthrie, who, in *The Causes of God's Wrath*[4], and in his speeches at his trial and on the scaffold[5], boldly maintained that the conduct of the government was such as to release its subjects from their debt of obedience. Even greater was the influence of *Naphtali*, which furnished a full account of the persecutions[6]. The government was frightened and pursued the work with the usual artillery of denunciation[7]. Undeterred by the storm he had aroused, one of the authors re-affirmed his position in *Jus*

[1] C. S. P. 1667–8, 270.

[2] *ib.* 306–10, 381. Even the existence of a small colony of the disbanded army in the Channel Isles was regarded with great apprehensions. C. S. P. 1670, 679, 682.

[3] It had been enforced in the sermon preached at the coronation of Charles II in Scotland, in 1651, the preacher, Douglas, little dreaming that the covert threat would so soon be put into practice. *Collection of Choice Tracts*, 1721, 234–61.

[4] See especially 52–9, ed. 1653.

[5] Wodrow's *Sufferings*, ed. 1837, I. 159–96.

[6] *Naphtali*, ed. 1845. A concise statement of principles occurs, 100–6.

[7] Wodrow, II. 100; and *Lauderdale Papers*, II. 88, C. S.

Populi Vindicatum. Since the *Lex Rex* of Rutherford, no such remarkable work had appeared in Scotland. It reviewed again the entire field of the theory of democracy. The basis of opposition lay in the 'law and light of Nature' to defend oneself against violence. What beasts may do men may do[1]. But further, as matter of history, despotism has no claim. When men are free and equal, they do not elect to change their condition for the worse. They choose what government they like, and reserve the power to alter it when they will[2]. The very conception of magistracy involves conditions. If the ruler break all or even the main conditions he becomes no prince and may be resisted, even by private persons[3]. To repeat that the primitive Christians did not resist tyranny is irrelevant, for different circumstances necessitate different conduct[4]. The entire work is eminently remarkable no less for its unreservedly democratic character than for its purely secular spirit. The doctrines of resistance spread to the body of the people, and the Cameronians in sending forth their *Declaration of Sanquhar* placed the deposition of the king in the forefront of their programme[5]. It was common to hear it said that it had become lawful to kill the king[6].

Far less radical was the principal literary champion of the opposition in England. Though a friend of many of the republicans, Andrew Marvell had remained throughout the Interregnum an adherent of the principle of monarchy[7]. He regarded Charles I as a good king[8], and spoke of the Restoration as a happy event[9].

---

[1] Ed. 1669, 40–6.   [2] 80–94.
[3] 95–144.   [4] 294–305.
[5] Wodrow, III. 212–13.
[6] Skene's Case, *State Trials*, VIII. 123. Carstairs was closely connected with the Whig Plots of the time. Story's *Carstairs, passim.*
[7] Poem on the death of the historian May, etc.
[8] *Growth of arbitrary government, Works*, ed. Grosart, IV. 385.
[9] *Rehearsal Transposed*, III. 212.

But the Restoration brought a danger of its own. To substitute a Commonwealth for the Monarchy was admittedly treason; but to make the Monarchy absolute was no less a crime[1].

The political writings of Sir William Temple reveal in an interesting manner the compromise which royalists found it necessary to make between the old doctrines and the new. As Burnet's charges of republicanism were scattered indiscriminately, we need not accept his account of Temple's views[2]; but that they were strongly impregnated with liberal thought is beyond doubt[3]. He was not ashamed to own his acquaintance with Sydney and his regret at his exile[4]. He made no secret of his belief that the progress of wealth and civilisation made men 'harder to be subjected,' and that 'conversation sharpened men's intellects and made too many reasoners in matters of government[5]. Though unwilling to accept the notion of a Social Contract as the origin of government, he readily admits that 'contract governments soon followed[6].' Further, though condemning the atomistic nature of the Dutch system[7], and the constant flux of *Oceana*[8], he borrows perhaps the most far-reaching suggestion of Harrington, and declares that the only remedy for the degeneration of the nobility and gentry is to limit the accumulation of wealth[9]. But the time of moderate men on both sides was drawing to a close.

[1] *Works*, IV. 248–61, etc.   [2] Burnet, II. 60–1.
[3] His biographer admits that some of his suggestions might have been ascribed to a leaning to republicanism. Courtenay's *Temple*, I. 382–3.
[4] *Works*, I. 265.   [5] *The Original and Nature of Government*, I. 4–5.
[6] *ib.* 9–18.
[7] *Observations on the United Provinces*, ch. 2, *Works*, vol. I.
[8] *Popular Discontents*, III. 36.   [9] *ib.* 59–60.

II

The discovery of the Popish Plot in 1678 ushered in a new period of protracted struggle. Driven by their inability successfully to combat the danger to the national religion by ordinary methods, the Whig leaders found themselves obliged to assume the power of the people to alter the succession. The spirit which animated the movement is seen in the writings of Samuel Johnson, Dryden's *Ben Jochanan*, whose support was of special value owing to his being a clergyman of the Church of England. The chaplain of Lord Russell[1] expounded a frankly Whig theory of government. Christianity had no special teaching in connection with politics. St Paul had said nothing about tyrants, and the law of the land was the best exposition of the 13th chapter of *Romans*[2]. Men were naturally free and could be bound only by their own act and deed. The king existed simply in order to protect the people, and Parliament must share in the work[3]. Resistance for the safeguarding of religion was as lawful now as in the time of Julian[4].

From the beginning of the Exclusion controversy the gravity of the crisis was foreseen, and intentions were attributed to the Whigs to attack the institution of Monarchy itself. 'Believe me,' wrote James to the Prince of Orange, 'it is republicanism which is at the bottom of all these affairs in England, and not

---

[1] See Lady Russell's *Letters*, vol. II.

[2] *Reflections on the History of Passive Obedience, Works*, ed. 1713, 253; cp. *Of Magistracy*, chs. 2 and 3.

[3] *Parliaments at a certainty*, 277–90; *Letter from a Freeholder*, 208.

[4] *Julian the Apostate*. Although published at various times, the crisis of 1678–81 forms the central point of Johnson's writings. Coleridge's high eulogy of this thinker will be remembered. *Table Talk*, May 15, 1833.

religion¹.' Shaftesbury, declared the duke, had been a republican
from 1673². Since, however, opposition to the Court was con-
founded with republicanism³, this does not prove anything very
definite; yet the opinion was widely held. Barillon thought that
the Whig leader might be playing a still deeper game. 'Perhaps
his principal end is to endeavour the establishment of a republic
of which he would aim at being chief⁴.' The first article of the
impeachment attributed to him anti-monarchical principles⁵, and
the accusation was supported by the genius of the Court poet⁶.

On the other hand, neither Shaftesbury nor his followers
admitted any other design than that of securing the maintenance
of the Protestant religion⁷. Though certain of the members of
the Oxford Parliament may have been republicans⁸, the spokesmen of the opposition cannot fairly be charged with republicanism.
Even Slingsby Bethel, labelled by Burnet 'a known republican⁹,'

¹ *Archives de la maison d'Orange*, v. 437–8. Cp. Grey's *Debates*, VII. 251,
405; VIII. 329, etc.
² Clarke's *Life of James II*, I. 488.
³ 'When I had the ill-luck,' said Bennet in 1678, 'to displease the Court,
they said, "There goes a rogue; he is for a Commonwealth."' Grey's *Debates*,
VI. 256. Cp. the charge against Osborne of 'saying that a Commonwealth is
the best government and that kings may be as safely destroyed as preserved,'
Hist. MSS. Comm. *9th Report*, 75, with the very moderate section 'Government'
in the *Advice to a Son*. North's remarks on the Coffee-houses must be understood in the same way. *Life of the Lord Keeper*, § 226.
⁴ Dalrymple, I. 341.
⁵ *State Trials*, VIII. 55. Cp. *Our Anti-monarchical Authors*, 737–8, ed. 1699.
⁶   'Others thought kings an useless, heavy load,
          Who cost too much and did too little good;
          They were for laying honest David by,
          On principles of pure good husbandry.'
Absalom and Achitophel. Cp. above all *The Medal*, with preface.
⁷ The great Whig manifesto, *The Vindication of the last two Parliaments*,
State Tracts of C. II, I. 165–87, indignantly disclaims the charge of
republicanism.
⁸ Cp. Ferguson's *Life of Ferguson*, 72.   ⁹ II. 242.

in publishing his *Interest of Kings and Princes,* allowed no hint of commonwealth principles to escape him[1]; and when he was rumoured to have said that he would have executed Charles I himself 'if none other had been willing,' he sued the author of the report for slander[2].

With the dissolution of Charles' fifth Parliament and the flight of Shaftesbury, what had been almost exclusively a Whig movement comes to an end. The country was once more in a loyal mood, and the king's refusal to call another Parliament left the Whigs powerless to oppose the Crown constitutionally. But it is at this point that a new set of thinkers and actors makes its appearance. Such a crisis as that which had suddenly come to an end could not fail to leave a prolonged discussion of the principles involved behind it. The official declarations of such royalists as Jenkins[3] and Nalson[4] being reinforced by the publication of Filmer's *Patriarcha,* and the reprinting of Overall's *Convocation-book* and other anti-democratic works, writers to whom liberal and republican principles were of value began to arm themselves for the struggle. Among those who fought with their pen were two survivors from the stirring times that preceded the Restoration.

After the dispersion of the Rota Club and the mental aberration of its founder, Harringtonianism had almost disappeared for many years, though we can trace its influence in Locke's *Constitution of Carolina* and in the *Popular Discontents* of Sir William Temple[5]. But the crisis called from their hiding place such of his followers

[1] He confines himself to a desire for greater freedom in trade and religion; but he strongly approves the Venetian constitution, 219–29, ed. 1680.

[2] Luttrell's *Diary,* I. 187.

[3] Wynne's *Jenkins,* I. 99–104, etc. Speeches on Exclusion Bill.

[4] *The Common Interest of King and People,* 1677. [On this and similar books cp. J. N. Figgis, *The Divine Right of Kings,* chs. VIII. and IX., and Appendix B. H. J. L.]

[5] *Works,* III. 29–65.

as still remained alive[1]. Nevile, the chief of them, who had lived on unobserved, came forward with a re-statement of his master's principles which evidently secured a good deal of attention, and which it was thought worth while to examine at length twenty years later[2]. It is characteristic that his creed should be put into the mouth of a noble Venetian on a visit to England; and the opportunity which this affords for the Englishman in the dialogue to eulogise the Constitution of the republic is naturally seized. There is, in fact, as the preface warns us to expect, a great deal of the *Oceana* in the book. He accepts Hobbes' account of the state of nature, but argues that by the social compact individuals consented to be debarred of but a part of their hitherto universal right. The discussion of the Venetian constitution is also of some interest. Had not strangers flocked in, it would have been a democracy[3]. Had the State, too, dreamed of conquests, it would have necessitated some form of popular government. But since the desire of the citizens was rather to preserve their wealth, they pitched on aristocracy. If, on the other hand, they had allowed their Doge or any other magistrate a negative voice, they would have been unable to call themselves a free people[4].

Of far greater importance was a second champion of democracy. When Sydney revisited England in 1677 to witness his father's death, he had found everything quiet, and told Furly that nothing was left but to return to the continent[5]. A longer residence soon convinced him that the country was less tranquil than he had thought, and he determined to re-enter public life. A similar resolution had been forced on the second founder of Quakerism,

---

[1] One of them contended that freedom was impossible without the ballot. *The Benefit of the Ballot, Tracts of C. II,* i. 443–7.
[2] *Remarks on Anti-monarchical Authors,* 145–350.
[3] *Plato Redivivus,* ed. 1681, 24–79.   [4] 122.
[5] *Furly Corresp.* 80.

and for some time Sydney is closely linked with Penn. Three
years previously, the son of the great admiral of the Commonwealth had come forward with a vigorous statement of the
delegation theory of Parliament[1]. He now warned his countrymen
to choose wisely in the forthcoming elections; 'for, to be plain
with you, all is at stake[2].' To give a practical illustration of his
meaning he supported the candidature of his friend in his two
successful contests, and took such a prominent part that he was
represented by Barillon as joint leader of the popular party[3].
Sydney's elections, however, were cancelled and the Court party
was victorious.

Penn withdrew in disgust from English politics, and sought
relief from his discouragement in elaborating a constitution for
his new province. It was now Sydney's turn to lend assistance.
Penn shewed the outlines of his scheme to his friend, and Sydney
took the draft back with him to Penshurst. The respective shares
of the two authors in the Constitution of Pennsylvania may
therefore be presumed to have been about equal. The sovereign
power was to reside in the governor and freemen of the colony[4].
Two legislative chambers, a council and an assembly, were to be
elected by universal suffrage. The members of the council were
chosen for three years, twenty-four of the members retiring each
year; those of the assembly for one year. The country was to be
divided into constituencies according to the population, and votes
to be taken by ballot. No religion was to be established, and all
opinions were allowed which did not interfere with social order.
Every man of twenty-one, unconvicted of crime, could elect and
be elected. All trials were to be conducted by jury. Education

[1] *Works*, ed. 1723, I. 683-4, etc.
[2] *The Choice of a new Parliament*, II. 678-82.
[3] Dalrymple, I. 282.   [4] Ewald's *Sydney*, II. 197-200.

was to be cheap, and facilities for its attainment to be secured. The fees of lawyers were to be reduced and fixed. Not the least remarkable feature of the system was the suggestion of various laws which should remain in force only till the council had been elected.

Foiled in his efforts to enter Parliament Sydney set himself to cope by a different method with the recrudescence of absolutist teaching. The *Discourses on Government* suffer from the same disadvantage which besets *The Religion of Protestants*. The exposition of the author's thought is obscured and retarded by a multitude of petty controversies which have lost their importance and to a great extent their interest. The more successful it was as a polemic, the less can it pretend to the title of a philosophical treatise.

Society, declares Sydney, owes its foundation either to consent or to force; but if to the latter, it cannot properly be called society. Its object is primarily to guarantee the liberty to which man has a natural love, tempered and guarded by reason[1]. The prince elect enters into a treaty before he becomes fully prince. Rulers may be deposed for misgovernment or if they differ in religion from the majority of their subjects[2]. Passing from the general principles of the relations of the governor and the governed, in which Sydney occupies common ground, he proceeds to manifest distinctly aristocratic preferences. 'As to popular government in the strictest sense, that is, pure democracy, where the people by themselves perform all that belongs to government, I know of no such thing[3].' The people, though *de jure* sovereign, are subject to the ruling of their representatives in all but extreme cases. Democracy,

---

[1] Sydney's *Works*, ed. 1772, 162–5.

[2] 94–7. Deposed but not executed. He opposed the death of Charles I. Blencowe's *Sydney Papers*, 233–40.

[3] 147, 160.

however, in the sense in which the liberty of the individual is the least restrained, and where the people retain the supreme power, is the most just and natural of forms[1]. There is, indeed, an almost infinite variety of choice between mere democracy and absolute monarchy; but any good form of government must have a monarchical element. Changes are inevitable, but good governments admit of changes in the superstructure while the foundations remain unchangeable[2].

Such is the outline of a system by no means remarkable for originality and interest, and disfigured by fundamental confusions of thought. The people are sovereign; but in every state an arbitrary power exists, and in England it is the Parliament. The author hastens to add that it is only arbitrary within certain limits, and unjust laws are not to be recognised as laws at all. The chief merit of the system lies in its method. Burnet declares that Sydney had studied the history of government beyond any man he ever knew[3], and indeed we hear far more of the historical sanction than of the law of nature. The keynote of the attack on absolutism is the coincidence of the teaching of facts and instincts.

So far from being, in the words of Burnet, 'stiff to all republican principles and an enemy to everything that looked like monarchy[4],' the Sydney of the Restoration is, strictly, not a republican at all. Temple remarked to Lord Dartmouth that one passage of the *Discourses* explained the whole. If there was such a thing as Divine Right, Sydney had written, it was where one man was better qualified to govern others than they to govern themselves. 'Now I assure you,' said Temple, 'he looked on himself as that very man so qualified to govern the rest of mankind[5].' In his *Apology* he declared

---

[1] 163, 258. [2] 142–6. [3] *Own Time*, ii. 344. [4] *ib*. ii. 344.
[5] Dartmouth's note to Burnet, ii. 341. The mysterious sentence in his description of his conduct at the time of the king's death, 'I had an intention

that he had from his youth upward merely endeavoured to uphold 'the common rights of mankind and the laws of the land[1].' If the earlier Sydney belongs to the first revolution, the later belongs to the second. He forms the transition between the thinkers of the Interregnum and Locke.

In addition to the publicists there was a considerable number of men who had not forgotten the trade of arms[2]. Walcot and Ferguson, old Cromwellian officers, Rumbold, who had stood on the scaffold of Charles I, Major Holmes, a Fifth Monarchy man and a personal friend of the Protector, Wildman, the indefatigable Leveller, emerged from their long obscurity[3]. Little groups of the Cromwellian army signified their readiness to bear arms[4]. Though Essex and Russell were nothing more than constitutional democrats[5], to the majority of the Rye House conspirators the goal of the enterprise was the re-establishment of a Commonwealth[6]. At the trials, however, there was a general indisposition to make a definite declaration of republican principles. Rumbold, for instance, regarded kingly government as the best 'when justly executed with the aid of Parliament[7]'; but he was sure that 'there was no man born marked of God

which is not very fit for a letter,' Blencowe's *Sydney Papers*, 240, is too slight a basis for any supposition. [Sydney's eulogy of the man fitted by capacity to rule is nothing more than the general Platonism which comes out in many parts of his book. H. J. L.]

[1] *Apology*, 3.
[2] Cp. the interesting account of old Captain Marshal in Dunton's *Life and Errors*, I. 126.
[3] The fullest catalogue in Bishop Sprat's *Rye House Plot*, ed. 1685, 20–8.
[4] North's *Examen*, 389.
[5] Confession in Russell's *Life of Russell*, 338–56. Cp. Lord Grey's *Secret History of the Rye House Plot*, 23, ed. 1754.
[6] Ferguson's account is printed in the *Life of Ferguson*, 409–37. Cp. Hist. MSS. Comm. *7th Report*, 363–8.
[7] Ralph, *Hist.* I. 872, Scaffold Speech.

above another, for none came into the world with a saddle on
his back, neither any booted and spurred to ride him[1].' From
the prosecutions for sedition we can tell little; but we may
safely infer that their number at this time points, if not to the
fact of a wide acceptance of republican principles, at least to the
prevalence of a body of very advanced ideas[2].

With Russell and Sydney dead[3] and the Cromwellians dispersed,
with the condemnation by the University of Oxford[4] of 'every
principle on which the constitution of this or any other free
country can maintain itself[5],' it might well seem that the cause
of liberty was dead. The mood of the time is revealed in the
semi-official *Jus Regium* of Sir George Mackenzie, an unusually
violent statement of the royalist theory, fitly dedicated to the
University of Oxford. The adherents of limited monarchy are
denounced as republican[6], and resistance to a tyrant is justified
only when he is an usurper[7], an article inserted to meet the objection that the royalists rebelled against the yoke of the Protector.
The accession of a professing Catholic, however, put a new face
on affairs. In the Monmouth movement there were two parties,
the one desiring to set the Duke on the throne, the other to use
him as a cloak for republican designs[8]. A considerable number
of his adherents joined him on the assumption that he would of
his own will set up a republic as soon as victory was won[9].

While the memories of the rising were still fresh, Thomas Hunt,
an old churchman and royalist, declared that if the royal line

[1] *State Trials*, XI. 873–81.
[2] Cp. Luttrell's *Diary*, ed. I. e.g. 109, 292, 323, etc.; *Memoirs* of Papillon,
186–7, etc.
[3] Hampden turned apostate. *State Trials*, XI. 479–94.
[4] *Tracts of Charles II.*   [5] Fox.
[6] Ed. 1684, 43.   [7] 24.
[8] *Letters of James*, Dalrymple, II. 53.
[9] Wade's Information, *Hardwick S. P.* II. 323.

became extinct the people might make a new king on any conditions they pleased, or make none if they thought best, since
the polity was not destroyed if no king was created[1]. The chief
factor in the declining vogue of absolutist ideas was the conduct of
the king, yet the Revolution was Whig and not Republican.
There is no evidence that anybody proposed that the monarchy
should come to an end. In Evelyn's classification of parties the
most extreme are 'the republicans who would make the Prince
of Orange like a Stadtholder[2]'; and of these there seems to have
been but one literary champion. The government was to be
carried on by a Grand Committee of Lords and Commons,
consisting of at least forty of each, of whom half were to be
elected for life and half for two years. The Prince of Orange or
his deputy was to preside and to have at least ten votes[3]. A few
days later, the author, finding his suggestions neglected, felt
moved to advise his fellow-countrymen before it was too late[4].
He urged once more that they had a golden opportunity, bringing
as they did the crown in one hand and their terms in the other.
To surrender the negative voice in such circumstances would
be base treachery. Frequent mention was made in the debates
of the French and Dutch jurists who had authorised the people
to look after their own safety; but no republican sentiment is
reported and no republican writer is cited[5].

Indeed it was a commonplace of oratory to assert that England
could never become a Commonwealth[6]. If we turn to the great
collection of tracts which the revolution produced we find the
same phenomenon. The Social Contract theory is deemed a

[1] *Apology for the Government of England,* 1686, 43.
[2] Jan. 15, 1689.   [3] *Somers Tracts,* x. 197.
[4] *Good Advice before it is too late, Somers Tracts,* x. 199–202.
[5] Somers' Notes, *Hardwick S. P.* II. 401, 25.
[6] Grey's *Debates,* IX. 238, 240, etc.

sufficient weapon both of offence and defence. 'The extent of the magistrate's power owes its original to the grant of the people; and what he cannot derive from some such concessions remains still invested in the people. But to dream of reducing England to a democratic republic is incident only to persons of shallow capacities; for the mercurial temper of the English people is not to be accommodated to a democracy[1].' Even Major Wildman was willing to nominate William and Mary, 'to prevent anarchy[2].' A Harringtonian confines himself to inculcating the necessity of the ballot and rotation[3]. The temper of the time was revealed at the return of Ludlow. Instead of finding himself the object of reverence and attention, he was met by the request of Parliament to the king to issue a proclamation of reward for his arrest, as 'attainted for high treason for the murder of Charles I'; to which the king replied that the desire was so reasonable that he had pleasure in granting it. Nobody desired or at least dared to say a word in his defence[4]. Ludlow had lived into an age in which there was no place for him, an age that was Whig, not Republican.

The philosophical basis on which Whiggism was to rest was two-fold. There was the old theory of natural right, implied in the notion of the social contract, and there was the new doctrine which approached the philosophy of politics without assumptions. Of these two positions the most illustrious representatives were Locke and Halifax. In Locke we see the struggle of first principles with the promptings of the sense of practical requirements[5].

---

[1] *Brief Justification of William's descent, State Tracts of W. III*, I. 141.
[2] Grey's *Debates*, III. 70.
[3] *Tracts of W. III*, I. 149–62. [4] *C. J.* X. 280, 282.
[5] [On Locke's political ideas see Sir F. Pollock's *Essays in Law*; H. J. Laski, *Political Thought from Locke to Bentham*, ch. II.; G. P. Lamprecht, *The Moral and Political Philosophy of Locke*. Locke is hardly less a Utilitarian than Halifax. H. J. L.]

G

Having drunk deep at the well of natural right, he has to throw consistency to the winds in addressing an age in which appeals to it had largely gone out of fashion. Men are born free and equal, and the individual may choose his own government and country; for subjection rests on consent, and nobody can be said to be born a member of any particular society. This logic leads straight to anarchy, and the theory is patched up by the assumption of a tacit consent to submit to the form of government established by the majority, provided it be not absolute monarchy. What, in the next place, is the relation of society as a whole to the government? The community retains the supreme authority, in abeyance indeed while its fiduciary faithfully executes the duties entrusted to it, chief among them the preservation of property, but ever ready to intervene when the trust is misused or betrayed[1]. Locke thus added the weight of his great name to that form of the theory of contract which alone is logically compatible with liberty[2].

The notion of a social contract had taken three distinct forms. With the Huguenots and Buchanan it retained the influence of its origin in the Bible, in Roman law and in the theory of Feudalism. The compact was between subjects and their rulers. In another form of the theory, introduced into England by Hooker, the compact was between the members of a group. As developed by Hobbes, the individuals parted irrecoverably with the whole of their rights to the sovereign they elected. As interpreted by the thinkers of the Interregnum and by Locke, the

[1] It is worth noting that Locke with a view of minimising the probability of such a betrayal insisted on Parliamentary Reform and the periodical redistribution of seats. *Second Essay on Civil Government*, § 157.

[2] I speak only of the different forms of belief in the contract as an historical fact. The interpretation outlined by Kant and Fichte and in our own day by Fouillée and others could not appear till the historical basis was given up.

community retained the supreme power in their own hands. The executive is the agent of the legislature, and the legislature the delegate of the people. They refuse to be like the recruit in battle who, fearing to be hit by the gun of the enemy, shoots himself with his own[1]. What they had really done by the social contract was simply to cease to share directly in the common affairs of government. The legislature is practically supreme for the period of its election, but it is never strictly sovereign. Nothing, commented the critics, could be more vague and therefore more dangerous. The reply to the indictment does not consist in a logical defence of the position, but in an appeal to experience. As a matter of fact, mixed governments do exist without involving anarchy. The sovereignty of the people is compatible with social order, owing to the existence of that fact of supreme importance, the inertia of mankind[2].

Far different is it with Halifax, the first Utilitarian in the history of English political thinkers[3]. His opposition to the Exclusion Bill had nothing in common with that of the royalists with whom for the moment he found himself acting in agreement, and he privately explained to the Whig leaders that his position was in effect the more liberal of the two, since the terms on which he proposed to allow James to succeed to the throne really amounted to republican government[4]. So clearly was this aspect of his thought seized that he was sometimes considered as a republican[5]. The truth was that Halifax occupied a position different from that of any other thinker of the age. In his system there were no fundamentals except the axiom that every supreme

[1] Bluntschli.
[2] See above all the admirable passage in the *Second Essay*, § 168.
[3] [See Foxcroft, *Life and Letters of Halifax*. Sir Walter Raleigh has reprinted the chief political works with an Introduction. H. J. L.]
[4] Burnet, II. 201.   [5] Burnet, I. 405; cp. Ralph, I. 637–8.

power is arbitrary. '*Salus Populi* comes nearest to a fundamental, but is not altogether immoveable,' while property is only an innovation sanctioned by time[1]. The idea of an historical contract is a superstition. The excellence of forms of government depends on their adaptation to circumstances. The Trimmer 'owns a passion for liberty[2],' and believes that, as Victor Hugo once said, republics are crowns for white hairs. 'A Commonwealth is not fit for us because we are not fit for a Commonwealth[3].' 'Monarchy is preferred by the people for the bells and tinsel; there must be milk for babes since the greatest part of mankind are and ever will be included in that lot[4].' To this he returns again and again. 'The people are generally so dead they cannot move, or so mad they cannot be restrained; to be neither quite cold nor all in a flame requireth more reason than great numbers can ever attain[5].' At times the tone is openly cynical. 'The lower sort of men must be indulged in the consolation of finding fault with those above them[6].' Principles of legislation there are none. 'All laws flow from that of nature; but by this nature is not meant that which fools and madmen misquote to justify their excesses[7].' We are clearly in a new generation of thought.

III

It is a difficult question how far the republican tradition continued after 1688. It remained fashionable for Tories to describe their opponents as republicans, but they were never at pains to produce any evidence of the assertion[8]. When the king

---

[1] *Political Thoughts and Reflections*, ed. 1750, *Fundamentals*, 63–77.
[2] *Miscellanies*, 1700, *Trimmer*, 22.
[3] *ib. Draft of a New Model at Sea*, 13.   [4] *Trimmer*, 9.
[5] *Thoughts*, 'The People,' 86–9.   [6] *ib.*   [7] *Trimmer*, 2.
[8] *Tracts of W. III*, III. 259; *Somers Tracts*, XII. 662, etc.

excused himself to Sunderland for not employing the Whigs more by declaring that they did not love monarchy, he meant nothing more than that they were by no means submissive to his will[1]. On the other hand we read, for example, in a letter of Hoffmann to the Electress Sophia, that the Lower House was so far gone on the way to a republic that, after the death of the king and queen, the monarchy would have difficulty in upholding itself, even if it did not fall with the king[2]. Burnet declares that some members of his own party had 'republican notions[3].' There can be no doubt, however, of the decline of the republican party and ideas. Writing at this time, Rapin declares that the number of republicans was small, and declining every day[4]. Whig writers declared that the country must always remain monarchical, the Interregnum having destroyed the chances of any other form of government[5]. It was asserted that the statement that a third party was constituted by Commonwealthsmen had no meaning[6]. Halifax, a trustworthy witness, declared in 1694 that although he could not pronounce a Commonwealth to be impossible, 'he gave it as his humble opinion that it was very improbable. Instead of a leaning to it, there is a general dislike to it[7].'

The most remarkable sign of the disappearance of republicanism is found in the so-called republican party itself. In the last years of the century Toland collected the works of three of the great

---

[1] Burnet, IV. 5, Onslow's note.

[2] Klopp, *Der Fall des Hauses Stuart*, IV. 483–4. [Hoffmann's letter merely represents the inability of the foreign observer, like Sorbière in the previous generation, to understand the violence of English party conflict. H. J. L.]

[3] *Own Time*, IV. 23.

[4] Tract on *The Government of England*, in Ker's *Memoirs*, II. 154. It would be interesting to know who was the author of the remarkable vindication of Cromwell against Ludlow, printed in the *Somers Tracts*.

[5] *Tracts of Will. III*, II. 268, 9; cp. *Memoirs* of Papillon, 375, 6.

[6] *State of Parties*, *ib.* II. 208.

[7] *Draft of a New Model at Sea*, 10–13.

thinkers of the last generation and wrote appreciative biographies. The political works of Milton had of course seen the light before; but they had been to a great extent forgotten, and the notices of him that appeared dwelt upon his poetry alone[1]. Sydney's *Discourses on Government* were published for the first time, and their appearance was justified on the ground that it was necessary for nations to be well-informed of their rights[2]. In 1699 Toland collected most of the published works of Harrington, explaining that, though he regarded Harrington as the greatest commonwealthsman in the world, he had written his history without being answerable for his opinions[3]. Those, however, once invidiously nicknamed commonwealthsmen were by this time sufficiently cleared of that imputation by their actions; for they 'not only unanimously concurred to fix the crown on the most deserving head in the universe, but also settled the monarchy for the future, not as if they intended soon to bring it to a period, but under such wise regulations as are most likely to continue it for ever[4].'

That these sentiments were not professed merely to shield himself from odium Toland proceeded to prove by repeating them in a separate work. Speaking on behalf of his party the author of *Anglia Libera* lays down its position with perfect clearness. 'Liberty under any form was the only thing they aimed to obtain. They have now eternally secured and fixed that which they more than once began to despair of seeing in this nation, the cause of Liberty. They will pay all good kings not only obedience but honour[5].' So far from the Whigs being Republicans, the Republicans had become Whigs. When Toland, so courageous

---

[1] Godwin, *Lives of Edward and John Philips*, 282–97, collects the testimonies throughout the period.

[2] *Discourses*, ed. 1698, Preface.

[3] Cp. *Amyntor*, ed. 1699, 159, etc.   [4] Preface, ed. 1699.

[5] *Anglia Libera*, ed. 1701, 87–93.

in maintaining unfashionable opinions and so enthusiastic a student of the great teachers of the past generation, confessed that his party had nothing to ask which the Whigs did not give, it is evident that republicanism is at an end. This does not mean to say that charges of republicanism came to an end. The Calves' Head Club, for instance, appears very frequently in controversial literature between the Revolution and the death of Anne. Stories were current that it had been instituted by Milton, and songs supposed to be received with applause at its convivial gatherings were printed[1]. Its very existence, however, was denied by the Whigs. Whatever the value of this denial, the charge brought against the Dissenting academies of educating their pupils in republican principles[2] was altogether without foundation[3].

If we turn to Scotland, we find a similar state of things. It was needless for the Scotch to justify what they had had no share in effecting, and the Revolution passes without leaving any trace in the literature of politics. It is not, indeed, till some years later that the one genuine thinker of the time appears. Fletcher of Saltoun, almost exclusively known as an opponent of the Union, is equally deserving of study for his contributions to political thinking. A great traveller, and, in the words of Lockhart, 'a great admirer of ancient and modern republics[4],' Fletcher inclines to a species of aristocratic rule that recalls the proposals of Milton. It being impossible to safeguard liberty even in a constitutional monarchy, it was necessary to remove everything but the insignia of royalty[5]. Nor would this be an innovation; for until the

---

[1] *Secret History of the Calves' Head Club, Harl. Misc.* VI. 596–605.
[2] South's *Sermons*, III. 409–10, etc.
[3] De Foe's *Answer to Samuel Wesley*, in the *Genuine Works*. Denunciations of republicanism occur frequently in the volumes of the *Review*.
[4] *Memoirs*, 60; cp. Burnet, 'a violent republican,' III. 24.
[5] Speeches of 1703, *Works*, ed. 1737, 203–6.

intrusion of the principles of Divine Right, no monarchy was more limited. That the true principles of government should be once more implanted it was necessary to remodel the system of education, substituting for the ordinary curriculum moral and civil knowledge[1]. In Fletcher's specific proposals we seem to find traces of the influence of Aristotle, the governing classes being designed to repose on a basis of state-organised serfdom[2].

In England, at the opening of the new century, the preposterous behaviour of Parliament in connection with the Kentish Petition brought to light much discontent with the prevailing Whig theory of the relation of Parliament to the people. A series of pamphlets pointed out that members of Parliament were primarily delegates[3], and the more far-sighted proposed to take practical measures for securing their end by the establishment of annual Parliaments[4]. Traces, too, of republican sympathies are still to be met with. The new edition of Harrington was a good deal circulated[5], and Sydney was still widely read[6]. Lord Spencer professed himself a disciple of Fletcher and made the collecting of similar political works the main business of his life[7]. Even the University of Oxford had to expel one of her members for anti-monarchical principles[8].

If in relation to the people the Whigs were not very democratic, towards the crown their attitude was independent. The revival of absolutist teaching from pulpits and elsewhere[9] con-

[1] *Right and Regulation of Governments*, 379.
[2] *First Discourse of Scotch Affairs*, 108.
[3] *Tracts of Will. III, Jura Populi Anglicani, The Claims of the People*, etc.
[4] *Tracts of Will. III*, 289–94. Cp. *Legion Memorial, Parl. Hist.* V. 1252–6.
[5] *Furly Corresp.* 105; *Corresp. de Leibnitz avec l'Electrice*, II. 208–10.
[6] Locke's *Thoughts concerning Reading and Study*, 1703.
[7] Cunningham, I. 201.
[8] Hearne's *Collections*, I. 85. Cp. Swift's 35th and 39th *Examiner*.
[9] It was at this time that Sprat obliterated that part of the epitaph of

sequent on the accession of Anne called for some response. Of the more liberal side of the Whig doctrine Sir James Tyrrel may be taken as the representative. Unlike several of his predecessors, who in defending their party from the charge of republicanism thought it necessary to declare decidedly that monarchy was the best form of government, Tyrrel never fears to record his conviction of the superiority of certain aspects of a republican system[1]. A monarchy, however, is satisfactory enough if certain principles are well understood. Tyrants may be driven out, and foreign help may be obtained if needful; for it is no alleviation to the subjects' misery to be told that their prince will be damned in another world. A long civil war itself is not so bad as slavish submission, which has been provided against by the Social Contract[2]. Once let these axioms be generally accepted, and there will be no need to give practical demonstration of them[3]. Further than this the Whigs did not go, and the reports that Tories endeavoured to make the Court of Hanover accept, when the death of the queen came within sight, had no more truth in them at this time than before[4]. Indeed it is from the Tories that the few democratic proposals,—of questionable sincerity though they were,—to which the time gave birth proceeded, for Wyndham and the High Church party contended for annual Parliaments and the ballot. In the tremendous struggle of the latter part of

Phillips that contained the hated name of Milton. Stanley's *Westminster Abbey*, 262.

[1] *Bibl. Politica*, ed. 1710, *Dialogue* II.

[2] 733-9.   [3] *Dialogue* XIV.

[4] Macpherson's *State Papers*, Strafford to Sophia, II. 344-51. Cp. an ironical pamphlet of 1712, *Vindication of Cromwell and the Whigs of* 1641: 'Our present Whigs as far surpass their fathers in everything but success, as their fathers everyone before them....Must we always have 1641 hanging over us?' p. 12. Leibnitz was brought to believe in a republican party. *Correspondance avec l'Electrice*, II. 218-19, 333-4.

Anne's reign only one writer is found to plead the cause of Commonwealth principles, and this solitary advocate seems to base his hostility to monarchy chiefly on the unworthy character of its representatives[1].

With the accession of the House of Hanover the chronicle of democratic thinking in England becomes silent for half a century. But we may find the influence of the speculation that had now ceased in the cool attitude assumed towards the Monarchy. Whig principles became dominant both in the theory and practice of the Constitution. That divinity no longer hedged a king may be seen in the writings of Gordon, the brightest of the pamphleteers of the decade succeeding the retirement of Swift[2]. In the following generation efforts were made by Ralph and Mrs Macaulay in their able narratives to do justice to the popular party of the seventeenth century. About the same time the works of Milton and Harrington, of Sydney and Nevile found enthusiastic editors, and Hollis spent the greater part of his useful life in ensuring the circulation of the works of his beloved republicans[3]. Horace Walpole, Baron, Dyson, Earl Stanhope, Lord Clare, Lord Sandys and others professed themselves, at least during part of their life, adherents of the republican idea[4]. Even Hume, though he had no wish to see a republic in England, was a convinced republican in theory[5]. During the seventy years of

[1] *A Cat may look at a King, Somers Tracts*, XIII. 509–21.

[2] Gordon's *Tracts*, especially *Dissertation on Old Women*, and *Character of an Independent Whig*, in vol. I. Cp. Hist. MSS. Comm. *2nd Report*, 112.

[3] Blackburne's *Hollis, passim*; Nichols' *Literary Anecdotes*, III.; Ralph's Preface to his edition of Sydney, etc.

[4] Horace Walpole's *Memoirs of George II*, I. 116, 376–8; Forster's *Goldsmith*, II. 204; Wilkes' *North Briton*, No. 33; Cartwright's *Works*.

[5] 'The republican form of Government is by far the best.' Burton's *Hume*, II. 480–1. Cp. Rousseau's judgment, 'Il avait une âme très républicaine.' *Confessions*, Livre XII. His 38*th Essay* contains his Idea of a Perfect

Tory domination which preceded the Reform Bill, the democratic tradition was carried on by Priestley and Price, by the societies that owed their existence to the revolt of the American colonies, and by the writers who drew their inspiration from the French Revolution.

IV

Fully to estimate the importance of the English thinkers of the seventeenth century in the subsequent history of political thought, and, indeed, we may say in the history of the world, we must briefly glance at their influence in the two countries which in the eighteenth century, in respect to political thinking, occupied the place which had been held by England in the seventeenth.

The constitutions of several of the American colonies were drawn up by the Independents, and that of Pennsylvania and Delaware owed its origin to Algernon Sydney himself. It is significant of the abiding influence of English ideas that in Connecticut and Rhode Island the constitutions created in the revolutionary era were confirmed at the Restoration, and remained unaltered, the one till 1818, the other till 1842[1]. Passing to the specific influence of individuals, Harrington occupies the foremost place. His principle of rotation was specially welcomed, for it testified that office was a trust. Even the ballot was tentatively introduced in the New York Constitution of 1777[2]. John Adams,

Commonwealth. [An interesting result of Hollis' activities was the presence of the writings of the English republicans, as his gift, in Harvard University Library, where they were read by students like John Adams and Otis. H. J. L.]

[1] Poore, 256, 1603–13.

[2] New York, 1777, Article 39. Some additional examples are also collected by Dwight, *Political Science Quarterly*, March, 1887. [For a full discussion of Harrington's influence in America see Russell Smith. H. J. L.]

who had studied the thought of the seventeenth century with
peculiar care, bears frequent witness to his debt to the same writer in
his *Defence of the Constitution of the United States* against Turgot's
attack[1]. The more democratic school of thinkers were also indebted
to the thought of the seventeenth century. The outspoken cleric,
Jonathan Mayhew, denounced Charles I as a lawless tyrant and
commended his execution[2], and explained his opposition to the
Stamp Act by asserting that he had been initiated into the principles
of freedom by Milton, Sydney and Locke[3]. The regicides were
eulogised by his friend Otis[4], and their conduct was held up in
warning by Paine[5].

The influence of the speculations of English thinkers before
Locke on the political thought of France was very small[6]. Until the
end of the seventeenth century the French remained in complete
ignorance of the neighbour country. The earliest guide-book
informed travellers that the land was peopled by demons and
parricides[7], and St Amant told his countrymen that the nation

---

[1] *Works,* VI. 210–11, etc.
[2] *Discourse concerning unlimited submission,* 40–54, ed. 1749.
[3] Tudor's *Life of Otis,* 142. Cp. Franklin, *Works,* II. 288–95.
[4] The Speech in Tudor, 327.
[5] *American Crisis,* Letter 8.
[6] [On English influence on French political ideas in the eighteenth century
there is much of interest in Joseph Dedieu, *Montesquieu et la Tradition
Politique Anglaise en France.* So small was the influence in the seventeenth
that only Bacon and Hobbes, among political writers, received the honour
of translation, though Sorbière also translated More's *Utopia* in 1643.
Sydney appears to have been known to, and honoured by, the French
Parlementaires of the eighteenth century; cp. Dedieu, *op. cit.* 319, note 1.
Sydney's *Discourses* were translated into French by Samson in 1702. A
special article was devoted to Toland's edition of Harrington in the *Biblio-
thèque Britannique* for September, 1700, and again in 1737. Montesquieu's
references to him suggest that he knew these articles rather than the original.
H. J. L.]
[7] 1654. Texte's *Rousseau et les origines du cosmopolitisme littéraire,* 5.

was composed of fanatics[1]. Even to Gui Patin, a keen student
for those days, the English were 'crudeles et feroces, de genere
lupino[2].' When Cominges arrived as ambassador in 1663 he
would have given no thought to anything but his diplomatic work
had it not been for the lively curiosity manifested by the Foreign
Secretary. After a month in England he set to work to draw up
a report on the Constitution, and Lionne could not find words
to express his delight at the thought of receiving information on
the subject[3]. Gourville did his best during a six weeks' visit to
gain acquaintance with the Constitution, but found his ignorance
of the language a fatal obstacle[4]. Even Saint-Evremond, who
spent 40 years of exile in England, never learned the language,
and seems to have known of no political writer but Hobbes[5].
Not till the expulsion of the French Protestants was interest
aroused. Correct knowledge began to be spread abroad by the
works of Rapin, Boyer, Dezmaizeaux and other settlers in England,
and by Le Clerc and many indefatigable contributors to the
Bibliothèques and the *Nouvelles* on the Continent[6]. With the
journey of Muralt in 1696 the taste for visiting the country
commenced, and through the exertions of Prévost and Voltaire
became universal. It was therefore the England of the second
revolution, not of the first, that became known[7]. Except for
Sydney, indeed, who was well known to Montesquieu[8] and

---

[1] *L'Albion, Œuvres*, ed. 1855, II. 452, 471, etc.   [2] *Lettres*, III. 133.
[3] Jusserand's *Cominges*, 100-3.   [4] *Mémoires*, 370.
[5] *Œuvres*, ed. 1866, II. 383-8.   [6] Hatin's *Gazettes de Hollande*, etc.
[7] The great crisis of the seventeenth century was known in France chiefly
through the queen's story as recorded by Mme de Motteville, the account
that Salmeron wrote for De Retz, the oration of Bossuet on Henrietta
Maria, Père D'Orléans' *Révolutions d'Angleterre*, and other unreliable sources.
Voltaire himself is a type of the prevailing ignorance, *Dict. Phil.* 'Cromwell,'
etc. Even the learned Bayle was hardly better informed. *Avis aux Refugiez*,
Œuvres, II. 592-611.   [8] *Esprit des Lois*, XI. 6.

Condorcet[1], none of Locke's democratic predecessors seem to have been studied by the French political thinkers of the eighteenth century[2]. But in studying Locke they were studying Locke's teachers; and when it is remembered that there is little in Rousseau that was not in Locke[3], and little in Locke that he did not find in the thinkers of the Interregnum, the connection of the French Revolution with the thought which we have been surveying becomes apparent[4].

A final contribution to thought from the English writers of the seventeenth century must not be forgotten. The thinkers who looked beyond mere rearrangements of political machinery were not without successors. Locke himself provides the theoretic basis of socialism. 'The labour of man's body and the work of his hands, we may say, are properly his. Whatsoever, then, he removes out of the state that nature hath provided and left it in, he hath mixed his labour with it and joined to it something that is his own, and thereby makes it his property[5].' A few years later, John Bellers published a pamphlet entitled *A College of Industry*, wherein he set forth the outlines of a reconstruction of society. The resemblance to the scheme of Peter Cornelius is too striking to be accidental,

[1] *Progrès de l'Esprit humain*, 9ème époque. The appearance of a French translation of the *Discourses* in 1702 materially contributed to their circulation on the Continent.

[2] Montesquieu's reference to Harrington does not suggest that he had studied his works.

[3] [This statement is too strong; cp. Vaughan, *The Political Writings of Rousseau*, Introduction. The organic state of Rousseau is essential to his thesis, and it is not in Locke. H. J. L.]

[4] On the eve of the Revolution Franklin presented a French copy of the *Constitutions of the American States* to Louis XVI. A new French edition of the *Discourses on Government* appeared in 1789, making the fourth within the century.

[5] *Second Treatise on Civil Government*, § 27. [On Locke and the labour theory of value see H. J. Laski, *Political Thought from Locke to Bentham*, ch. 11, and Beer, *op. cit.* 102 f.]

and the fact that he was a Quaker[1] tempts us to believe that some traditions of the great socialist who had died a member of that body had floated down over a generation. Groups of individuals are to form 'Colleges of Industry,' and these associations are to produce and consume in common[2]. Three years later Bellers issued a volume of essays on economic subjects, modifying his scheme by declaring that the colleges were not designed for all, but only for those in want[3]. Many years after a third plea for cooperative production appeared. It is obvious that the labouring classes produce more than they require for subsistence; were it not so, every gentleman would needs be a labourer. With such organisations the poor would no longer be in want; there would be a constant market among the members of the society[4].

For half a century after the last pamphlet of Bellers no socialist speculation is to be found[5]. But in 1775, Thomas Spence, a schoolmaster of Newcastle, read to the Philosophical Society of his native town a discussion of the question 'if the members of human society reap all the advantages from their natural and equal rights of property in land and liberty which they may and ought to expect,' and concluded in the negative[6]. A few years after Spence's lecture, *The Right of Property in Land*, the work of Ogilvie, an Aberdeen professor and a friend of Reid, laid

[1] *Essays about the Poor*, etc. 20–6.
[2] *College of Industry*, ed. 1696. [Bellers' *College of Industry* has been reprinted by the Swarthmoor Press. There is a study of his social theories by P. S. Belasco in *Economica* for 1925–6. Cp. also Beer, *op. cit.* 7 f. H. J. L.]
[3] *Essays about the Poor, Manufactures*, etc., ed. 1699, 5.
[4] *Essay for the Employing the Poor to Profit*, ed. 1723.
[5] *Gulliver's Travels*, Part IV. shews traces; but nothing can be inferred. Nor have we enough information about the 'Enthusiastic Levellers who pulled down enclosures and sought equality,' in 1724 (Tindal's *Continuation of Rapin*, IV. 682), to estimate their significance.
[6] Reprint of 1882, 5–14.

down the outlines of a complete scheme of land nationalisation[1].
With the outbreak of the French Revolution appeared the *Political
Justice* of Godwin, urging the same change[2]. Charles Hall quickly
added new elements to Godwin's legacy, and in 1817 Owen
published his *New View of Society*, relating the results that had
been attained at New Lanark, and recommending the formation
of associations[3]. The modern socialist movement had begun, and
England produced in Gray and Thompson, Edmonds and the
Brays, the links that connected Owen with Proudhon and
Marx.

The father of modern English Socialism declared that the
principles which he expounded had no claim to originality. He
had found a work in which they were all combined, though it
was written a hundred and twenty years earlier. 'Any merit due
for the discovery calculated to effect more substantial and permanent benefit to mankind than any ever yet contemplated by the
human mind belongs exclusively to John Bellers[4].' But Owen
post-dated the origination of collectivism. Though he did not know
it, the earliest socialist of the nineteenth century was directly
descended from the thinkers of the Interregnum.

[1] Reprint of 1891, esp. 7–42.   [2] Book VIII. chs. 1, 2, 4.
[3] Ed. 1817, 3.   [4] *New View of Society*, ed. 1817, 14.

APPENDIX A

The Influence of Harrington in America

WHILE it is difficult to prove any direct connection between Harrington's ideas and the constitutions of colonial America, certain broad resemblances are worthy of remark. *Oceana* is built upon three basic principles, the written constitution, the wide use of the elective principle, and the separation of powers; while minor features are (1) short terms of office, (2) popular approval of constitutional change, (3) the use of the ballot and of petitions, (4) special safeguards for religious freedom and popular education. These ideas, generally, became a settled part of American constitutionalism in the century after *Oceana* was published. While many of them were, of course, simply adaptations by Harrington either of historic practice or of experiences garnered during his wide foreign travel, there is no other book in which they are in the juxtaposition he gave them. There is, moreover, plenty of evidence that Harrington was widely read and discussed both by Englishmen engaged in the plantation of colonies, and by Americans concerned in their governance. In an age of constitutional experiment, it does not seem unduly far-fetched to argue that the influence of Harrington in the new world was important.

Oceana was published in 1656; and in 1669 the recently founded colony of Carolina was given a new constitution. Among its features are (1) the association of political power with the ownership of land; (2) the division of legislative power between two councils, one of which was to propose, and the other to decide upon, measures; (3) the ballot for elections; (4) religious toleration;

G

20

(5) civil marriage; (6) universal military training; (7) a distinction between constitutional and ordinary legislation, and the right to veto unconstitutional acts. Each of these proposals was Harringtonian in substance; and if, as is reported by several observers, the constitution was the work of Locke or Shaftesbury, it was made by a man who is known to have been acquainted with Harrington's writings. Perhaps it should be added that the constitution proved unworkable in practice and was reorganised in 1719.

In 1676 William Penn acquired an interest in New Jersey and began there a system of constitutional experiments notably resembling those of *Oceana*. (1) The legislature was forbidden to alter the constitution; (2) the ballot was to be used in elections; (3) the land was divided on a decimal system. This was in the west of the province. Three years later, in 1679, Penn purchased Sir George Carteret's interest in the eastern section, and a new constitution was drawn up in 1682. Among its essential features are (1) that the governor is to be ineligible for consecutive terms of office; (2) that the council, which is divided into committees, has administrative, but not legislative, power; (3) that one-third of the Grand Council (the legislative body) retired annually and were not re-eligible for two years; (4) that religious toleration and civil marriage are introduced; (5) that a distinction is made between ordinary and constitutional legislation; (6) that a limit is placed on the amount of land any citizen may hold.

It is not known decisively that Penn was acquainted with Harrington's works, though the probability is very nearly complete; and a first edition of *Oceana* was in the library of his friend and secretary, Logan. In the constitution of Pennsylvania itself there are many Harringtonian features. (1) The Provincial Council retires by one-third, who are ineligible for a further consecutive term, each year; it proposes the legislation to the Assembly; and for administrative purposes it is divided into committees. (2) The Assembly considers the Council's proposals and votes by ballot. (3) There are religious toleration and civil marriage. (4) Ownership of land is the basis of a share in government. (5) There is to be no constitutional change without the assent of six-sevenths of the Assembly. The constitution of Pennsylvania is the fourth made in forty years from the publication of *Oceana* which shews a striking resemblance to its details. The failure of the scheme does not seem to have impeded interest in Harrington, for Professor C. H. Van Tyne[1] has shewn that he was frequently quoted with respect by influential writers at the time of the American Revolution. Though Locke, Montesquieu, and Hume were more widely known, Harrington seems to have been widely respected; and the influence of Harrington on Locke and Hume, and, through Locke, on Montesquieu, was, of course, profound.

A full account of Harrington's influence on America, of which this note is a bare summary, will be found in Russell Smith, *Harrington and his Oceana*, Chapters VII. and VIII.

[1] *The Causes of the War of Independence*, p. 343.

The Movement for Law Reform under the Commonwealth

EVERY great popular movement in English history has been accompanied by a demand for law reform and the exhibition of hostility to the legal profession. The rebellions of Tyler and Cade, the Commonwealth itself, the search for parliamentary reform in the eighteenth and nineteenth centuries, are all examples of this temper. Roughly speaking, the Commonwealth movement may be divided into three groups: (a) There is a small and unimportant party who desire the abolition of the Common, and its replacement by the Civil, Law. A typical example of this attitude is R. Wiseman, whose *Law of Laws, or the Excellency of the Civil Law above all other humane laws whatever* (1656) is an attack on the existing system for its complexity and lack of uniform principle, together with an eulogy of the Civil Law for its neatness and elegance. Wiseman was a civilian who practised in the Court of Admiralty and became, first, Advocate-General and, later, Deputy-judge in the Court of Admiralty, under Cromwell. His book may be called the swan-song of the Civilians, as he himself seems to recognise that it was a dying profession. (b) The definite opponents of the Common Law who regard it as complex, oppressive, and unnecessary. These are of various types. One school desires the abolition of all laws except the law of God; of this Winstanley, discussed above (Chap. VII.), is a good example. Others, especially Levellers like Walwyn and Lilburne[1], regarded the Common Law as expressive of the Norman Con-

---

[1] E.g. in the *Just Man's Justification* (1646); and for eulogy of Anglo-Saxon law see *Vox Plebis* (1646).

quest, and, as such, a conspiracy against the freedom of the Common man; they therefore desired a return to the simplicity of the pre-Conquest period. The best statement of their views is perhaps that of John Warr, *The Corruption and Deficiency of the Laws of England* (1649)[1]. Another group desires amendment in the direction of simplicity and uniformity. These are mainly benevolent amateurs interested in the law, but without any real sense of the complexity of the issue. Perhaps the best of them is 'An Impartiall Well-wisher to the Peace and Well-beeing of All' who, on August 17, 1648, published an *Experimentall Essay touching the Reformation of the Lawes of Englana*. We may, perhaps, briefly summarise his views, as it typifies a large number of similar pamphlets.

The 'Impartiall Well-wisher' begins by desiring to reduce the laws to brevity. To this end, he suggests, 'let all those matters which are the occasion of so many laws be taken away, and let every one that shall sustain any damage in the Commonwealth by it, have just recompense and satisfaction.' 'If,' he says again, 'there were a law made that whosoever did hurt another by word or deed should make recompence to the party hurt, according to the quality of the offence, people would be more careful how they hurt any than now they are.' He desires the abolition of all local customs in the interest of uniformity. He would make all tenure freehold and have immediate compounding for tithe. Intestacy is to be dealt with by 'indifferent men,' who are 'to dispose of the estate according to equity.' He would deal very simply with all; trespasses by word or deed are to be settled locally by 'conscientious men,' who are to have full power to make the parties come *viva voce*, and settle the dispute. All written agreements are to be brief and 'without words of forme, but plainly to expresse the matter.' They are to be entered in a parish record

---

[1] Reprinted in *Harleian Miscellany* (ed. of 1808), III. 250.

book within a week or else to be void; by this means, the Well-wisher thinks, there will be 'no need of going to London about suits, nor any expense in law at home, no need of Court of Common Pleas, nor Chancery, nor Duchy Court, nor any Court of Law but a Court of Parliament.' The latter body is to deal with unjust judges, and public rates; it is to establish equal weights and measures throughout the kingdom; and it is to abolish the death-penalty for any offences except treason, rebellion, or murder. For felony, men are to make four-fold restitution; if this is impossible 'they might be made to work in some place of restraint until some satisfaction be made. Then men might not lose their lives for so triviall matters, but have time to live and repent.' Such a law 'would be full of mercy to men's souls, agreeable to the law of love.' If these changes are made, we should have, 'instead of the vast body of the law, a few plain briefe laws, like a new Magna Charta...to conclude that every one may have their right according to the law of the land and the law of charity; this is *salus populi* and *suprema lex*.' Well-wisher, it may be added, was an optimist, for he felt that 'the main of these things may be settled in a quarter of a year without any great trouble to anybody.' Other pamphlets on similar lines, notable in each case for their interest in justice for the poor, are Henry Parker's *Reformation in Courts* (1650) and Henry Robinson's *Certain Considerations* (1651); the latter was answered by Walwyn, the famous Leveller.

(c) The third group consists of reforming lawyers of whom the most notable were William Sheppard[1] and William Leach[2]. Their

---

[1] *England's Balme, or Proposals by way of Grievance and Remedy towards the Regulation of the Law* (1656).

[2] *Questions Propounded or Quaeres concerning Remedies* (1646); *Bills proposed for Acts or Proposals Concerning the Principall Courts of England* (1651). Though the first is not signed by Leach its resemblance to the latter makes its authorship practically certain.

work was two-fold. On the one hand they pointed out the just grievances that could be brought; on the other they proposed a body of specific remedies many of which notably anticipate the reforming legislation of the last hundred years. Many of their suggestions were adopted by the government though the Restoration prevented their translation into practice. As this group has been fairly fully discussed in the standard treatises, no analysis of it will be attempted here. See Holdsworth, *History of English Law*, VI. 412 ff.; Robinson, in *Essays in Anglo-American Legal History*, I. 481; Inderwick, *The Interregnum*, Chap. IV. For Cromwell's support of the proposals see Carlyle, *Letters and Speeches*, IV. 33, 209. From the *Clarke Papers* (vol. III. 64) it appears that Sheppard was called into consultation by the government. The chief proposals are printed in the *Somers Tracts*, vol. VI. p. 177 f.; and the actual legislation is in Firth and Rait, *Acts and Ordinances of the Interregnum*. Professor Holdsworth, *op. cit.* VI. 429, gives good reasons for thinking that had the changes demanded been brought into operation, the result, in the growing state of a rapidly changing law, might have been harmful to its development. But Professor Holdsworth does not deal with the sentiment hostile to the Common Law as the badge of slavery. That is the aspect of the movement which still needs exploration. The dissatisfaction, it may be added, did not die down; for there are faint echoes in each decade of the next seventy years. As late as 1706 proposals were being made to the House of Commons for reform which repeat the ideals of the earlier movement; cp., for example, *Proposals...for Remedying the Great Charge and Delay of Suits at Law and in Equity* (1706), the writer of which is unknown.

APPENDIX C

The Influence of the Revolution of 1688 *in France*

IT has been pointed out in the first chapter of this book how largely the political controversies of the French civil wars influenced English democratic evolution in the seventeenth century; and it is perhaps worth while to note the influence of the English civil wars on French development. That influence is due, not to 1649, but to 1688. The Cromwellian period, especially after the execution of Charles, seems merely to have aroused horror abroad, as the controversy between Saumaise and Milton makes evident; and, in the reign of Charles II, despite the presence of French exiles like Saint-Evremond at his court, England was still something of a barbarous curiosity to her neighbour. But the Revolution of 1688 met a very different temper. The bitter memories of the Revocation of the Edict of Nantes were still fresh in the minds of French Huguenots; and the victory of William III inspired them to hope that he might prove their saviour. The result is seen in books like the famous *Soupirs de la France Esclave* (1689)[1] which, after a bitter attack on the despotism of Louis XIV, points to English freedom as a model worthy of imitation. The *Lettres Pastorales* of Jurieu (1686–9), is, especially in its third part, an open eulogy of William, and the expression of a hope that he will come to the aid of French Protestants. Its open expression of disloyalty pricked Bayle into writing, or aiding to write, his *Avis aux Refugiés* (1690),

---

[1] Probably the work of Michel Levassor.

which insists that the duty of Huguenots, even when oppressed, is loyalty to their legitimate sovereign. This, together with the work of Jurieu, divided the Huguenots into two parties, with the English Revolution and its consequences as the touchstone of division. On the English side were Jurieu, and Abbadie, whose *Defense de la Nation Britannique* (1692) is a work of interest and ability; on the other side were Bayle himself, Isaac Papin (*La Tolérance des Protestants et l'Autorité de l'église*, 1692), and an anonymous but skilful writer of a *Defense des Refugiez* (1691)[1]. Broadly, it is not unfair to say that the Revolution persuaded the French Huguenots to recover that contract theory of the State which had been their mainstay in the civil wars of the sixteenth century. On the influence of the Huguenot refugees in making English ideas generally known in France after 1688 the reader should consult C. Bastide, *Anglais et Français du XVIIme Siècle*, Chaps. VII. and VIII., and Texte, *J. J. Rousseau*, Chap. I. Up to 1695 no less than fifteen histories of the English Revolution were published in Paris; and much was published on the character of William III and his policy up to 1704. From then, however, until the *Lettres sur les Anglois* of Muralt (1725) there is nothing published on the internal politics of Great Britain.

[1] Possibly the work of Isaac de Larrey on whom see Haag, *La France Protestante*.

INDEX

CAMBRIDGE: PRINTED BY
W. LEWIS, M.A.
AT THE UNIVERSITY PRESS